James Alison and a Girardian Theology

James Alison and a Girardian Theology

Conversion, Theological Reflection, and Induction

John P. Edwards
Foreword by James Alison

t&tclark
LONDON • NEW YORK • OXFORD • NEW DELHI • SYDNEY

T&T CLARK
Bloomsbury Publishing Plc
50 Bedford Square, London, WC1B 3DP, UK
1385 Broadway, New York, NY 10018, USA
29 Earlsfort Terrace, Dublin 2, Ireland

BLOOMSBURY, T&T CLARK and the T&T Clark logo are
trademarks of Bloomsbury Publishing Plc

First published in Great Britain 2020
This paperback edition published in 2021

Copyright © John P. Edwards, 2020; Foreword © James Alison, 2020

John P. Edwards has asserted his right under the Copyright, Designs
and Patents Act, 1988, to be identified as Author of this work.

For legal purposes the Acknowledgments on p. xii–xiv constitute
an extension of this copyright page.

All rights reserved. No part of this publication may be reproduced or
transmitted in any form or by any means, electronic or mechanical,
including photocopying, recording, or any information storage or retrieval
system, without prior permission in writing from the publishers.

Bloomsbury Publishing Plc does not have any control over, or responsibility for,
any third-party websites referred to or in this book. All internet addresses given in
this book were correct at the time of going to press. The author and publisher
regret any inconvenience caused if addresses have changed or sites have
ceased to exist, but can accept no responsibility for any such changes.

A catalogue record for this book is available from the British Library.

A catalog record for this book is available from the Library of Congress.

ISBN: HB: 978-0-5676-8905-4
       PB: 978-0-5676-9901-5
       ePDF: 978-0-5676-8906-1
       ePub: 978-0-5676-8908-5

Typeset by Integra Software Services Pvt. Ltd.

To find out more about our authors and books visit www.bloomsbury.com
and sign up for our newsletters.

In loving memory of my father, Anthony Nicholas Edwards ("Papa Tony").

*Dad, in so many ways this was written for you and because of you.
With much love, your son always.*

Contents

Foreword by James Alison — x
Acknowledgments — xii
Acknowledgment of Copyright Permissions — xiv

1 Introduction: James Alison's Life and Theology — 1
   1.1 James Alison—Catholic Priest, Theologian, and Preacher — 2
   1.2 Discovering Girard and Developing a Theological Method — 6
      1.2.1 Conversion, Theological Reflection, and Induction — 8
   1.3 Locating Alison's Girardian Theology — 10
   1.4 The Organization of the Work — 14

Part One The Beginnings of a Christian Mimetic Anthropology

2 Continuity and Development in René Girard's Understanding of Mimetic Desire and Conversion — 19
   2.1 René Girard's Experiences of Conversion — 21
   2.2 *Deceit, Desire and the Novel* (1961): Girard's Discovery of Conversion as Freedom from (Rivalrous) Desire — 24
      2.2.1 "Triangular Desire" — 25
      2.2.2 The Desiring Subject and the Selves of Desire — 28
      2.2.3 Conversion as Freedom from Rivalrous Desire — 31
      2.2.4 The Process of Conversion—From the Illusion of Absolute Autonomy to the Discovery of Relative Freedom — 33
   2.3 *Things Hidden since the Foundation of the World* (1978): Identifying the Contexts of the Modern Form of Desire — 35
      2.3.1 Imitating Acquisition — 37
      2.3.2 The Formation of Human Consciousness in Rivalry — 38
      2.3.3 The Rise of Human Culture and Desire — 40
      2.3.4 The Judeo-Christian Scriptures and the Emergence of Metaphysical Desire — 42
      2.3.5 Conversion—Freedom from the Metaphysical Form of Desire — 47
   2.4 Girard's Mature Thought: Mimetic Desire in a Gospel Perspective? — 49
      2.4.1 Mimetic Desire and Human Freedom — 50

	2.4.2 The Christian Character of Conversion	52
	2.4.3 The Converted Subject as the Norm of Subjectivity	53
	2.4.4 A Gospel or "Revealed" Anthropology in Place of Theology	55

Part Two An "Inductive" Theological Method and a *Theological* Anthropology Informed by Mimetic Theory

3 From "Conversion" to Theological Reflection: Receiving a "Revealed" Perspective through the Forgiveness of Sins   65
    3.1 Alison's Epistemology—An Overview   67
    3.2 The Disciples' Experience of Meeting the Risen Jesus as the Beginning of "Conversion"   72
       3.2.1 Girard's Influence on Alison's View of the Disciples' Resurrection Experiences   73
       3.2.2 Alison's Method for Exploring the Disciples' Experience of Jesus' Death and Resurrection   76
       3.2.3 An Imaginative Reconstruction of the Disciples' Post-crucifixion Experience   78
       3.2.4 The Resurrection Narratives as the Key to Alison's View of the Whole of Scripture   80
       3.2.5 The Conversion of the Disciples upon Meeting the Risen Jesus   85
          3.2.5.1 The Emotional/Affective "Valence" of the Disciples' Experience of the Resurrection   87
          3.2.5.2 The Spiritual/Immaterial "Valence" of the Disciples' Experience of the Resurrection   89
          3.2.5.3 The Intellectual/Cognitive "Valence" of the Disciples' Experience of the Resurrection   93
          3.2.5.4 Intelligence Operative in the Mind of Christ   95
          3.2.5.5 Intelligence Operative in the Minds of the Disciples   97
          3.2.5.6 Subversion from Within   101
    3.3 From "Conversion" to Theological Reflection   106

4 From Theological Reflection to (Ongoing) Conversion: Sharing a Received Perspective through an Act of Witnessing   111
    4.1 Distinguishing between the Order of Discovery and the Order of Logic   112
       4.1.1 The Status of Doctrines and Apologetics in Alison's Conception of Theology   114
       4.1.2 The Status of Theoretical Understanding and "Mimetic Theory"   118
    4.2 From Theological Reflection to Conversion through Witnessing   123

  4.2.1 The History of a Chain of Witnesses   126
  4.2.2 The Variability of Place   129
  4.2.3 Theological Reflection and Theological Texts as a Form of Witness and Place of Encounter   131
    4.2.3.1 Alison's Experience of Encounter via Girard's Text   133
    4.2.3.2 Turning to Ricoeur—Texts as Occasions of Encounter   135
    4.2.3.3 The Protagonist of the Encounter via the Text   136
    4.2.3.4 Distinguishing Theological Texts—Composition vs. Effect   138
    4.2.3.5 The Fruits of the Encounter via the Text and the Possibility of False Witness   139
4.3 From Theological Reflection to Ongoing Conversion: An "Inductive" Theology   145
  4.3.1 Alison's Own Theological Texts as "Inductive"   146

5 Theology "in the Order of Discovery" or an Inductive Theology   149
 5.1 Depicting the Inductive Aim of Theology   150
  5.1.1 "A Beneficent Understanding of Natural Law"—An Apologetic Excerpt   151
  5.1.2 "An Atonement Update"—A Historical Excerpt   155
  5.1.3 The Structure of Jesus' Creative Imagination and the Trinity—A Systematic Excerpt   159
  5.1.4 Original Sin in a Framework of Forgiveness—A Constructive Excerpt   162
  5.1.5 A Gay Catholic Heart—A Pastoral Excerpt   166
 5.2 A Theological Anthropology Informed by Mimetic Theory   171
  5.2.1 Clarifying Girard   174
 5.3 Contributions to Contemporary Christian Theological Questions   180
  5.3.1 An Inductive Theology of Doctrines?   180
  5.3.2 The Doctrine of Revelation as a Safeguard of Human Knowing   186
 5.4 Conclusion   190

Bibliography   193
Index   199

Foreword

You are about to embark on a highly professional book. One for which I am extremely grateful. John Edwards has done a brilliant and delicate job at explaining certain things both about the work of René Girard and about my own. Even if it has been a little weird reading about myself in the third person!

Let me explain the reason for my gratitude. I received a quite extraordinarily privileged foundational education in theology and its philosophical underpinnings from the English Dominicans. Anyone who has read the writings of Herbert McCabe, Fergus Kerr, Simon Tugwell, or Timothy Radcliffe begins to get a sense of what it might have been like to live with them for four years and be taught by them regularly, both in the classroom and from the pulpit. However, it was not only the quality of these minds that I was receiving, but a shared culture of reading, based both loosely and really around the thought of Aquinas. That shared culture of theological reading and learning amounted to something genuinely pre-modern, whose very special quality I didn't become aware of until I went to study my theology degree with the Jesuits in Brazil.

The special quality is, if I may say so, that of an organic quality of the whole of theology being one discipline. Of course, some of my then teachers were (and are) interested in philosophy, others ethics, others history, others doctrine, and others Scripture. But in all cases, there was an awareness that these were all enrichments to a whole. And it is not surprising that it should be thus, since the approach of being on the inside of an organic whole had as its purpose the formation of preachers: people who could pass on the fruits of contemplation; people who could, at a moment's notice, preach the Gospel of Grace.

I mention this here because only later did I come to understand why people referred to the Dominicans (with, I think, genuine affection) as "glorious amateurs." What happened after my time of formation with the Dominicans was my receiving the equally enormous, but psychologically very different, privilege of studying for my theology degree proper with the Jesuits in Brazil. With them I sensed that the shared sacrament that bound them together was the Spiritual Exercises, and that a shared perception of theology as an organic whole was not needed for their group belonging. The result was that they were much happier for theology to be subdivided into a whole variety of branches, like for instance fundamental theology, biblical theology, moral theology, and so forth, each with its particular questions, methods, and exigencies. Psychologically I struggled with this. I have no doubt that it was my reading of Girard's work before beginning my theology degree that gave me a way of both learning from the more professional understanding of theology that my Jesuit teachers were imparting, and holding onto the wholeness of vision with which my English Dominican teachers had blessed me. Girard's insight (well explained by Edwards here) was, as it were, my ongoing Spiritual Exercises. I can remember clearly being in class listening to my Jesuit teachers (João Batista Libânio and Ulpiano Vázquez Moro) and trying to translate theology through Girard's lens, from the world of Karl Rahner and modern adoptions of German idealism, into the pre-modern world to which I was trying to hold.

What John Edwards has done (and which I could never do) is make sense of what I was doing (and hopefully still am) in modern theological and philosophical idiom. John's theological study in a world in which Rahner and Bernard Lonergan are as much in the air breathed as Thomas and Wittgenstein were in my world have enabled him to make sense analytically of something of which I could only make sense synthetically. These two—the analytical and the synthetic—are different casts of mind and of soul, and there are few (certainly not including me) who are able to bring both together.

John has done this with unfailing fairness. I could never have offered an analytical account of my method, and yet John has taken it apart and put it back together again in such a way that at no stage do I feel that I am being short-changed, or misinterpreted. Even if there are one or two points (such as the final parts of his reading of "the intelligence of the victim") where I'm not sure I understand, such has been his sharpening of my amateurism!

Another sign of the delicacy of John's work is that he has researched my biography, and reported the links between events in my life and things that I have written, or talks I have given, in a way that is both accurate and leaves me feeling comfortable with how someone else has told my story—by no means something to be taken for granted.

In addition to being delighted with John's treatment of my own work, I'd like to bring out how he has done a favor to all of us who are students of Girard's thought. Amongst Girard scholars there are often confusions of terminology owing to words not meaning the same in one discipline as in another; for instance, "metaphysical desire" in literary criticism and theology. I think John does us all (both Girardians and Christian theologians) a valuable service in showing how René's own use of words shifted over time as he found himself explaining his insight in different contexts and to different interlocutors. In my own work I had, perhaps rather blithely, simply assumed what John has actually shown, and Girard studies are the richer for it.

This book is a serious contribution to the fundamental change in the paradigm of Christian thought that René Girard opened up for us; one that I had the good fortune to get in on in its relatively early days, and that, as John demonstrates, is acquiring ever more breadth and heft as it allows itself into interlocution with wider theological traditions and methods.

James Alison
Madrid, September 2019

Acknowledgments

It would be difficult to put into words the journey of mind and heart that has made this book possible and I will not attempt to do so here. I understand better now than I did at the time an insight James Alison once shared with me when I was first grappling with the work of René Girard. I was struggling to piece together what Girard had written about his own experiences of conversion and Alison remarked to me that "the line between self-disclosure and self-indulgence is very thin."

Gratitude, of course, is the antidote to self-indulgence. And self-disclosure is never accomplished by the self alone. It has been with the support of many people that I have been able to bring this book into existence; I would like to express my gratitude to a few of those who have served as vehicles of grace along the way.

I can still remember the day, almost fifteen years ago now, when I first came across James Alison's *Faith beyond Resentment*. Reading that collection of essays furthered an internal process of becoming untied from a series of theological knots—knots in which for many years I had become so entangled that I did not know how I would survive them. And I can remember just as clearly the day, almost four years earlier, when the loosening began. I was listening to a homily when I heard something that hit me with so much force that it was as if I were hearing God speak directly into my innermost self. Fr. Martin Laird, O. S. A., speaking gently, slowly, and clearly in his usual manner, said, "God is waiting to embrace us, in the places inside ourselves, that we find most despicable." The impact of these two moments remains within me still. I must also thank both Martin Laird and James Alison for being more than vehicles of these particular moments of grace, as profoundly transformative as each has been. This project, which first began as a dissertation while I was studying at Boston College, would not have been possible without the encouragement, engagement, and support that I received from each of them over many years. They each also provided invaluable feedback on the drafts and revisions that brought that original project into its current form.

The conversation partners and mentors involved in the dissertation phase of this project were many. Mary Ann Hinsdale, IHM, Charles Hefling, Brian Robinette, Fr. Robert Daly, S. J., Fr. John Baldovin, S. J., and Brad Rothrock all played essential roles throughout my doctoral studies, as well as in the writing of my dissertation. Conversations with many members of the Colloquium on Violence and Religion (COV&R), including Ann Astell, Susan Wright, Suzanne Ross, Grant Kaplan, Matthias Moosbrugger, Wolfgang Palaver, Scott Cowdell, Betsy Hansborough, Lee Cheek, Adam Erickson, and Andrew McKenna, also provided me encouragement along the way.

My dissertation would never have found its way to becoming *James Alison and a Girardian Theology* without the persistent encouragement of a few key supporters. First among them is John Immerwahr, a friend and former professor at Villanova, whose continued interest in the project never allowed the idea of finding a publisher to be extinguished. His multiple rounds of feedback on the introductory chapter made it much stronger than it would have been otherwise. Robert Daly's support was also significant in pushing me toward publication. Brian Robinette's and Grant Kaplan's feedback on the manuscript proposal were both invaluable. I am especially grateful to Robin Baird-Smith, Editor at Bloomsbury Academic, for his eager support of my proposal and his efforts to get it into the hands of the right person. Anna Turton, Senior Theology Editor at T&T Clark, provided feedback that improved the manuscript greatly, as did the proposal reviewers. Paul Camacho's and Kathryn Getek Soltis's consistent presence and friendship through my writing and revising kept me moving forward. Amanda Osheim provided much-needed moral and editorial support as I navigated the publication process. Suzanne Ross's careful and caring feedback on a close-to-final version of the manuscript made my evaluation of both Girard's and Alison's thinking clearer in several places.

All of my colleagues in Campus Ministry at Villanova showed me patience and kindness as I worked on this manuscript over the last two years. Linda Jaczynski gave me a listening ear and gentle reassurance during a time of disorientation. Fr. Art Purcaro, O. S. A., has been a mentor and trusted friend who allowed me to take the time I needed to pray and write. Finally, Suzanne Wentzel, another colleague and friend at Villanova, very graciously volunteered her editorial expertise and an undisclosed number of hours to make my over-explanatory and sometimes convoluted prose exceedingly more readable and concise.

I owe much to Jared May, who has opened my eyes and my heart to experience God in places that I never may have come to on my own. He always found new ways of helping me to find hope in the life that would be possible beyond the dissertation. And, in the past two years of working on this manuscript, his patient confidence and enthusiastic encouragement often made up for what was lacking in myself and enabled me to keep taking another step forward.

I have chosen to dedicate this book in memory of my father partly because he taught me to value education and clear, careful thinking. I also received from him the desire to integrate deep psychological insight and sincere theological questioning, which formed the background against which Girard and Alison so thoroughly captivated my imagination. In so many ways, my desire and effort to think through the relationship between conversion and theological reflection with Alison's work can be attributed to my dad's ongoing struggle to do this for himself. Dad, I hope at least one or two of those who continue in this struggle after you might find some nourishment in the pages that follow.

My mother has been a model of faith throughout my life. If I have any ability to trust in the goodness of the One who says to all of us "Have life and have it abundantly," it is because of the simplicity and the depth of my mother's trust. Friedrich Schleiermacher depicted piety as consisting of awe, surrender, and joy; more than anyone else in my life, my mom has shown me a faith that embodies all three. For that I will be forever grateful.

Acknowledgment of Copyright Permissions

Several excerpts from James Alison's works are used with permission of the publishers. James Alison, excerpts from *The Joy of Being Wrong: Original Sin through Easter Eyes*. Copyright © 1998 by James Alison. Excerpts from *Raising Abel: The Recovery of the Eschatological Imagination*. Copyright © 1996 by James Alison. All reprinted with the permission of The Permissions Company, LLC, on behalf of The Crossroad Publishing Company, Inc., crossroadpublishing.com.

James Alison, excerpts from *On Being Liked* © 2004 by James Alison. Excerpts from *Faith beyond Resentment: Fragments Catholic and Gay* DLT, 2001 by James Alison. All reprinted with permission of Dalton, Longman & Todd Ltd (UK) and Crossroad Publishing Company, Inc. (the United States and Canada).

1

Introduction: James Alison's Life and Theology

James Alison and René Girard are unfamiliar names in most Christian circles today. Even among Christian theologians, few have more than a surface acquaintance with their work.

My own introduction to Alison's theology (and subsequently to Girard's work) came about by chance when I was intrigued by a passing reference to Alison's *The Joy of Being Wrong: Original Sin through Easter Eyes* in an article I was reading for a graduate course in theology. My curiosity led me to spend the entire summer before I began my doctoral studies slowly digesting that book one page at a time from cover to cover. As a result, a foundational insight pierced through all of my previous theological reflection and began to transform my view of myself and the world: We can only ever see sin clearly as that which we are being freed from through an experience of receiving forgiveness. Alison provided theological language and context for what I already knew to be true in a deep but implicit way.

After I came to this discovery, my ongoing effort to integrate theology with my own experiences of God had a new point of departure. Girard's mimetic theory presented me with language for articulating the interdependence of human beings at a pre-conscious, pre-linguistic level. While human beings tend to see our desires as indications of our uniqueness, mimetic theory holds that we desire according to the desires of others; in other words, our desires are always imitations of the desires of those who act as our models. Alison's use of mimetic theory to shed light on the process of religious conversion and theological reflection refined and offered hope of resolution for an internal struggle with the disconnection I had long felt between experiences of faith and reflection on the content of Catholic faith. As I read more of Alison's work, it became increasingly clear to me that the resolution I was seeking lay in a deeper understanding of the disciples' experience of receiving forgiveness from the crucified and risen Christ, who was their friend and teacher.

This book connects the mimetic theory of René Girard—a French historian, student of modern novels, and cultural anthropologist-turned philosopher and biblical hermeneut—to the practice of theological reflection within Christian theology. It presents the work of James Alison, a contemporary, Catholic theologian and student of Girard, as an under-examined bridge for bringing mimetic theory into conversation with Christian theology. While Alison's theological corpus has grown steadily over the last twenty-five years, little work has been done to articulate his theological method. This book contributes to the study of Girard by arguing that Alison applies mimetic theory to theology in a way that Girard was unable to do, despite writing about the Bible and Christianity for over thirty years. I argue that an explicit Christian theological perspective is necessary for providing a fully coherent account of the meaning of "conversion" and "mimetic desire" within a Girardian perspective. I also believe that many Christian theologians who have had an initial exposure to mimetic theory have sometimes been deterred from investigating it more fully due to what can appear to be a fuzziness or slipperiness around the use of several of its key terms. An apparent lack of systematization and consistency around descriptions of dynamics of "mimetic desire," "mimetic rivalry," and "conversion" (even if this consistency is not actually lacking) can make it more difficult to see the lines of connection to Christian theological discourse.

James Alison's work is unique among theologians who make use of Girard and mimetic theory. I will argue throughout this book that, from the beginning of his theological engagement with Girard, Alison focused primarily on bringing mimetic theory to bear on his understanding of the very nature of theology, theological reflection, and conversion. I have found Alison's approach to be extraordinarily fruitful both for Christian theology and for an understanding of mimetic theory. In the pages that follow, I hope to convince Girard scholars, Christian theologians not yet engaged with mimetic theory, readers of Alison's work, and other interested Christians that an investigation into Alison's theological application of mimetic theory is well worth the effort.

1.1 James Alison—Catholic Priest, Theologian, and Preacher

Both James Alison and René Girard recognize that one's life is the inescapable context within which one's thinking and writing take place. Indeed, the theological method that Alison practices, partly as a result of Girard's influence, is grounded in an assertion that one's own life story, that is, the narrative history of one's most formative relationships, constitutes the fundamental context in which one's faith and understanding of the content of that faith are perceived, reflected upon, and articulated. Neither Girard's nor Alison's thinking and writing are exceptions. While it is beyond the scope of this work to offer more than a brief biographical introduction to each of these figures, such an introduction is necessary to more fully appreciate their thinking.

The next chapter, which is devoted to Girard's thought, will begin with a sketch of some of the experiences that provided the immediate context to his work. But now, before presenting Alison's discovery of Girard and a summary of the theological method that Alison has developed, I will offer a short biography of Alison focused on the experiences and relationships that tilled the soil and prepared Alison to be profoundly changed through his reception of Girard. Several interrelated experiences from Alison's childhood and up to the beginning of his vocation as a priest and teacher created a constellation of theological and personal questions that Girard's writing would powerfully illuminate and integrate. These experiences included Alison's gradual affirmation of the Catholic faith, his grappling with his own sexuality, his ordination to the priesthood as a Dominican, his pastoral work with AIDS patients, an entanglement with ecclesiastical authorities over a teaching post, and the death of a friend with whom he was in love. Without this particular network of experiences, we may not have the theological work and method that are the subject of this investigation. The interconnectedness of these experiences influenced Alison's self-understanding and his perception of God throughout his young adult years.

James Alison was born in England in 1959 to a strict Evangelical Anglican family. He was soon baptized by the well-known leader of the international Anglican Evangelical movement, Rev. John Stott. As Alison is known for his pastoral care of Catholic and ecumenical groups of gay and lesbian men and women around the world, it is not surprising that his ongoing reflection upon the interplay between his experience of faith and sexuality shaped much of his growth and development. Alison recalls that as early as the age of eight or nine after having been immersed in biblical stories, he fell in love with a boy at school and clearly sensed that the language of love in the Bible had something to do with what he felt toward that boy.[1] In his teen years, Alison fell in love with another boy who happened to be Catholic. He says that he sensed a degree of warmth about this boy that he somehow linked to the boy's being Catholic and that he had never felt in his own evangelical Protestant world. This warmth was a felt part of Alison's attraction to him.

But it wasn't until the age of eighteen that, as Alison describes it, he was able to "come out" as a gay man while living in Colombia in early 1978. Alison's subsequent decision to tell his family was followed by a period of depression. During this time, he happened upon and read a biography of Padre Pio. The love in the midst of physical and social suffering embodied in Padre Pio's life was a source of comfort and deep joy for Alison, and that joy moved Alison to become Catholic later that year. Over the next six or seven years, while living in Mexico and then Oxford, Alison received an understanding of love and grace that was much warmer than what he had known in the religious practice of his childhood. Into this fertile soil the work of René Girard fell and took root.

Alison discovered Girard in 1985 near the beginning of his philosophy studies with the English Dominicans in Blackfriars, Oxford, as he was preparing for ordination to the priesthood. His intellectual and personal engagement with Girard altered his own theological perspective. The influence of Girard's thinking led Alison to see that confessing the Christ required more than the merely intellectual; it also included the "visceral," that is, the deeply personal and existential. Between 1987 and 1994, Alison was engaged in his formal theological study at the Jesuit Faculty in Belo Horizonte, Brazil. Most of his professors were students of Karl Rahner or of the Liberationist school. He was also in formation and residence with the Dominican community in Brazil, and he was ordained a Dominican priest in 1988 in Oxford.

From 1987 to 1990, and again in 1992, Alison was engaged in regular pastoral work with people dying of AIDS in Brazil. He accompanied AIDS patients to their deaths and ensured that they were buried. Through this work, Alison says, the full

---

[1] The brief sketch of Alison's childhood and young adulthood that follows is drawn partially from an interview I conducted with him on August 23, 2011.

force and truthfulness of Girard's scapegoating thesis became clear to him. One of his earliest articles, published in 1991, was the direct fruit of this experience. The English translation of the Portuguese title is "AIDS as a Place of Revelation: Girard and a Pastoral Theology."[2] His pastoral work with those dying of AIDS also provided the context for the lectures that Alison gave at Blackfriars in 1991, which were later published as his first book, *Knowing Jesus*, in 1993.[3]

In February 1994, after Alison took a teaching post at a graduate institute in Chile, multiple religious superiors (who supplied the majority of the students for the course) complained about Alison's "militancy" in seeking out and insisting upon open conversation about sexual orientation and faith within ecclesiastical circles, and they sought his removal.[4] Although Alison's local boss, a heterosexual Frenchman, held firm and kept him in the post, the violence of this clear rejection by the South American superiors led to a period of personal devastation.

In April 1994, Alison was able to make a month-long retreat that proved to be pivotal in his faith journey. Alison describes undergoing a transformation from a largely intellectual understanding of his own relationship to the human mechanism of victimization, which had been made clearer to him through his study of Girard's reading of the Judeo-Christian Scriptures, to a "visceral" one. As he found himself reflecting upon his anger toward the complaints of the religious superiors (most of whom he had never met or spoken to), Alison was enabled to consider honestly for the first time the "deep resentment" that had put him on "a sort of crusade" against the ecclesiastical structures that were refusing him the open conversation he was demanding.[5] In this time of pain, he was able to see that it was actually God whom he resented because deep down he still believed that God was on the side of the ecclesiastical authorities and could not love gay people as they were. After Alison finally experienced that God had nothing to do with the violence directed at gay people by various Christian churches, his dependence on his fundamental belief in God's rejection of him began to crumble. During this time, Alison developed the material for a course that he would give later that year entitled "Fix Your Minds on the Things That Are Above," which eventually became the basis of his second book, published in 1996, as *Raising Abel: The Recovery of the Eschatological Imagination*.[6]

A few months after this pivotal retreat experience, in November 1994, a friend with whom Alison was in love became ill with AIDS. This friend died about a month later. Alison says that through this relationship and the loss and grief that followed,

---

[2] James Alison, "A AIDS como lugar da revelação: René Girard e uma teologia pastoral," in H. Assmann, ed. *René Girard com os teólogos da libertação* (Petrópolis: Vozes, 1991).

[3] James Alison, *Knowing Jesus* (London: SPCK, 1993; Springfield, IL: Templegate, 1994).

[4] The experiences recounted in this paragraph are drawn from my interview with Alison on August 23, 2011. He gives his own partial account of these experiences in *Faith beyond Resentment: Fragments Catholic and Gay* (London: DLT, 2001; New York: Crossroads, 2001), 36–41.

[5] Alison, *Faith beyond Resentment*, 39.

[6] James Alison, *Raising Abel: The Recovery of the Eschatological Imagination* (New York: Crossroad, 1996).

particularly in the light of his deepening experience of God's love for him, he discovered fully for the first time that real love was present at the root of his being a gay man.[7]

Realizing that he had entered religious life partly at the prompting of his shame-bound conscience regarding his own sexual orientation, Alison left the Dominican Order in 1995, although his ordination to the priesthood remained sacramentally valid.[8] The years 1995 and 1996 were very low years of depression and unemployment. But from 1997 to 2001, Alison held various teaching and business posts in the United States, Chile, the UK, and Brazil.

Since 2001, Alison has worked as an itinerant preacher, lecturer, and retreat giver. He is currently a Fellow of Imitatio, an international foundation devoted to promoting scholarship that applies the mimetic theory of René Girard to the social sciences.[9] He accompanies a wide variety of audiences through academic lectures; undergraduate, postgraduate, and professors' seminars; adult catechesis courses; and retreats for priests and parish groups. He is known internationally for his extensive pastoral outreach in support of Catholic and ecumenical groups of gay and lesbian men and women.

Alison is now the author of three book-length monographs, including *The Joy of Being Wrong*; four collections of essays, including *Broken Hearts and New Creations*; and an adult Christian formation course entitled *Jesus the Forgiving Victim*.[10] Several editions of these books have been published in or translated into Spanish, Italian, Dutch, French, Russian, and Portuguese. He has also co-edited with Wolfgang Palaver, *The Palgrave Handbook of Mimetic Theory and Religion*.

Alison's theological work has received high praise from leading Christian figures. James Keenan, SJ, a Catholic moral theologian and virtue ethicist, says of Alison's work, "Not since C.S. Lewis has an English Christian summoned his readers into such holy conversations."[11] Stanley Hauerwas lauds Alison's theology as "almost frighteningly profound."[12] Richard Rohr describes *On Being Liked* as "intellectual dynamite and spiritual joy."[13] Monica Furlong writes, "James Alison is the most fascinating theologian I have read for ages, both courageous and intellectually irresistible ... a David before Goliath!"[14] And Sebastian Moore: "To touch the nerve of life and find the words that

---

[7] From a personal interview with Alison on August 23, 2011.

[8] Alison has recently given his own account of this departure from the Dominicans and his subsequent journey toward clarifying the status of his ordination and his self-understanding—a journey that culminated in a personal phone call from Pope Francis in July 2017 giving Alison the freedom to live priesthood honestly and in good conscience. "This Is Pope Francis ...," *The Tablet* (September 28, 2019): 14–16.

[9] See www.imitatio.org.

[10] *Jesus the Forgiving Victim: Listening for the Unheard Voice* (Glenview, IL: Doers Publishing, 2013). This course includes four volumes covering an introduction to Christian theological anthropology, trinitarian theology, Christology, and ecclesiology. It is supplemented by a set of videos, a facilitator's guide, and a participant workbook that includes overviews, summaries, reflection questions, and corresponding scriptural passages. These materials can be found at https://www.forgivingvictim.com/.

[11] From the back cover of James Alison's *On Being Liked* (New York: Crossroad, 2003).

[12] From the back cover of James Alison's *Undergoing God: Dispatches from the Scene of a Break-in* (London: DLT; New York: Continuum, 2006).

[13] From the front cover of *On Being Liked*.

[14] From the back cover of *Faith beyond Resentment*.

say it, is exceptional. To do it again and again is more like genius. And Alison does just this."¹⁵ These are not ordinary statements of praise from ordinary Christian figures. Instead, they signal that we may have in James Alison a theological imagination powerful enough to reawaken and invigorate many in our present age who have grown weary of or indifferent to Christian faith.

1.2 Discovering Girard¹⁶ and Developing a Theological Method

Alison's ecclesial, personal, and theological seeking prior to his encounter with Girard's work prepared the way for the impact that would follow, and this impact goes far deeper than Alison's intellectual approach to theological questions. Alison's initial discovery of Girard caused Alison to understand himself in a way that previously had been hidden from his own view and, once revealed to him, allowed Alison to make much clearer sense of himself, his narrative history, and his relationship with the God in whom he professed faith. The impact of this discovery also led Alison to spend the next thirty-five years (and counting) reading and thinking with Girard. That continued reading and accompanying self-reflection brought about a fundamental shift in Alison's practice of theological reflection and in his understanding of the nature of theology, or theological method.

To show the nature of this shift in his theological perspective and its relationship to the deeper transformation in Alison's self-understanding, I will consider one of Alison's most illustrative descriptions of his discovery of Girard's work and the impact it had on him. This description of Alison's experience also gives an initial glimpse into the shift in theological perspective that began to shape the trajectory of Alison's own work. In a short article published in 1996, Alison writes,

> A series of coincidences in early 1985 led me to René Girard's *Things Hidden since the Foundation of the World*. As I staggered through its third part [in which Girard develops his reading of Scripture] I found myself being read like an open book, feeling like the woman at the well of Samaria, as she returned to her compatriots to say: "Come and meet someone who has told me everything I ever did." Eleven years on, I am still struggling to put into words the fecundity of what continues to be a completely unexpected and extraordinary access to Christ that is absolutely concentric with, and illuminating of, the central tenets of the Catholic faith.¹⁷

---

¹⁵ Ibid.
¹⁶ I should acknowledge that "Discovering Girard" is the title of an introduction to Girard written by Michael Kirwan (*Discovering Girard* [London: DLT, 2004; Cambridge: Cowley Publications, 2005]). This is not a particular reference to Kirwan's work here, however. Instead, now that we have a brief introduction to James Alison's life, I will turn to describing Alison's experience of discovering Girard for the first time.
¹⁷ James Alison, "Girard's Breakthrough," *The Tablet* (June 29, 1996): 848–9. This article can also be found on Alison's website at http://www.jamesalison.co.uk/texts/eng05.html (link last tested on May 23, 2014).

As is clear from Alison's comparison of his experience to the New Testament story of the woman at the well of Samaria, Alison's discovery of Girard was at least as much of an encounter with Christ as it was with Girard. Or, as I have suggested before, it was an experience of being "encountered by Christ at Girard's well."[18] For Alison, deep personal and theological insight converged; his self-understanding and his understanding of God became more deeply intertwined. His pastoral work with AIDS patients in Brazil, the interpersonal and ecclesiastical dynamics surrounding the loss of his teaching post in Chile, and the death of the friend who he loved dearly clarified these newly intertwined insights.

While the next chapter will examine the elements and development of what is referred to in Girardian circles as Girard's theory of mimetic rivalry and scapegoating, I offer here a brief overview of Girard's "mimetic theory" to illuminate how the content of Alison's changing understanding of himself and of God relates to the biographical material in the last section. Girard's corpus elaborates a view of how particular human desires arise through largely pre-conscious imitation of the desires of others (i.e., mimetically) and then provides a reading of the history of human conflict as the consequence of rivalry generated through this preconscious imitation. In addition, his corpus expounds his view that the texts of the Judeo-Christian Scriptures can fully expose how this rivalry is generated and how it has created innocent human victims throughout history.

As Alison's own description above tells us, his reading of the culmination of Girard's thinking in the third part of *Things Hidden* caused him to feel that he was "being read like an open book." In each of the pivotal life circumstances that followed Alison's discovery of Girard, the impact of Girard's understanding of human desire, rivalry, and Scripture enabled Alison to observe in his immediate surroundings and, indeed, in his own psyche the dynamics of rivalry and scapegoating that Girard was describing and thereby to confirm Girard's observations for himself. As a result, both Alison's own relationship to rivalry and the dynamics of the larger societal and ecclesiastical structures in which he was operating were laid bare to him, without the distortion of seeing himself as the primary victim. Rather, he could begin to see honestly his own engagement in rivalry and his own participation in scapegoating. He could also perceive for the first time "the absolute non-involvement of God in all that violence," an insight accompanied by the beginnings of a felt belief "that God loves us just as we are."[19] Thus, Girard's theory of the mimetic workings of desire and the scapegoat mechanism, especially as it is sharpened through his reading of the Judeo-Christian Scriptures, provided for Alison the medium for coming to perceive clearly both his own formation via desire and his relationship to social and ecclesiastical others and to God.

Through this growing personal and theological insight, which we have seen Alison describe as the fruit of "a completely unexpected and extraordinary access to Christ" granted at Girard's well, the seeds of Alison's theological method began to take root.

---

[18] John P. Edwards, "From a 'Revealed' Psychology to Theological Inquiry: James Alison's Theological Appropriation of Girard," *Contagion* 21 (2014): 127.

[19] Alison, *Faith beyond Resentment*, 39–40.

In the passage above, he offers a helpful initial description of that method. It is an experience of "being read like an open book" followed by a "struggling to put into words" the access to Christ that one has been given. The primary aim of this study will be to articulate in detail this theological method, which Alison consistently employs throughout his theological corpus. By examining his understanding of the disciples' experience of the resurrection while also presenting systematically Alison's many short descriptions of his conception of theology, I will be able to show that Alison's theological method operates according to the fundamental theological conviction that the believer's experience of conversion to Christ (i.e., the experience of receiving faith) and his or her engagement in the activity of theological reflection have an ongoing and reciprocal relationship. The reciprocal dynamic between conversion and theological reflection within the believer fosters his or her gradual induction into a new way of relating to others.

1.2.1 Conversion, Theological Reflection, and Induction

Throughout this study, I will develop Alison's usage of two terms that are foundational to his understanding and practice of theology, "conversion" and "theological reflection," in order to articulate the nature of the reciprocal relationship that Alison sees between them and to demonstrate the "inductive" character of theology as Alison understands it. "Conversion" for Alison refers both to pivotal moments of transformative encounter in the life of an individual or community, in which the believer(s) gain "unexpected and extraordinary access to Christ," and to the subsequent ongoing process by which that access, or receptivity, to Christ develops and deepens into a new and ever-evolving perception of self, God, humanity, and the whole of creation. Alison sees all of our human capacities of perception, imagination, memory, and understanding, as well as our capacity for relating to others, as inextricably interwoven such that an evolution or transformation in one or more of them is inevitably preceded by and follows from an evolution or transformation in the rest. We could say then that, in Alison's usage, "conversion" is the transformation of the subject's perception, imagination, memory, understanding, and relationality as a fruit of her reception of "an unexpected and extraordinary access to Christ."

Correspondingly, the activity of theological reflection is the believer's "struggling to put into words" both her experience of encounter with Christ and her changing perception and understanding of self, God, and others that result from that encounter. The basic activity of theological reflection as a "struggling to put into words" these two aspects of one's experience of conversion is a participation in the communicative and unveiling action of the Spirit of Christ toward humanity.

To express this recognition that authentic Christian theological reflection arises out of an experience of encountering Christ, Alison uses the phrase "theology in the order of discovery." The intellectual engagement with Girard's work that resulted from Alison's own transformative encounter via *Things Hidden* gradually enabled Alison to gain insight into the dynamic of conversion and transformation that he found himself undergoing. As Alison says, his reading of *Things Hidden* made him an open book to himself and simultaneously gave him access to the meaning made incarnate in Christ. Girard's understanding of human beings (i.e., his anthropology), which allowed Alison to make sense of his own history, also gave him access to Christ and the perception of God that Christ made discoverable through his life, death, and resurrection. We can see from Alison's brief description of his experience above that the richness and depth of this new perception of God have required of Alison much more than a purely intellectual grasp of its meaning. Rather, it has involved almost thirty-five years of reading his own story and the Gospels in the light of Girard's anthropology, of reading his own story and Girard's anthropology in the light of the Gospels, and even of reading the Gospels in the light of the self-understanding that Alison has gradually received via his encounter with Christ at Girard's well. The continual interplay among these layers of reading and interpretation has driven Alison's "struggling to put into words the fecundity" of his ongoing, revelatory experience of encounter with Christ. The theology "in the order of discovery" that he advocates similarly consists of the believer's ongoing effort to articulate the meaning that she finds herself discovering as she comes to understand anew her own identity, the love of God, and all of creation in light of the forgiveness being offered her by the crucified and risen Christ.

Because Alison sees the dynamic of reciprocal formation between the believer's experiences of conversion to Christ and the activity of Christian theological reflection to be constitutive of the nature of theology, I will argue that Alison's theological method is most helpfully described as "inductive." I use the term "induction" primarily as it refers to a process of receiving and forming someone into belonging to a particular group. Alison himself describes faith as induction in this sense, saying, "supernatural faith is the induction into the historical body and its practices whose underlying structure is faith ... it is [the] induction into these actions and practices *as* stretching [the subject] out of the worldly self and into the beginnings of a new ... self, whose full ramifications are not yet known."[20] Induction, then, refers to a process of transformation that occurs in and through a subject as she leaves behind a formerly constitutive way of belonging and is received into a new form of belonging.

Alison's theological method is inductive in this sense because it identifies the activity of theological reflection among those actions and practices that "stretch" the subject out of an old form of belonging and into a new one. Alison sees the believer's participation in the revealing action of the Spirit (i.e., theological reflection) as following upon and deepening her participation in an ongoing experience of conversion. As the believer struggles to articulate her ongoing experience of relational transformation as well as the evolving perception and understanding of God and creation that accompanies it, she is, in and through her engagement in this activity, gradually and simultaneously being inducted into a new, peaceful mode of being in the world, which consists in a new mode of perceiving, imagining, remembering, and relating to God and all of creation. Alison richly describes of this transformation as it unfolds in the life of the believer:

---

[20] James Alison, *The Joy of Being Wrong: Original Sin through Easter Eyes* (New York: Crossroad, 1998), 59; Alison's emphasis.

The process of faith in the life of the person is therefore precisely [the] learning to relax into the suggestion of [the divine] "Other," a process that is arduous because what is being undone is the way in which our selves are formed and constituted by the "worldly" other, which is at many points in denial of the peaceful mimesis, which is the new "Other's" way into us.²¹

This arduous process of learning to relax into being given a new identity from a new Other who appears to be more trustworthy than many of the others who have formed us previously is facilitated in part by the subject's effort to grapple with and articulate the perception of the divine Other into which she is being inducted.

1.3 Locating Alison's Girardian Theology

While James Alison's theology is unique in its application of Girard's work, he is not the first theologian to employ Girard's mimetic anthropology to articulate a Christian theological perspective. Before beginning my investigation into Alison's theological method and its development from his ongoing engagement with Girard, I want to locate Alison's work among those Christian thinkers who have used Girard's theory within their own theological, biblical, and ethical contributions. Locating Alison's work this way will allow me to explicitly recognize the fact that Alison's "Girardian theology" has not been generated in a vacuum by acknowledging the significant contributions of these other Girardian scholars. It will also allow me to articulate the uniqueness of Alison's application of Girard and the value of giving it sustained attention. I will rely on Grant Kaplan's recent mapping of Girardian theologians to locate Alison's work among them.²² The present study will develop Alison's unique contribution both to a clearer understanding of Girard's thought and to showing the usefulness of mimetic theory for Christian theological method.

The list of Christian theologians and biblical scholars working to demonstrate the usefulness of Girard's work for developing a Christian theological perspective includes figures spanning the 1970s to the present, namely, Raymond Schwager, James Williams, Gil Bailie, Robert Hamerton-Kelly, Wolfgang Palaver, Michael Kirwan, Mark Heim, Robert Daly, Scott Cowdell, Robert Doran, and Brian Robinette. With his recent book, *René Girard, Unlikely Apologist*, Grant Kaplan must be added to this list of Christian theologians substantially engaging mimetic theory. In his "Introduction," Kaplan sketches the terrain that has been covered by the most significant efforts to bring Girard's work into sustained dialogue with Christian theology.²³ He argues that these efforts fall into two categories: (1) efforts to bring mimetic theory into dialogue with particular theological questions, such as atonement theory and soteriology more

---

²¹ Alison, *The Joy of Being Wrong*, 60.
²² Grant Kaplan, *René Girard, Unlikely Apologist: Mimetic Theory and Fundamental Theology* (Notre Dame, IN: University of Notre Dame Press, 2016), 1–16.
²³ Ibid., 4–7, 10–14.

broadly, biblical hermeneutics, original sin, the resurrection, and the Trinity,[24] and (2) efforts to bring mimetic theory into dialogue with various topics within the discipline of fundamental theology, which, as Kaplan deftly describes it, is concerned "not so much [with] *faith seeking understanding* [as the rest of theological inquiry is] but rather *unbelief seeking belief.*"[25] In other words, this second category tries to address the more "fundamental" questions of the nature of religious knowing as compared to other forms of knowing to provide a context for talking about how believers might understand particular doctrines of faith. Kaplan rightly notes that the vast majority of the works by Girardian theologians to date fall more readily into the former category than the latter.

Kaplan's sorting of Girardian theologians into these categories derives from his own training in fundamental theology which leads him to distinguish between two basic theological operations: (1) "making reasonable revealed objects of faith," and (2) giving "greater rationality to the tenets of faith, or [lending] power to [faith's] worldview and fundamental assumptions."[26] Kaplan brings mimetic theory into further dialogue with both of these theological operations, but he places his primary focus on the dialogue between mimetic theory and fundamental theology, which has received less attention.

Kaplan places Alison's work in the first category, that of using mimetic theory to help make more reasonable particular revealed objects of faith. He cites Alison's most thorough-going work of systematic theology, *The Joy of Being Wrong: Original Sin through Easter Eyes*, which employs mimetic theory to help deepen our understanding of the doctrine of original sin, as well as grace, the Trinity, the resurrection, and redemption.[27] In a chapter entitled "Imagining a Mimetic Ecclesiology," Kaplan draws

---

[24] In this category, Kaplan specifically mentions the following as noteworthy examples (ibid., 5): Raymond Schwager, *Jesus in the Drama Salvation: Toward a Biblical Doctrine of Redemption* (New York: Crossroads, 1999); Raymond Schwager, *Must There Be Scapegoats* (New York: Crossroads, 2000); Alison, *The Joy of Being Wrong*; Mark Heim, *Saved from Sacrifice: A Theology of the Cross* (Grand Rapids, MI: Eerdmans, 2006); Brian Robinette, *Grammars of Resurrection: A Christian Theology of Presence and Absence* (New York: Crossroads, 2009); and Robert Doran, *The Trinity in History: A Theology of Divine Missions* (Toronto: University of Toronto Press, 2012).
  To this list, I would add the following: Robert Hamerton-Kelly, *Sacred Violence: Paul's Hermeneutic of the Cross* (Philadelphia, PA: Fortress Press, 1991); Robert Hamerton-Kelly, *The Gospel and the Sacred: Poetics of Violence in Mark* (Philadelphia, PA: Fortress Press, 1993); James G. Williams, *The Girard Reader* (New York: Crossroad Herder, 1996); Gil Bailie, *Violence Unveiled: Humanity at the Crossroads* (New York: Crossroad, 1995); Raymond Schwager, *Banished from Eden: Original Sin and Evolutionary Theory in the Drama of Salvation* (Leominster, Herefordshire: Gracewing Publishing, 2006); and Robert Daly, *Sacrifice Unveiled: The True Meaning of Christian Sacrifice* (New York: T&T Clark, 2010).

[25] Kaplan, *René Girard, Unlikely Apologist*, 7. In this category, Michael Kirwan's *Girard and Theology* (New York: T&T Clark, 2009) is the only previous book-length project devoted to mimetic theory and the discipline of theology. And Kaplan sees his own book as advancing Kirwan's project. See *René Girard, Unlikely Apologist*, 6.
  Two more recent works include particular chapters that would also fall into this category: Scott Cowdell's *René Girard and Secular Modernity: Christ, Culture, and Crisis* (Notre Dame, IN: Notre Dame University Press, 2013) and Wolfgang Palaver's *René Girard's Mimetic Theory* (East Lansing, MI: Michigan State University Press, 2013).

[26] Kaplan, *René Girard, Unlikely Apologist*, 6. This distinction fits well with the classical theological distinction between *fides quae* and *fides qua*, which I have developed at length in order to articulate the relationship between Girard's work and Alison's. See John P. Edwards, "From a 'Revealed' Psychology to Theological Inquiry: James Alison's Theological Appropriation of Girard," *Contagion* 21 (2014): 121–30.

[27] Kaplan, *René Girard, Unlikely Apologist*, 5.

significantly on Alison's work to develop an understanding of grace and of the church that is grounded more fully in the self-offering of Jesus the forgiving victim.[28]

While Kaplan is correct to identify and develop a few of the many contributions that Alison's theology makes toward bringing mimetic theory into dialogue with particular aspects of Christian theology, my aim will be to show that the primary contribution of Alison's theology lies in the realm of theological method, or fundamental theology. A persistent curiosity about the very nature of theological inquiry guides the body of Alison's theology, beginning with his first book *Knowing Jesus*, and continuing to his recent essays in *The Palgrave Handbook of Mimetic Theory and Religion*, a volume he co-edited with Wolfgang Palaver, and his "Introduction" to the edited volume *The Practice of the Presence of God: Theology as a Way of Life*.[29] He delves into mimetic theory to clarify the questions of the nature of Christian conversion (i.e., the believer's reception of faith) and the activity of theological reflection—in other words, questions regarding the nature of religious knowing or of "knowing Jesus." Of what does this knowing consist? How does one come to participate in such a knowing? And what impact does this knowing have on persons and communities? These are questions of theological method, or fundamental theology. Thus, my investigation into Alison's work will show that Alison would be more appropriately understood in the second category of "Girardian theologians" that Kaplan identifies.

By giving sustained attention to Alison's theological corpus as a whole to develop systematically his conception of theological method, this study will demonstrate that Alison's work should be viewed primarily in the category of bringing mimetic theory into dialogue with fundamental theology and, further, that Alison's work makes a strong case for seeing the primary contribution of mimetic theory within the realm of fundamental theology. Only as a result of this primary contribution does Alison's theology (and mimetic theory generally) have the secondary capacity to help elucidate other theological questions, such as soteriology. Alison's understandings of conversion, theological reflection, and induction, as informed by his ongoing engagement with Girard, undergird his approach to every other theological and ethical discipline. In other words, Alison's use of mimetic theory to develop an operational theological method led him to apply mimetic theory to other theological questions.

After I develop Alison's understanding of the reciprocal relationship between conversion and theological reflection in Chapters 3 and 4 of this book, I will show in Chapter 5 how this understanding operates within Alison's approach to a range of theological questions spanning multiple disciplines, including an apologetic for natural law, to a historical retrieval of the Jewish liturgy of atonement, Christology, Trinitarian theology, theological anthropology, and soteriology. We will see that Alison's understanding of theological knowing as made possible by a personal and social conversion to Christ the forgiving victim is grounded in a Girardian epistemology that

---

[28] Ibid., 139–52.
[29] James Alison, *Knowing Jesus* (Springfield, IL: Templegate, 1993); James Alison and Wolfgang Palaver, eds. *The Palgrave Handbook of Mimetic Theory and Religion* (New York: Palgrave Macmillan, 2017); Martin Laird and Sheelah Treflé Hidden, eds. *The Practice of the Presence of God: Theology as a Way of Life* (London: Routledge, 2017).

views our various social others as the mediators of our desire and shapers of the lens of our perception. This epistemology is formed by and formative of Girard's and Alison's reading of the Judeo-Christian Scriptures. As a result, it guides Alison's approach to all of his theological queries.

As I seek to demonstrate the primary theological impact of Alison's work and of mimetic theory more broadly in the area of theological method, the question of origin with regard to mimetic theory and the Judeo-Christian Scriptures comes to the fore. Through my developmental approach to Girard's writings and my efforts to show the relationships among Alison's discovery of Girard, the disciples' experience of the crucified and risen Christ, and Girard's formulation of mimetic theory, we will see that in Alison's view (and, I believe, Girard's as well), the source of the fruitful resonance between mimetic theory and Christian theology is in their shared origin within the disciples' experiences of the resurrection of Jesus. It is this shared origin or shared point of unveiling that presents mimetic theory as a particularly rich dialogue partner for Christian theology.

Demonstrating the primary contribution of Alison's appropriation of mimetic theory to theological method will also contribute to Girardian studies by clarifying a still unresolved confusion within Girard's usage of several of his key terms. Girard's tendency, which is more pronounced in the first half of his career, to use the terms "mimetic desire" and "mimetic rivalry" relatively interchangeably, along with his insistence on avoiding theological inquiry in favor of his anthropological approach to the biblical narrative, has led to a central confusion within the reception of Girard's work as to whether mimetic desire is inherently rivalrous or whether mimetic desire as such is actually neutral in its openness to being formed in either a negative or a positive mode. My developmental approach to Girard's work will allow me to make evident the source of this confusion and alleviate it through an application of Alison's theology. Because Alison develops mimetic theory within the arena of theological method, his theological perspective can be used to show that, despite the confusion generated by some of Girard's less-than-careful usage of his own terms and his disavowal of a theological approach, mimetic theory can be applied within a Christian theology that seeks to understand the process of religious conversion and the nature of religious knowing. By giving a coherent articulation of Alison's theological method, I will also be able to show how Alison's theological project does for the application of mimetic theory to theology something that René Girard was unable to do, despite writing about the Bible and Christianity for over thirty years, that is, fully develop the "Gospel anthropology"[30] that Girard set out to formulate in some of his later works, but which he is only partially successful in accomplishing.

Thus, this systematic investigation into Alison's theological method will further advance the conversation between mimetic theory and fundamental theology by demonstrating that Alison's theological method has been an application of mimetic theory to questions of fundamental theology from his first encounter with Girard to

---

[30] René Girard, *I See Satan Fall Like Lightning*, trans. James G. Williams (New York: Orbis Books, 2001), 191; René Girard, *Evolution and Conversion: Dialogues on the Origins of Culture* (London/New York: Continuum, 2007), 215.

the present. An investigation into Alison's engagement with Girard on the level of the fundamental theological questions of conversion and theological reflection will also clear up a central confusion within Girard's articulation of mimetic theory.

1.4 The Organization of the Work

Part One (Chapter 2) of this investigation into Alison's theological method and its contribution to Christian theological discourse, as well as to the study of mimetic theory, consists of a developmental look at René Girard's mimetic anthropology and sociology. This treatment of Girard will not attempt to repeat the growing engagement with his work, which was undertaken early in his career by scholars such as James Williams, Raymond Schwager, Eugene Webb, and Robert Hamerton-Kelly, and which has continued most recently with several major studies on his thought in relation to secular modernity and modern fundamental theology by Wolfgang Palaver, Scott Cowdell, and, as we have just seen, Grant Kaplan.[31] Instead, I will offer the first extended, systematic account of the historical development within Girard's writings of his usage of two of his central terms, "mimetic desire" and "conversion." I also will consider Girard's view of human history, which he believes was fundamentally altered by the Judeo-Christian Scriptures. In taking this approach, I will show that Girard's articulation of his understanding of conversion and his correlative understanding of desire has developed over his career. But I also will argue that Girard's explicit choice both to maintain a strictly anthropological, sociological approach in his treatment of the Christian Scriptures and to refrain from entering into theological discourse has created some terminological inconsistencies that remain even within his mature thought.[32] Identifying these inconsistencies in greater detail will help to isolate one of the most common sources of confusion within attempts to understand Girard's theory and its potential relevance for Christian theology.

My investigation into the development of Girard's understanding of desire and conversion will lay the foundation for Part Two, in which I will articulate Alison's theological method. I then will show how a fully explicit Christian theological perspective such as Alison's is necessary for bringing these terminological inconsistencies into relief and for providing a fully coherent account of the meaning of "conversion" and "mimetic desire" within a Girardian theology. I will proceed in Chapters 3 and 4 with my study of Alison's theological method and its underlying

---

[31] See notes 23 and 24 for full citations of most these works, with the exception of Eugene Webb's which interprets Girard within the disciplines of French philosophy and psychoanalysis. Eugene Webb, *The Self Between* (Seattle/London: University of Washington Press, 1993).

[32] Here I will draw on a previous essay of mine while also engaging with Wolfgang Palaver's, Grant Kaplan's, and Kevin Mongrain's positions on the theological character of Girard's work. See John P. Edwards, "From a 'Revealed' Psychology to Theological Inquiry," *Contagion* 21 (2014), especially 124–6; Palaver, *René Girard's Mimetic Theory*, 212–30; Kaplan, *René Girard, Unlikely Apologist*, especially 3–16; and Kevin Mongrain, "Theologians of Spiritual Transformation: A Proposal for Reading René Girard through the Lenses of Hans Urs von Balthasar and John Cassian," *Modern Theology* 28.1 (2012): 81–111.

assertion of the reciprocal relationship between the ongoing experience of conversion to Christ and the activity of theological reflection. Chapter 3 will develop Alison's implicit understanding of one movement in this reciprocal relationship, namely, the movement from conversion to theological reflection, and it will present theology as a fruit of conversion. Chapter 4 will develop Alison's implicit view of the movement from theological expression to the potential conversion experiences of others; that is, it will present theology as an occasion for conversion.

Chapter 3 begins with a summary account of Alison's epistemology. This will allow for a clearer presentation of Girard's influence on Alison's understanding of the New Testament accounts of the disciples' experiences of Jesus' death and resurrection. The primary aim of Chapter 3 will be to show that Alison's view of the New Testament accounts of the resurrection appearances, which he begins to develop very early in his theological career (around 1990), leads him to see and begin to understand the reciprocal relationship between conversion and theology that has guided his theological performance throughout his career thus far. The majority of the chapter will be spent examining what Alison describes as the "density" of the disciples' experiences of the crucified and risen Lord. I will consider Alison's description of the overlapping layers of the disciples' experience to articulate the dynamic process of conversion to Christ, which transforms the whole person and which Alison designates as a "subversion from within."[33] The chapter concludes by drawing out Alison's implicit understanding of the activity of theological reflection as part of the believer's response to the process of conversion that she finds herself undergoing.

Chapter 4 will begin by exploring what Alison's understanding of conversion to Christ and the activity of theological reflection implies for a few essential theological and epistemological categories, including "doctrines" and "apologetics." It then will relate the discussion of the reciprocal relationship between conversion and theological reflection to Alison's use of the phrase "theology in the order of discovery"[34] to clarify the meaning and significance of this term for understanding Alison's theological

---

[33] "Subversion from within" is Alison's preferred way of talking about how the intelligence operative in the mind of the subject undergoing conversion is gradually exposed, undone, and replaced by the clearer perspective operating in the mind of Christ. See especially *Raising Abel*, 30–3. I will consider it at length at the end of Chapter 3.

[34] As will become evident in Chapters 3 and 4, the phrase "the order of discovery" is more essential to Alison's theological project than one would likely observe when first reading Alison's work. I develop Alison's view of this contrast in some detail at the beginning of Chapter 4.

For a brief articulation of Alison's own contrasting of these two orders and of their implications for theological method, see *The Joy of Being Wrong*, 100. Alison gives some further insight into the motivation behind his use of the phrase "the order of discovery" in several places scattered throughout his writings. See, for example, *Raising Abel*, 55–6; "Theology amidst the Stones and the Dust," in *Faith beyond Resentment: Fragments Catholic and Gay* (London: DLT, 2001; New York: Crossroads, 2001), 27–55; "On Learning to Say 'Jesus Is Lord': A 'Girardian' Confession," in *Faith beyond Resentment: Fragments Catholic and Gay* (London: DLT, 2001; New York: Crossroads, 2001), 156–64; "Unpicking Atonement's Knots," in *On Being Liked* (New York: Crossroads/London: DLT, 2004), 20–2; "An Atonement Update," in *Undergoing God* (New York: Continuum/London: DLT, 2006), 52–5; "Doing Theology Is a Slow Business," in *Broken Hearts and New Creations* (New York: Continuum, 2010), vii–x.

Cf. John P. Edwards, "From a 'Revealed' Psychology to Theological Inquiry," *Contagion* 21 (2014): 121–30; see endnote no. 13.

method. The relationship between the origins of mimetic theory and Christian revelation also will be considered.

As a fruit of receiving faith in the risen Christ, theological reflection is what Alison described above as a "the struggling to put into words the fecundity" of the intelligence that the believer receives in and through her reception of forgiveness. The ongoing attempt to articulate this newly received perspective fosters the believer's induction into a new way of perceiving, imagining, remembering, and relating because it is part of the believer's affirmation of the truthfulness of this perspective. Chapter 4, then, will draw out Alison's implicit understanding of theology as an act of witness that becomes a new or renewed occasion for the Spirit of Christ to make the crucified and risen Christ present and able to be encountered repeatedly by the one giving witness and by those who receive that witness. It will rely considerably on Elizabeth Johnson's work on the communion of saints, Richard Bauckham's account of the New Testament witnesses, and Paul Ricoeur's understanding of texts.[35]

Chapter 5 will demonstrate Alison's "inductive" fundamental theology operative in several excerpts from his writings on particular theological questions. I will draw out its essential characteristics from instances of Alison's own practice of theological reflection. We will see that Alison's theological performance coheres with and operates according to the understanding of theology that is implicit in his reading of the New Testament accounts of the disciples' experiences of the death and resurrection of Jesus.

The chapter will conclude by showing how Alison's fully and explicitly theological employment of mimetic theory resolves a long-standing source of confusion within Girard's own articulation of mimetic theory. It will also develop the contributions that Alison's inductive theology can make toward a Christian theological anthropology, a theology of doctrines, and a theology of revelation.

---

[35] Elizabeth Johnson, *Friends of God and Prophets: A Feminist Theological Reading of the Communion of Saints* (New York: Continuum, 1999); Richard Bauckham, *Jesus and the Eyewitnesses: The Gospels as Eyewitness Testimony* (Grand Rapids, MI: Eerdmans, 2006); Paul Ricoeur, *From Text to Action: Essays in Hermeneutics*, II (Evanston, IL: Northwestern University Press, 2007).

Part One

The Beginnings of a Christian Mimetic Anthropology

2

Continuity and Development in René Girard's Understanding of Mimetic Desire and Conversion

James Alison's substantial and still growing theological corpus makes a strong case for the value of René Girard's work and of mimetic theory in providing an illuminating new framework for working out a contemporary Christian theological anthropology. The impact of Girard's thinking on Alison's ongoing experience of conversion and his approach to theology is such that, without it, it would be difficult to imagine the emergence of anything like what we have in Alison's theological corpus thus far. We saw in the last chapter that Alison describes his own engagement in theological reflection as an ongoing attempt to unpack the fecundity of the Gospel to which he has been given "unexpected and extraordinary access" as a result of his discovery and continued reading of Girard's work.[1]

Therefore, to draw out Alison's understanding of conversion and reflect systematically on his theological method, I will first investigate Girard's work. This chapter will consider the continuity and development of Girard's understanding of "mimetic desire" and the kind of "conversion" that discloses to persons their own formation in and through the "mimetic" operation of desire. Many commentators on Girard's work have observed that Girard is much more of a "hedgehog thinker" than a systematic one, since his writings attempt to articulate repeatedly and in a variety of academic contexts (literary criticism, cultural anthropology, biblical hermeneutics, psychology, philosophy, political theory, etc.) his keen and ever-deepening perception of "a single intuition" or insight, which leading Girard scholar Wolfgang Palaver labels "the encompassing concept of the *mimetic cycle*."[2] This way of thinking and writing is quite effective as a means of communicating the depth of Girard's intuition, as well as its descriptive force. Girard's approach reveals the capacity of his understanding of this

---

[1] Alison, "Girard's Breakthrough," 849.
[2] Palaver, *René Girard's Mimetic Theory*, vii (Palaver's emphasis). Palaver points to Girard's own summary of the core of his thinking in which he uses this phrase "the mimetic cycle." See *I See Satan*, 30.
  Girard has been described as a "hedgehog thinker" by many other scholars who have tried to communicate the significance of his thought as well. See, for example, Roberto Calasso, *The Ruin of Kasch*, trans. William Weaver and Stephen Sartarelli (Cambridge: Harvard University Press, 1994), 157–8. Also see Michael Kirwan, *Girard and Theology* (London/New York: T&T Clark, 2009), 19.

concept to provide access to the meaning being communicated, either explicitly or implicitly, by a wide range of texts.[3]

However, this same approach creates some difficulties in following Girard's usage of many of his key terms. When Girard uses the terms "mimesis," "mimetic desire," "mimetic rivalry," "acquisitive mimesis," "conflictual mimesis," and "metaphysical desire," it is not always clear in each particular instance of his use of one of these terms to what extent their meanings are intended to overlap or to what extent Girard uses different terms to distinguish between different aspects or modes of the "mimetic cycle" as he understands it.[4] This lack of clarity with regard to the overlap or distinction in the meaning of these various terms for mimetic desire produces a correlative lack of clarity with regard to Girard's understanding of conversion.

To isolate Girard's intended meaning for each of his different terms for mimesis and desire, and thereby come to a fuller grasp of his understanding of conversion, I will examine his usage of these terms across four of his major texts, which were written at three different points in his academic career. This approach will show that Girard's usage of these terms has developed as his articulation of his understanding of mimetic desire, conversion, and the scapegoat mechanism has become increasingly more precise through his continued reflection and application of it within various contexts.

For the purpose of focusing my investigation, I have chosen to examine the following texts: *Deceit, Desire and the Novel* (*DDN*) (original French edition 1961, English translation 1968), *Things Hidden since the Foundation of the World* (original French edition 1978, English translation 1987), *I See Satan Fall Like Lightning* (original French edition 1999, English translation 2001), and *Evolution and Conversion: Dialogues on the Origins of Culture* (original French edition 2004, English translation 2007). These works represent major achievements within Girard's intellectual life and his academic career. They also depict the emergence of important nuances in his account of mimetic desire.[5]

I will argue that Girard's initial understanding of mimetic desire (articulated in *DDN*) focuses almost exclusively on his discovery of what he calls "mimetic rivalry," which he eventually comes to describe as a negative or rivalrous mode of mimetic desire. This focus causes Girard to tend toward identifying "mimetic desire" with "mimetic rivalry" in his earlier writings. As his articulation of mimetic theory gradually becomes more nuanced, Girard makes increasingly clearer distinctions between "mimesis" as

---

[3] For an excellent account of how Girard's thought provides access to the meaning being communicated (unveiled), or obfuscated (veiled) by particular texts, see Jeremiah Alberg's *Beneath the Veil of the Strange Verses: Reading Scandalous Texts* (East Lansing: Michigan State University Press, 2013).

[4] There are several good lexicons of Girardian terminology available. I recommend one created by longtime Colloquium on Violence and Religion member, Sherwood ("Woody") Belangia, which is available online at http://woodybelangia.com/2014/01/09/the-mimetic-theory-of-rene-girard-part-i/#more-290 (accessed July 9, 2014). The Colloquium on Violence and Religion is the first and still primary professional organization dedicated to the study and ongoing application of Girard's work. They can be found online at http://www.uibk.ac.at/theol/cover/ (accessed February 28, 2015).

[5] Palaver's account of Girard's life and work locates each of these four texts within the development of Girard's corpus and attests to the intellectual significance of each for the development of mimetic theory. See Palaver, *René Girard's Mimetic Theory*, 8–14. Scott Cowdell's biographical sketch is also helpful in this regard. See Cowdell, *René Girard and Secular Modernity*, 2–6.

a fundamental capacity for imitation that both human beings and animals possess, "mimetic desire" as a name for mimesis as it is operative in human cultures, and two modes of mimetic desire, one negative ("mimetic rivalry") and one positive (which Alison and some other Girardians often refer to as "pacific mimesis").

My treatment of *Things Hidden since the Foundation of the World* will show how Girard's articulation of his understanding of mimesis and mimetic desire in relation to history and the process of hominization helps to provide the context for recognizing the meaning of the distinctions that he intends among all of the terms listed above. And my consideration of two of Girard's later works (*I See Satan* and *Evolution and Conversion*) will show his increasing, but never fully realized, capacity to articulate mimetic theory as a Christian anthropology, that is, as an understanding of human desire and human culture most fully disclosed in the Judeo-Christian Scriptures. I conclude with an extended discussion of the question as to whether Girard's treatment of the biblical narrative is in fact exclusively "anthropological" (i.e., psychosocial) as he claims, or whether it crosses into the domain of theology and if so in what senses, which has been the subject of ongoing debate among some theologians who employ Girard's work. This discussion will lay the foundation for the investigation of Alison's work in Part Two and for the contribution of that investigation to both mimetic theory and fundamental theology.

2.1 René Girard's Experiences of Conversion

Before moving to a treatment of these four works, a brief consideration of Girard's reflections on two of his own pivotal experiences of conversion will help to provide the context for the investigation that follows, and it will offer an initial articulation of his understanding of conversion. According to Girard's account, his own experiences of conversion are directly connected to his discovery of the mimetic operation of desire. This discovery came about in the late 1940s and early 1950s during his preparations to teach a course in French literature while completing his doctoral work in history at Indiana University.[6] As part of this preparation, he devoted extensive time to reading the novels of Stendhal, Flaubert, and Proust. The study of these French novelists, combined with his reading of Dostoyevsky and Cervantes' Don Quixote (the latter of which Girard first began reading as a child), led him to his first moment of real discovery regarding "triangular" or "mimetic" desire.[7]

Because Girard did not have academic training in French literature or literary criticism, his reading of these texts was not guided by standard disciplinary methods. He sees his lack of training in literary criticism as a great advantage and even as contributing to his intellectual discovery. He says,

---

[6] Kirwan, *Discovering Girard*, 10; James Williams, ed. *The Girard Reader* (New York: Crossroads, 1996), 1–2.
[7] Girard, *Evolution and Conversion*, 24–6.

I did not realize that [literary] critics were supposed to look for differences, singularities, and not similarities, in the works they studied. Similarities... contradict the romantic fetish of originality and novelty at any price.[8]

Girard believes that his lack of formal training made it possible for him to come to perceive strong similarities among these five European novelists. *DDN* argues that these similarities converge around each novelist's portrayal of the arduous journey culminating in a certain kind of conversion of each of the novel's protagonists.[9] Girard sees the clarity of this portrayal becoming more pronounced in each novelist's later works.

Because of his observations of similar depictions of the process leading to conversion in the works of five different novelists, as well as his observation that their depictions become more pronounced in the novels written later in this lives, Girard concludes that each novelist is attempting to depict and communicate an ongoing and demanding process of conversion that each one has found himself undergoing in his own life and that is being enacted through their very efforts to depict it in their novels.[10] Girard sees this conversion as the discovery of each one's own constitution in and through the dynamics of mimetic (or "imitative") desire, which ultimately leads the novelists to an increasing degree of freedom from enslavement within a negative mode of that desire.

Girard's growing discovery of, and conviction about, the depth and the commonality of the experience of conversion undergone by each of the novelists had an increasingly profound effect upon him. The process of writing *DDN* brought about a deep existential discovery within himself. Girard says that as he began writing it, he was "very much in the pure demystification mode: cynical, destructive... [and] engaged in debunking."[11] However, through the process of his own effort to make explicit the novelists' similar intention to reveal the structure of desire in which they discovered themselves to be formed, Girard found himself undergoing "his own version" of the transformation that he saw unfolding in the novelists and their heroes.[12] The transformation occurred as Girard recognized that the imitative, and also rivalrous, operation of the desire of the other (primarily that of the novelists) was equally descriptive of his own desire. Girard describes this initial insight into the triangular operation of his desire as an "intellectual-literary" conversion.[13] By this he means that his insight into his own desiring was a change in his understanding of

---

[8] René Girard and Rebecca Adams, "Violence, Difference, Sacrifice: A Conversation with René Girard," *Religion and Literature* 25.2 (1993): 12. This interview is the opening article in a special issue of *Religion and Literature* devoted to mimetic theory.

[9] Girard, *Deceit, Desire, and the Novel: Self and Other in Literary Structure*. Translated by Yvonne Freccero (Baltimore/London: Johns Hopkins University Press, 1976), see especially chapters 7 and 12. Going forward I will regularly refer to this text as *DDN*.

[10] René Girard and James Williams, "The Anthropology of the Cross: A Conversation with René Girard," in James Williams, ed. *The Girard Reader*, 284.

[11] Ibid., 283.

[12] Ibid., 285.

[13] Ibid., 285.

himself and his relationship to desire. As Girard describes it, it was a "conversion in which you accept that you are part of the mimetic mechanism which rules human relationships."[14]

Girard recounts that he experienced this change in his self-understanding as enjoyable, comfortable, and even self-indulgent.[15] In recognizing intellectually his own relationship to desire, Girard did not have to go through the painful process of the crumbling of denial and self-justification that he observes in the heroes of the novels. Instead, without personally struggling through the process of trying to avoid an honest acknowledgment of his own relationship to desire, Girard grasped the intellectual content of the conversion undergone by these heroes, and he was convinced of the truth of the novelists' key insight that oneself is never the exception to the rule of imitative desire. Girard came to a new intellectual understanding of himself through the experience of the novelists as depicted in the lives of their various protagonists. Thus, it seems that this initial conversion was vicarious. It changed Girard's self-understanding, but, as he admits, it "did not imply any change of life … [,]" and " … it entailed no demands or commitments which I perceived at the time[.]"[16]

Even if Girard's initial recognition and acknowledgment of his own relationship to desire did not change his life significantly, the discovery provoked a new interest in reading the Judeo-Christian Scriptures, particularly the Gospels.[17] This new program of reading, in turn, "prepared the way" for a deeper conversion to Christianity. His reading of the Gospels while writing *DDN* coincided with a potential health scare that moved him to a period of genuine repentance during Lent of 1959. When on Holy Wednesday his doctor gave him the news that he did not have cancer, Girard received the sacraments of penance and Eucharist. He felt that he had been "liberated … just in time … to have a real Easter experience, a death and resurrection experience."[18] The period of interior penitence followed by an experience of resurrection deepened Girard's intellectual discovery and new self-understanding into a real conversion of life, an interior conversion that he describes as "serious," "definitive," and "religious."[19]

Asked again about that experience in 2004, Girard emphasized that his "religious" conversion would not have been possible if the "intellectual" conversion had not preceded it. As Girard says, "[I]t was my work that oriented me towards Christianity and convinced me of its truth. It is not because I'm Christian that I think as I do; it is because of my research that I became Christian."[20] Girard's understanding of his own experience of conversion, then, affirms that it is possible for persons to come to an authentic conversion of life, to which the Gospels give witness, via a path of intellectual inquiry that becomes a source of a new self-understanding.

---

[14] Girard, *Evolution and Conversion*, 45.
[15] Girard and Williams, "The Anthropology of the Cross," 285–6.
[16] Ibid., 285–6.
[17] Ibid., 284.
[18] Ibid., 286.
[19] Ibid., 285–6.
[20] Girard, *Evolution and Conversion*, 44–5.

2.2 *Deceit, Desire and the Novel* (1961): Girard's Discovery of Conversion as Freedom from (Rivalrous) Desire

This sketch of the circumstances surrounding Girard's own experiences of conversion provides the context of the origin and development of Girard's first book. In his preparations to teach a literature course, Girard recognized that the plot of Dostoyevsky's *Eternal Husband* was essentially the same as that of a short story in Cervantes' *Don Quixote*, which, in turn, had significant similarities to the plots of the novels of Flaubert, Stendhal, and Proust.[21] The line of reflection begun by this insight led Girard to believe that the same basic movement and intention underlie the works of these five modern novelists. As we have just seen, Girard asserts that these novelists are, through the medium of their art, attempting to reveal the imitative, or triangular, operation of desire that they observe in various realms of social and family life and that they come to see as operating no less fully in themselves. This triangular operation of desire, as the novelists depict it, always leads to illusion, rivalry, and, in its most vicious forms, death.[22] The similarity in the fundamental aim of these novels is demonstrated most clearly by the underlying constancy of their conclusions. The hero undergoes a conversion in which he is finally freed from his entanglement in a system of triangular desire because he repudiates the "mediator(s)" of his desires.[23] According to Girard, the consistent presence and common pattern of these conversions demonstrate that the writing of these novels results from, and is the culmination of, a similar spiritual or existential journey undertaken by each of the novelists. The authors came to recognize fully the workings of imitative desire in themselves through their efforts to reveal this operation of desire in the novels they created. The very process of attempting to depict this triangular operation of desire through the writing of their novels became an essential component of each novelist's journeys toward insight and conversion.

In his interview with James Williams, Girard vividly describes the novelists' experience of their writing as leading to a real, interior conversion. He says,

> I think this has been the case with a number of great writers. Their first conception of their novels was very different from what it became ultimately. The author's first draft is an attempt at self-justification, which can assume two main forms. It may focus on a wicked hero, who is really the writer's scapegoat, his mimetic rival, whose wickedness will be demonstrated by the end of the novel. It may also focus on a "good" hero, a knight in shining armor, with whom the writer identifies, and this hero will be vindicated by the end of the novel. If the writer has a potential for greatness, after writing his first draft, as he rereads it, he sees the trashiness of it all. His project fails. The self-justification the novelist had intended in his distinction between good and evil will not stand self-examination. The novelist comes to

---

[21] Ibid., 25; *DDN*, 49–51.
[22] Girard, *DDN*, 3.
[23] I will use masculine pronouns throughout this chapter when referring to the heroes of the various novels because almost all of them are in fact male figures with the exception of Emma Bovary in Flaubert's *Madame Bovary*.

realize that he has been the puppet of his own devil.... *The novelist of genius thus becomes able to describe the wickedness of the other from within himself*....This experience is shattering to the vanity and pride of the writer. It is an existential downfall. Very often this downfall is written symbolically, as illness or death, in the conclusion. In the case of Proust and Dostoyevsky it is explicitly presented as a change of outlook. Or to take Don Quixote, on his deathbed he sees finally his own mimetic madness, which is also illness and death. And this existential downfall is the event that makes a great work of art possible.[24]

Girard's study of these novelists, combined with the experience of conversion that this study gradually effects in himself, leads Girard to conclude that the process of writing is part of a process of an interior conversion for any "novelist of genius."

Girard uses the term "novelistic" to designate works of literature that are created out of this "genius" and that, as a result, are able to disclose the pervasiveness of the imitative operation of desire.[25] He opposes to it the term "romantic," which he uses to describe works that "reflect" (i.e., operate according to) the workings of imitative desire without containing the personally experienced insight that makes it possible to disclose those workings. In treating the works of five "novelistic" novelists, Girard attempts to show that, beneath their differences in literary strategy, the levels of society they depict, and the character traits they develop, the authors are driven by the common aim to reveal the pervasiveness of triangular desire and its inevitable movement toward emptiness and death. Their ability to do this is the direct fruit of the "existential downfall" and conversion that they experience when they recognize that their discovery of the vanity of others requires an honest appraisal and recognition of their own vanity and its resulting "wickedness."

2.2.1 "Triangular Desire"

Girard begins *DDN* by describing "triangular" (i.e., "imitative" or "mediated") desire as an intersubjective system. Of triangular desire, Girard writes, "[Its] real structures are intersubjective. They cannot be localized anywhere; the triangle has no reality whatever; it is a systematic metaphor, systematically pursued."[26] Girard then describes what he is doing in this book in relation to the novelists' pursuit of this systematic metaphor by saying, "A basic contention of this essay is that the great writers apprehend intuitively and concretely, through the medium of their art, if not formally, the *system* in which they were first imprisoned together with their contemporaries. Literary interpretation...should formalize implicit or already half-explicit systems."[27] Thus, for Girard, triangular desire is a system or network that operates intersubjectively. By employing the triangle as a metaphor (one not explicitly present in the novels) to illustrate how this system of desire operates, Girard sees himself as giving an explicit,

---

[24] Girard and Williams, "The Anthropology of the Cross," 284; emphasis added.
[25] Girard, *DDN*, 16–17.
[26] Ibid., 2.
[27] Ibid., 3; emphasis added.

expository description of that which the novelists are attempting to reveal systematically (i.e., thoroughly and persistently) by various literary methods. The metaphor is "systematic," according to Girard, because it adequately represents the results of the novelists' thorough pursuit. All the forms or modes of desire that the novelists pursue in their novels can be represented by means of the metaphor of the triangle.

Girard sees a triangle as an apt metaphor because its three vertices can be used to illustrate the three "points" in the operation of desire as the novelists understand it: the mediator or model, the desiring subject or imitator, and the desired object. The novelists have come to recognize that desire, as it is constitutive of the identity of the subject, is always generated and always operates through the influence of a mediator/model. The mediator/model actively or passively attracts the attention of various others (the desiring subjects) and suggests to them what is worth desiring. Girard acknowledges that the "source" of desire (by which he seems to mean the potential capacity for desiring) is within the subject, but this "spring" of desiring opens up only when it is struck by the mediator.[28]

Girard further depicts his understanding of triangular desire by contrasting it with the commonly held, but false, perception of "linear" or "spontaneous" desire. Most works of fiction, according to Girard, are "romantic" in that they cling to the illusion that each person's desire is individual and unique. They portray characters whose desire is "simpler" in that there is no mediator; desire arises spontaneously within the subject and moves linearly toward the object that the subject desires.[29] The great novelists have been disabused of this illusion not only in their perceptions of the desires of others, but eventually in their recognition that not even their own desires are spontaneous, original, or linear.

Within the realm of mediated or triangular desire, Girard distinguishes between two forms of mediation. External mediation occurs when the "distance" between the subject and the mediator is sufficiently great so as to prevent any contact between their "spheres of possibilities."[30] By "possibilities," Girard means possibilities for attaining their desired objects and the identities that those objects represent. With external mediation, it is not possible for the subject and the mediator to enter into rivalry with one another because the subject and the mediator do not desire the exact same particular objects or identities. The subject chooses to desire particular objects that resemble the objects desired by the mediator in some significant way, but he does not choose to desire the exact same object or position as the mediator because of geographical, social, or

---

[28] Girard, *DDN*, 33. Here Girard actually says that the source of the transfiguration of the object is within us. But, it is the transfiguration of the object into something desirable by the apparent desire of the mediator that ignites the desire of the subject.

[29] Girard, *DDN*, 2. According to Girard, it is primarily Cervantes and Stendhal (and to a lesser extent Flaubert) who employ this method of contrasting depictions of triangular desire with depictions of linear desire, but they employ it in inverted ways. Cervantes depicts the crowd as desiring spontaneously (and thus this "form" of desire *appears* to be the norm) and he depicts the hero, Don Quixote, as desiring triangularly (which thus *appears* to be the exception). Cervantes's intention, however, is to bring the reader, primarily through the hero's conversion, to see that everyone actually desires triangularly. Stendhal inverts this approach by depicting triangular desire as the norm and spontaneous desire as the exception. Yet, his intention is the same. See *DDN*, 139–42.

[30] Girard, *DDN*, 9.

psychological barriers that prevent the subject from doing so. The mediation between Don Quixote and his imaginary hero, Amadis, is real but external. Don Quixote does choose the objects to desire based on what he imagines Amadis would desire, but he does not imagine that he and Amadis are actively trying to acquire the same objects or that he must eventually conquer Amadis to become chivalrous himself.

Accordingly, internal mediation occurs when the subject and the mediator are sufficiently "close" to each other that their respective spheres of possible identities intersect more or less extensively. As it is depicted in the novels, internal mediation inevitably leads to some degree of rivalry between the subject and the mediator, because the subject perceives the maintenance or realization of his own identity, or the acquisition of a particular object, as in conflict with that of the mediator. "Metaphysical desire" in *DDN* refers to this rivalrous mode of internal mediation, and it indicates the source of the rivalry that arises from this mediation. Internally mediated desire is "metaphysical" for Girard in that it is ultimately a desire to *become* the mediator. It is a desire to possess the mediator's *being*, which the subject perceives to be more substantial and self-sustaining than his own.[31]

This desire to possess the being of the other arises out of a basic intolerance of one's experience of one's own desire. The subject experiences his own desire as indicating a fundamental lack of being within himself. The subject's intolerance of this perceived lack leads him to misperceive particular others as lacking desire and, therefore, as possessing a more substantive form of being than he possesses. This perception of a particular other, who is able to portray himself as fully satisfied within himself, makes him a model for the subject. In the eyes of the subject, the model transfigures any object associated with himself into something that the subject believes to be able to convey the being of the model.

Within the novels that Girard has been studying and, thus, within Girard's own conception of desire at this point in his career, all internally mediated desire is *de facto* metaphysical and rivalrous. Every mediator/model with a sphere of possible identities that overlaps with that of his imitator's is inevitably perceived as a rival. In the world of the novel, the subject desires the "being" of his rival—that is, the sense of autonomy and self-sufficiency that his rival *appears* to possess by appearing to securely possess all the objects and identities he wants and, therefore, to lack desire altogether.

The perception of the other as a rival is a two-way street. Girard uses the phrase "double" or "reciprocal mediation" to highlight the contagious and pervasive character of internally mediated desire, which moves back and forth between the subject and mediator and acts as "a veritable generator of desire."[32] The subject's perception of the mediator as a rival often induces the mediator to perceive the subject as a rival in turn. Each one acts as a mediator/model for the other, but each denies the influence of the other on herself. This denial of the subject's own desire for the being of the other

---

[31] Ibid., 53–5. Girard does not mean "being" in the technical sense of classical metaphysics. Rather, he uses it to describe the psychological illusion of autonomy or self-sufficiency that each individual wishes he possessed and which the subject's experience of desire for belonging and recognition suggests to be lacking.

[32] Girard, *DDN*, 173.

(which Girard refers to as "dissimulation"), along with her very inclination toward desiring the other's being, arises out of the subject's basic intolerance of her own lack of self-sufficiency.[33] Each subject/mediator must deny her own desire so as to project an illusion of self-sufficiency. An admission of desire would reveal the subject's lack of self-sufficiency and validate her misperception of the mediator as possessing a more substantial and autonomous being than herself. If either subject/mediator reveals her desire, the "generator" breaks down, and a new mediator is necessary to keep desire alive. Thus, both subjects actively hide their desire to keep the generator running because each one sees this reciprocally mediating relationship as the source of her identity as she experiences it.

With both subjects/models hiding their imitation of the other, each subject has to try harder to appear to be satisfied and without desire. Thus, as the mediating relationship continues, the degree of dissimulation enacted by each subject gradually increases as the subject renounces more and more of his desires to imitate the other. That is, he prevents himself from attempting to satisfy those desires. Eventually, both subjects/models progress toward an attempt to renounce all desires to imitate the other. This extreme renunciation is the subject's self-deluded attempt to convince himself that he alone has moved beyond desire. Yet, even renunciation of desire does not free the subject from desire as he hopes it will, for his identity is still determined by the system of desire over and against which he now rigorously and relentlessly attempts to maintain himself, and without which he would feel that he lacked an identity. When the subject appears to have renounced all desires, his desire for complete renunciation of desire is still mediated to him either by a group of lowly and reverent disciples or by a model who is equally intent on renouncing all desires for the being of the other.[34]

Thus, at this early point in Girard's development, he views desire as a system that operates intersubjectively. Desire constitutes the essence of the subject's identity because identity is formed within and by this system of desire. More importantly, desire, in Girard's treatment of it in *DDN*, is always rivalrous because, in the subject's mind, it indicates a fundamental lack of being that he or she ought to possess but does not. Through this lens, then, the subject is (mis)guided by various models into desiring the apparent being of others. In this context, Girard is concerned only with depicting the dynamics of metaphysical desire.

2.2.2 The Desiring Subject and the Selves of Desire

To follow the novelists' and Girard's depictions of desire, one must recognize that desire is an intersubjective network. This means that each subject is always already in

---

[33] Ibid., 107.

[34] Girard sees this extreme renunciation of desire most clearly in the character of Stavrogin in Dostoyevsky's *The Possessed*. He describes Stavrogin as no longer having a mediator himself, yet his identity is derived from the desire of others that he attracts to himself. Girard writes, "Stavrogin is beyond desire. It is not clear whether he no longer desires because Others desire him or whether Others desire him because he no longer desires. Thus is formed a vicious circle from which Stavrogin cannot escape. No longer having a mediator himself, he becomes the magnetic pole of desire and hatred" (*DDN*, 162–3).

the act of desiring. It is not as if a subject comes into existence and then begins to be formed by the patterns of desire of various models that influence him or her. Rather, it is the reception and imitation of the desiring of others that engender a sense of a self in the subject; it makes subjective awareness possible.

In Girard's view, the subject consists primarily of the capacity to receive and imitate the (metaphysical) desires of those who have become his or her models, and then to acquire the (rivalrous) identity resulting from the desires received and imitated.[35] Therefore, it is the activity of desiring that makes the subject a subject. Participation in the system of desire effects subjectivity. Desire is the connectivity that relates subjects to each other and thereby makes them subjects. Through participation in the intersubjective network of desiring, subjects become conscious of themselves and others. Because this constitution of the subject takes place within a system of desire that is at least partially rivalrous, the subject also receives a capacity and an inclination to hide from herself her own basic structure as a receiver and an imitator of the desires of others. That is, the subject learns from the beginning to deceive herself and others about the kind of creature she is; therefore, her own original self-understanding is always, at least in part, a self-deception.

A "self," which can be understood as interchangeable with "identity," is for Girard (in agreement with Proust) the world of possibilities projected by or generated within the subject's relationship with a particular mediator or group of mediators.[36] That is, the subject's various "selves" together represent the horizon of possible identities that the subject is able to imagine for himself. These selves are received by the subject through his imitation of his various mediators. With each change in mediator, the subject's world of possibilities changes accordingly and, thus, "a new self replaces the old."[37] Yet, this replacement of the self (i.e., the subject's horizon of possibilities) does not constitute a replacement of the desiring subject, who is continually choosing more or less consciously and freely to desire according to the desires of this or that mediator. The "desiring subject" indicates the individual (which Girard, along with Jean-Michel Oughourlian, later comes to describe as "interdividual") who is constituted within the system of desire and has a fundamental capacity to imitate the desires of others, whereas "selves" indicate the horizon of possible identities received by the subject as the result of his imitation of his various mediators.

Proust's and Dostoyevsky's literary strategies are particularly helpful for illustrating this relationship between the desiring subject and the various selves it acquires because both depict heroes who are continually reshaped, or "re-selved," in the changing winds of the desires of their mediators.[38] The other novelists depict protagonists with relatively constant identities received through the protagonist's imitation of a single mediator.[39]

---

[35] Telling instances in which Girard uses the phrase "the desiring subject" are found at *DDN*, 8, 35, 73, 164. They demonstrate his understanding of desire "preceding" subjectivity.
[36] Girard, *DDN*, 90.
[37] Ibid., 237.
[38] Ibid., 238.
[39] Ibid., 236. Speaking of Stendhal and Flaubert, Girard writes, "[they] never really needed the future or the past, since their characters were as yet neither divided within themselves nor split into several successive selves."

These novelists use other means to show their readers the imitative operation of the protagonists' desires and to draw the readers into seeing the same degree of imitation within their own desiring.[40] But Proust and Dostoyevsky attempt to lead their readers to a similar recognition by developing characters who become fragmented into a series of completely isolated selves as they continually shift from one mediator to another.[41] Girard remarks that Dostoyevsky takes this method to an extreme by depicting characters who change mediators so rapidly that

> [W]e can no longer even speak of distinct Selves. The periods of relative stability, separated by violent crises or intervals of spiritual emptiness, which we have seen in Proust, are supplanted in Dostoyevsky by a perpetual crisis.... In fact the man from the underground is often torn between several simultaneous mediations.[42]

In Proust, the series of "successive about-faces" between the various distinct selves is hidden from the subject by the duration of each self and the gradual transitions between them.[43] The subject believes himself to be consistent in pursuing what he believes to be his own desires. He fails to perceive the imitative structure of his own desiring and his continuous "choosing" of various mediators. In fact, he "protects" himself from perceiving this truth about himself through a series of increasingly absurd lies. The subject lies to protect the illusion of the "autonomous self" as true of himself no matter how clearly he comes to see it as untrue for others. For Girard, Dostoyevsky represents the height of novelistic genius because, beginning with *Notes from the Underground* and ascending to the "peace and serenity of *The Brothers Karamazov*," he depicts a range of characters who are in the painful process of coming to see through their own intricate system of lies and self-deceptions.[44]

Dostoyevsky also shows his readers that, before beginning to see through the illusion of autonomy, the subject clings to it more and more desperately with increasingly elaborate lies, even to the point of desiring death as the only remaining means of affirming the "originality" and "spontaneity" of his own desire. Thus, Girard writes,

---

[40] Girard devotes two chapters of the book to an investigation of the various methods of the novelists (chapters 6 and 10). As I have described above, Cervantes and Stendhal employ inverted forms of a method of contrast. Flaubert uses this method of contrast to a much lesser degree and instead uses "a style of false enumerations and false antitheses" which confront each other in "impassive juxtapositions" that reveal the emptiness of the oppositions (*DDN*, 150–1).

[41] Proust provides an inventory of the "successive about-faces" of the characters (to which the characters themselves are blind) in order to reveal the truth about their desires (*DDN*, 236–8). And, "Dostoyevsky's method is to bring about confrontations which exhaust all possible relationships between the different characters in the novel.... No one scene can reveal the whole truth about a character" (*DDN*, 245). Dostoyevsky intends the reader to recollect and compare these scenes in order to perceive the inconsistency of the characters' desires and, thus, of their distinct "selves" (*DDN*, 91).

[42] Girard, *DDN*, 91–2. "Underground" is Dostoyevsky's term for the world of consciousnesses formed in rivalrous desire. It is taken from his short novel translated as *Notes from the Underground* (1864). Girard uses this term to indicate the world explicitly explored by the whole of novelistic literature. He writes, "It is the 'underground' forms of the struggle of consciousnesses which are studied by the modern novelists" (*DDN*, 111).

[43] Girard, *DDN*, 236–7.

[44] Ibid., 260.

"[t]he affirmation of the self [that is, the affirmation of the 'autonomous self'] ends in the negation of the self."[45] Here, Girard uses the term "self" to indicate the illusion of autonomy. It is the "self" that the subject, formed in rivalrous desire, wishes that it was, which prevents the subject from perceiving the various "selves" that it actually has been, is, or could choose to be. This "autonomous self" is a false self because it does not represent a world of real possibilities for the subject. Instead, it purports to offer the subject that which the subject can never be—the autonomous source of its own spontaneous desires.

2.2.3 Conversion as Freedom from Rivalrous Desire

The world depicted and explored by these novelists and, in turn, by Girard, is the world of the "underground," or the world of consciousnesses formed in rivalry. Girard recognizes that this underground does not represent the totality of the modern world, but he also sees it as "the [region] of [modern] existence where spiritual energy has taken refuge."[46] With the exception of those novelists (primarily Cervantes) who give some attention to external mediation—that is, mediation in which there is no intersection between the possible identities of the subject and those of the mediator—authors of novelistic literature depict a world in which internally mediated desire is de facto always rivalrous.[47] As rivalrous, it necessarily gravitates toward self-destruction and death.

Girard sees Dostoyevsky's character of Stavrogin as a theoretical case depicting the "successful" fulfillment of metaphysical, or rivalrous, desire. This so-called "success" entails renouncing (i.e., actively denying the satisfaction of) all desires for easily attainable objects and identities, and renouncing them more stringently than anyone else within one's sphere of mediation, such that the subject's identity consists in making disciples or slaves out of all persons while *appearing* to be lacking any mediator himself. The continual subjugation of more and more persons as one's disciples never results in the satisfaction of the desire of "the master." This process of subjugation continues until the master eventually encounters a formidable obstacle— either a person capable of resisting his coercion or a lack of persons who have not already been subjugated to him. Both bring desire to an impasse. In either case, such an obstacle presents only two possible paths forward for the master: self-destruction (most fully enacted through suicide) or conversion. The first is a definitive enactment of the subject's secret belief that his internally experienced—though consciously hidden from himself and others—lack of self-sufficiency indicates an essential emptiness or lack of substantive existence. For the subject who cannot come to see the falsity of this belief and whose experience of desire can no longer be extended through the winning of more disciples, self-destruction appears to be the only viable path forward.

---

[45] Ibid., 287.
[46] Ibid., 111.
[47] Girard writes, "In the universe of internal mediation—at least in its upper regions—force has lost its prestige. The elementary rights of individuals are respected but if one is not strong enough to live in freedom one succumbs to the evil spell of vain rivalry" (*DDN*, 112). Internally mediated desire is an enslaving spiritual force, even if it lacks physical or legal instruments.

Yet, the novelists and Girard have discovered another path, namely, conversion. Girard writes, although "[t]he ultimate meaning of [metaphysical] desire is death[,]...death is not the novel's ultimate meaning."[48] Instead, the ultimate meaning of the novel is conversion.[49] But arriving at this meaning is difficult. The path of conversion is not directly within the power of the subject's choosing because conversion is not within the world of possibilities that the subject is able to conceive for herself if she understands herself through the imitation of exclusively rivalrous desires. The subject cannot conceive of conversion as a real possibility or a viable path, even if she is capable of seeing that her continual pursuit of metaphysical desires necessarily leads to a dead end. The words of the character Stepan as he finally finds himself undergoing conversion in Dostoyevsky's *The Possessed* convey this inability. Stepan says, "I've been telling lies all my life. Even when I told the truth I never spoke for the sake of the truth, but always for my own sake. *I knew it before, but I only see it now.*"[50] Before his conversion, Stepan knew that his whole life consisted of a series of lies, but in the midst of those lies, he could not see any alternative to lying for the sake of continuing his pursuit of desire. Only in the moment of his conversion when he conceives of the possibility of an identity outside of his pursuit of rivalrous desire does he see the possibility of putting an end to his lying.

Because, following the novelists, Girard has identified all internally mediated desire with metaphysical, or rivalrous, desire, conversion ultimately brings about the subject's *freedom from* desire. Above, or outside of, desire there is peace, tranquility, and aesthetic happiness, which Girard describes as "the delight of creation which wins out over desire and anguish."[51] Only outside of the subject's mimetic pursuit of the desire to possess identities that directly conflict with the identities of others can the subject know peace, happiness, and delight. The subject has no way of revealing this path to him or herself. This insight about the path leading to peace, like the subject's pursuit of an unattainable sense of autonomy, can be learned or received only through imitation.

Freedom from rivalrous desire begins as the subject, through some unexpected form of mediation; gains deeper and clearer insight into the rivalrous operation of her desires; and sees for the first time the non-necessity of this kind of imitation. While the subject may have previously had some awareness of this rivalry-producing dynamic within herself, conversion leads the subject to see for the first time the possibility of renouncing all rivalrous desires and repudiating all rivalrous mediators. The subject acquires a capacity to openly acknowledge the imitative structure of her rivalrous desires, which leads to the possibility of setting those desires aside.

Thus, conversion occurs if the subject chooses to renounce all of his or her rivalrous desires. This "absolute renunciation" is distinct from the renunciation depicted in the character of Stavrogin.[52] Girard's description of the effects of conversion is telling in this regard: "Every level of [the hero's] existence is inverted, all the effects

---

[48] Girard, *DDN*, 290.
[49] Ibid., 294.
[50] As quoted by Girard at *DDN*, 290; emphasis added.
[51] Girard, *DDN*, 22.
[52] Ibid., 272.

of metaphysical desire are replaced by contrary effects. Deception gives way to truth, anguish to remembrance, agitation to repose, hatred to love, humiliation to humility, *mediated* [i.e., rivalrous] *desire to autonomy.*"[53] Girard sees Stavrogin's renunciation of only those rivalrous desires that the subject has the capacity to satisfy as a hypothetical depiction of what "successful" metaphysical desire would look like. It is a renunciation aimed at keeping one's rivalrous desire alive by not allowing the subject to experience the disappointment that comes when he or she finds desire left unsatisfied by the acquisition of particular objects or positions of his or her various mediators. This renunciation does not effect freedom from rivalrous mediation. It is an attempt to conquer all rivals through an extremely rigorous effort at appearing indifferent to them and their desires. Such a renunciation and the identity that it provides the subject are formed *within* the system of rivalrous desire.

Conversion, in contrast, involves a relinquishing, rather than renouncing, of all desires to possess identities formed in rivalry. Conversion is a relinquishing of these desires made possible by an empowering discovery of *both* the "dead end" of rivalrous desire *and* an alternative to rivalry. This alternative is the possibility of acquiring through remembrance an accurate perception of oneself as an imitator and the subsequent capacity to consciously choose mediators who operate outside of the system of rivalrous desire.

2.2.4 The Process of Conversion—From the Illusion of Absolute Autonomy to the Discovery of Relative Freedom

The subject's freedom from rivalrous desire, which results from his relinquishing all rivalrous mediators, illuminates the subject's past.[54] As Girard says, "the absence of desire in the present makes it possible to recapture past desires."[55] Because the subject is no longer caught in the pursuit of the "being" of others, he is now able to look back over the past and perceive the imitative structure of his desires from the beginning, as well as the rivalry preceding and arising from the hiding of this imitation from himself and others. Girard employs Proust's depiction of *The Past Recaptured* to describe the remembrance that begins to take place as a result of conversion. The recaptured past is "a veritable river of *living memory*, a veritable resurrection of truth ... a rediscovery of 'time.'"[56] In recapturing the past, the subject recovers the process by which he had been deceived into perceiving himself as the source of his own desires:

> [To recapture the past] is to understand that the process of mediation creates a very vivid impression of autonomy and spontaneity precisely when we are no longer autonomous and spontaneous ... [it is] to recognize that one has always copied Others in order to seem original in their eyes and in one's own.[57]

---

[53] Ibid., 294; emphasis added.
[54] Girard, *DDN*, 297.
[55] Ibid., 298.
[56] Ibid., 37; Girard's emphasis.
[57] Girard, *DDN*, 38.

In recapturing the past, the subject is able to see clearly and distinguish the various, often conflicting selves he has received and tried to become over the course of his life.

By stringing together these various past selves, which the subject has tried to become but which have been hidden from her own view by her false perception of herself as "autonomous," the subject comes to a deeper and truer recognition of her relationship to desire. The subject comes to recognize that she is not and can never be the "autonomous self" that she had previously wished herself to be. She sees that she is not an original and spontaneous source of her own desires, but rather a constant imitator "on [her] knees before the mediator."[58] The subject comes to perceive and acknowledge the truth of her own imitating nature and thereby relinquishes her belief in an autonomous self.[59] In relinquishing the belief in a false sense of her autonomy—understood as a self who is the source of its own spontaneous and original desires—the subject paradoxically finds herself acquiring a true form of autonomy as she comes to discover her capacity to choose not to imitate rivalrous mediators and metaphysical forms of desire.

Although Girard does not say much about this paradox, I would suggest that we could understand it as a paradox of the illusion of absolute autonomy versus the discovery of relative freedom. The discovery and the stringing together of the various past selves lead the subject to acknowledge and accept the imitative structure of his own desire, which, in turn, allows the subject to unite and integrate, or to "re-member," those past selves into a single narrative history that represents who the subject has actually been. This re-collection and re-membering of the past have a profound effect on the subject's present and his future; it is, as Girard says, a *living* memory. In recognizing the coherence and continuity of his past, which have persisted despite his deepest fear that he had no substance at all, the subject can let go of his pursuit of an autonomous self and, instead, make choices in the present and for the future about who will serve as his models, and thus about who he will become. That is, the subject is now able to live in the worlds of possibilities that are actually presented to him by the various people who can act and have acted as his models. This is an acceptance of the relative freedom that is actually possible for human beings who are, by their very nature, imitators. Previously, the subject was bound by striving to live in a world of impossibilities that he believed to be possible and that were constructed by his fear-driven and imitated desire for complete independence and autonomy of desire. This attempt to acquire an absolute autonomy is simply not possible for human beings, who are, in fact, imitators.

In *DDN*, however, Girard does not elaborate upon this subject who has fully acknowledged him or herself as an imitator and who therefore becomes free to operate outside of the rivalrous forms of imitative desire. While the novelists (and, as a result, the heroes of their novels) are able to attain this authentic and relative freedom, they depict it only as a peace and a tranquility inevitably experienced as the absence of the only form of desire they had ever known previously, namely, metaphysical, or rivalrous,

---

[58] Ibid., 298.
[59] Ibid., 38.

desire. Here Girard does not explicitly identify this freedom from rivalrous desire as itself a form of non-rivalrous desire. Instead, he describes it only as a freedom from desire in accordance with the novelists' depiction of the conversions of their heroes.

Also like the novelists, Girard does not give much consideration to what might nudge the subject down a path of conversion rather than a path of self-destruction. Such a consideration would require a depiction of the subject, desire, and freedom as they might operate outside of rivalry. At the end of this chapter, however, we will see that, later in his career, his attention to the New Testament and its portrayal of Jesus will allow him to imagine more fully what desire looks like outside of rivalry, as well as how the subject might be led toward the process of conversion.

2.3 *Things Hidden since the Foundation of the World* (1978): Identifying the Contexts of the Modern Form of Desire

In *Things Hidden*, published sixteen years after the publication of the original French edition of *DDN*, Girard attempts, in part, to more clearly connect the subject of his first book, the triangular and rivalrous operation of desire as depicted by his select group of modern novelists, and that of his second book, *Violence and the Sacred* (1972), which presents his thesis concerning the intrinsic relationship between the "victimage mechanism" and the origin of religion and culture.[60] The reviews of *Violence and the Sacred* revealed to Girard that he had not yet made the connection sufficiently clear. In *Things Hidden*, Girard attempts to remedy this by providing what he sees as the missing link between the two, namely, a reading of the Judeo-Christian Scriptures that makes explicit their capacity to unveil the rivalrous operation of desire and its generation of the social mechanism of victimization.

The text itself is set up as a trialogue among Girard and two French psychiatrists, Jean-Michel Oughourlian and Guy Lefort, who are interested in the relevance of Girard's "mimetic theory" for their work. It is not the transcript of an actual series of conversations; rather, it is the fruit of their joint effort to complete, organize, and divide into questions and answers a manuscript that Girard himself had drafted after finishing the manuscript of *Violence and the Sacred*.[61]

The primary value of *Things Hidden* for the present investigation into the development of Girard's thinking about desire, conversion, and the self is that, in it, Girard contextualizes his understanding of mimetic, or triangular, desire within a more fully articulated cultural anthropology and he presents his hypothesis about how the modern world and its unique form of (metaphysical) desire have developed from earlier forms of human culture, which, in turn, developed from animal society.

---

[60] Girard says that *Things Hidden* is simply a continuation of the project begun in *Violence and the Sacred*, which was originally supposed to include a whole second part on Christianity, but which was shortened due to the amount of time it was taking to complete the book. Thus, Girard sees *Things Hidden* as the completion of his elaboration of a single and unified theory of rivalrous triangular desire maintaining a social mechanism of victimization (*Evolution and Conversion*, 38–9).

[61] Girard, *Evolution and Conversion*, 39–40.

The key for grasping both the continuity and the distinctness in these different forms of society/culture and instinct/desire is attention to the operation and effects of "acquisitive mimesis."

Although my presentation below of a schematic of Girard's understanding of the process of hominization and the historical development of mimetic desire into its modern form oversimplifies Girard's actual account in *Things Hidden*, it helps as an interpretive hypothesis for distinguishing among four sub-meanings of mimesis as Girard understands them.[62] Systematizing Girard's understanding of these four categories more clearly depicts how Girard's articulation of desire and conversion develops over his career. Each term or meaning within this schematic represents a further degree of specialization that operates within the preceding one without terminating or replacing it. Girard refers to the broadest degree of specialization simply as (1) "mimesis," which indicates imitation as the fundamental mechanism of all learning, socialization, and social cohesion in animal and human groups/societies. Girard associates this broadest meaning of the term with primarily positive developmental effects. Within this relatively positive meaning, Girard identifies (2) "acquisitive mimesis" as the imitation of behaviors aimed at acquiring material objects for the satisfaction of basic needs and appetites (most prominently, alimentary and sexual ones).[63] According to Girard, acquisitive mimesis, although it is not inherently conflictual, is the source of all rivalry and conflict in animal and human societies. (3) "Mimetic desire" represents a specifically human form of acquisitive mimesis directed primarily toward, not material objects, but symbolic objects that provide or maintain the identities of particular individuals and groups (as we saw in considering Girard's first book). As the human capacity for symbolization increases, these desires and identities become more complex. In Girard's view, both acquisitive mimesis and mimetic desire have operated in a conflictual or rivalrous mode from their origins. His account of the process of hominization and the subsequent development of human culture depends upon this assertion. Finally, Girard identifies (4) "metaphysical desire" as the particular form of the rivalrous operation of mimetic desire peculiar to modernity. He sees the Judeo-Christian Scriptures as playing an essential role in the development of this modern form of rivalrous desire, precisely in and through its disclosure of the "mimetic cycle."

For the present study, I will not be arguing in favor of the validity of Girard's claims regarding human history and culture; rather, I aim to elaborate Girard's view of human history so as to make explicit his understanding of these four key categories at this point in his career. Furthermore, I am primarily interested in his view of the historical development from (2) acquisitive mimesis to (3) mimetic

---

[62] I welcome other hypotheses for systematizing the key terms of mimetic theory as well. I believe that a lack of clarity and consistency in how Girard and Girardians define key terms contributes to lack of further engagement by many Christian theologians. The schematic that I offer in this chapter is in part an effort to overcome these inconsistencies.

[63] Suzanne Ross has helpfully expanded upon Girard's description of acquisitive mimesis for the satisfaction of alimentary and sexual appetites by exploring how acquisitive mimesis also shapes the domains of childhood learning and socialization. See Suzanne Ross, "The Montessori Method: The Development of a Healthy Pattern of Desire in Early Childhood," *Contagion: Journal of Violence, Mimesis, and Culture* 19 (2012): 87–122.

desire, which Girard refers to as the process of hominization, and from (3) mimetic desire to (4) metaphysical desire, which Girard believes to be largely the result of Judeo-Christian revelation in human history. Girard's view of these two phases of human history is fundamental for understanding the relationships that Girard sees among desire, the subject, and conversion. Thus, after briefly articulating Girard's distinction between (1) mimesis and (2) acquisitive mimesis, I will summarize and clarify his account of the development of (3) mimetic desire from (2) acquisitive mimesis and the development of (4) metaphysical desire from (3) mimetic desire. I will conclude by showing what his anthropological and historical account of the rise of metaphysical desire adds to his understanding of the process of conversion that I have just elaborated above through a treatment of *DDN*, as well as what Girard leaves unconsidered with regard to the process of conversion.

2.3.1 Imitating Acquisition

Girard begins to locate mimetic desire within the broader domain of animal and human activity (all of which is mimetic for Girard), at the outset of the discussion in *Things Hidden*, where he asserts that virtually all human and animal behavior is learned and that all learning happens through imitation.[64] Human beings and human culture as a whole are formed in and through imitation. Girard sees human imitation, or mimesis, understood most broadly, as playing a fundamental, formative role in being human. Mimesis is the necessary social and anthropological condition for the possibility of human intelligence and subjectivity, and it is the force that effects cultural integration.[65] Thus, for Girard, constructing an adequately scientific understanding of the human person (i.e., an anthropology) requires comparing human imitation with animal imitation and then, based on that comparison, identifying the specifically human modes of imitative behavior.[66]

It seems that, in Girard's analysis, carrying out such a comparison reveals that the theories of human imitation in the West starting with Plato have systematically overlooked the fundamental type of imitation—one that human beings have in common with animals, though we exercise it in a distinct way.[67] That is, we imitate each other's efforts to acquire the objects that we need or desire. According to Girard, this "acquisitive mimesis" provides the key for understanding both the basic similarity and the essential difference between animal and human societies because acquisitive mimesis, as well as the rivalrous effects it produces, initiates the evolution from the former to the latter. Girard points to the behavior of apes in imitating each other's attempt to reach for an object, as well as their counter inclination to resist such imitation, as evidence of acquisitive mimesis in animals and of their learned efforts to

---

[64] Girard, *Things Hidden since the Foundation of the World*. Research undertaken in collaboration with Jean-Michel Oughourlian and Guy Lefort. Translated by Stephen Bann and Michael Metteer (Stanford, CA: Stanford University Press, 1987), 7.
[65] Ibid., 17.
[66] Ibid., 7.
[67] Ibid., 8.

avoid or reduce potential conflict by avoiding the imitation of acquisitive behaviors. Girard writes, "[This effort to resist acquisitive imitation] makes the animal a sort of brother to us by showing it subject to the same fundamental rule as humanity—that of preventing conflict, which the convergence of two or several avid hands toward one and the same object cannot help but provoke."[68]

Girard chooses to use the term "mimesis" rather than "imitation" to designate animal and human imitative behavior because he believes that the term "imitation" tends to connote the positive, integrative effects of imitation to the exclusion of the conflictual effects that inevitably result from the mimicking of acquisitive behaviors.[69] This reasoning reflects Girard's inclination in *Things Hidden* to identify mimesis with acquisitive mimesis. In doing so, he does not intend to deny the positive side of imitation; rather, he intends to combat modern schools of thought that reject any and all talk of imitation/mimesis because they fear that it will minimize "the importance of everything that tends toward division, alienation, and conflict."[70] Thus, in *Things Hidden*, while Girard clearly acknowledges that mimesis plays a fundamental, formative, and positive role in human and animal development, he does not give any treatment of this role. Instead, he moves on to investigate the workings and rivalrous effects of acquisitive mimesis. As a result, although he asserts a clear distinction between "mimesis" and "acquisitive mimesis" at the outset of the work, his subsequent usage of "mimesis" throughout the text generally refers to acquisitive mimesis.

In the following two sections, I will examine Girard's understanding of the role of acquisitive mimesis in animal societies, in the crisis that led to human consciousness through victimage, and in the subsequent rise of human culture. Attending to the role of acquisitive mimesis in this way will elaborate the working anthropology that underlies Girard's "mimetic theory."

2.3.2 The Formation of Human Consciousness in Rivalry

I indicated above that, according to Girard, the conflictual, or rivalrous, effects of acquisitive mimesis upon animal societies initiate and control the process of hominization. Now, I would like to summarize Girard's account of hominization and the role of acquisitive mimesis in it since this forms the fundamental component of his anthropology and is essential for understanding Girard's view of acquisitive mimesis as coextensive with, and constitutive of, human consciousness.[71]

Girard observes two opposing behaviors in animals that lead him to discern within animal societies the operation of acquisitive mimesis and the rivalrous effects it inevitably produces. First, animals always seek to acquire the nearest available objects for satisfying their needs and appetites when there are no potential rivals present. Second, they defer "this satisfaction from the nearest objects to those that are more distant and

---

[68] Ibid., 8–9.
[69] Ibid., 16–17.
[70] Ibid., 7.
[71] For a more extensive treatment of Girard's account of hominization and the origin of culture, see Palaver's *René Girard's Mimetic Theology* (East Lansing, MI: Michigan State University Press, 2013), 136–52.

apparently less accessible" when they are in the presence of potential rivals.[72] According to Girard, the only plausible explanation for this divergence of behavior based on the presence or absence of a rival is that animals have learned to fear the outbreak of interminable violence that is likely to occur when their instinctual tendency to imitate acquisitive behaviors is not kept in check. Animal societies are structured in such a way as to prevent such an outbreak through prohibitions against the acquisition of the nearest and most accessible objects (particularly alimentary and sexual objects) and through the maintenance of whatever dominance pattern is first established among the members of the group.[73] These prohibitions and dominance patterns minimize rivalry within the group by placing strict limits on acquisitive behaviors.

Although Girard clearly asserts that acquisitive mimesis and the rivalry it produces affect the structure of animal societies and their patterns for allowing their members to satisfy their needs and appetites, he does not believe that acquisitive mimesis *generates* animal needs and appetites. These needs and appetites are innate. What is generated is the rivalry resulting from the inclination to imitate the acquisitive behaviors directed toward the objects necessary for satisfying those needs and appetites. The inclination toward acquisitive mimesis also helps to shape the animal's perception of *which* objects in particular are worth pursuing. The learned fear of rivalrous violence subsequently designates some objects as off limits or less preferable.

The process of hominization eventually begins because the prohibitions and dominance patterns in animal societies are not capable of keeping acquisitive mimesis and its rivalrous effects to a certain manageable threshold. The minimal amount of rivalry among members of a particular animal society, which can never be completely eliminated, gradually increases the inclination toward imitating acquisitive behaviors, which in turn generates more rivalry and leads members of the group to violate the prohibitions and dominance patterns aimed at minimizing intragroup violence. This cycle escalates until a "mimetic crisis" ensues. The animal group somehow senses itself to be on the verge of a return to interminable violence. To prevent the return of this feared state of violence, all the members of the group come to identify a vulnerable member of their own group or an outsider as an acceptable target for their rivalrous aggression. Such a "consensus" puts an end to the crisis and reconciles the group at the expense of the victim. Thus, the threshold of rivalry beyond which animal society can no longer function "corresponds to the appearance of the victimage mechanism and would thus be the threshold of hominization."[74]

Girard sees the contrast between the mimetic frenzy leading to victimage and the tranquility that follows as the conditions that give rise to human consciousness. His description of the scene is quite rich, so I quote him at length:

> I think that even the most elementary form of the victimage mechanism, prior to the emergence of the sign, should be seen as an exceptionally powerful means of creating a new degree of attention, the first non-instinctual attention. Once it has

---

[72] Girard, *Things Hidden*, 76.
[73] Ibid., 76, 90.
[74] Ibid., 95.

reached a certain degree of frenzy, the mimetic polarization becomes fixed on a single victim. After having been released against the victim, the violence necessarily abates and silence follows mayhem. This maximal contrast between the release of violence and its cessation, between agitation and tranquility, creates the most favorable conditions possible for the emergence of this new attention. Since the victim is a common victim it will be at that instant the focal point for all members of the community. Consequently, beyond the purely instinctual object, the alimentary or sexual object or the dominant individual, there is the cadaver of the collective victim and this cadaver constitutes the first object for the new type of attention.[75]

The unexpected unity and tranquility that result from the shared violence give rise to a prolonged and shared attention focused on the cadaver of the common victim. This new form of attention marks the beginning of human consciousness and language, which emerges out of the rivalry generated by acquisitive mimesis and the temporary cessation of rivalry accomplished through the collective victimization of a member of the group.

With this account of hominization through victimage in place, Girard later asserts that, in relation to modern society's fascination with the "end times," "violence has always been inherent in [humanity]. Yet at the same time the use of violence does not rest on an irresistible instinct."[76] Girard does not state explicitly what he means by "inherent" and "irresistible," but based on his understanding of hominization and the theory of culture that follows from it (which I will explore next), he seems to be saying that, as a matter of historical contingency, violence is inherent in humanity in the sense that human consciousness, as well as human culture and desire, arose through a collective act of violence and has been shaped by that violent act from the beginning. Yet, while Girard hypothesizes that the building rivalry within animal societies did in fact lead to such an act of violence, he does not see the collective inclination toward that act as having been irresistible in the sense that no other path for preventing a return to interminable violence could have been taken, however unlikely such an alternative path might have been. Nor can one conclude based on this hypothesis that human consciousness could have developed only through some violent act and not through any alternative means. Girard also seems to be suggesting that, although human consciousness arose from violence and, as a result, has some "inherent" inclination toward violence, it is still possible for persons and communities to resist that violent inclination however compelling it may appear to be.

2.3.3 The Rise of Human Culture and Desire

Girard then hypothesizes that the new attention and capacity for language that were formed in the tranquility following the founding murder initiate a second "consensus"—a consensus to prevent any return of the mimetic crisis by minimizing the rivalry produced by acquisitive mimesis. This united effort constitutes the beginning

---

[75] Ibid., 99.
[76] Ibid., 260.

of human culture, which is essentially a more sophisticated means of minimizing violence than was possible in animal societies. The three basic mechanisms of this effort to prevent violence, which Girard identifies as the three poles of culture, are prohibition, ritual, and myth.[77]

Girard describes the role of the first two, prohibition and ritual, saying:

> To understand human culture it is necessary to concede that only the damming of mimetic forces by means of the prohibition and the diversion of these forces in the direction of ritual are capable of spreading and perpetuating the reconciliatory effect of the surrogate victim.[78]

The prohibitions in the early forms of human culture are similar to those operating in animal societies, but they are also distinct in that they seem to be more explicitly held and more ardently and widely obeyed and enforced. The rise of ritual constitutes a new technique for combating rivalry by reenacting the victimage mechanism in a predetermined and controlled manner so as to harness the conciliatory effects of the mechanism while attempting to prevent conflict from becoming too widespread.

Myth, the third aspect of culture, both veils and keeps alive the memory of the founding victimage by retelling it as a story in which the violence is enacted by some divinity, absolving the members of the group of any responsibility for that violence, while still preserving both the fear of a return of violence and the community's solemn vow to prevent such a return.[79] Together prohibition, ritual, and myth express, embody, and enact a tension within human culture, which is always attempting to prevent the possible return of uncontrolled violence by enacting lesser forms of violence, namely, the violence of enforcing prohibitions, the controlled violence of ritual, and the truth-concealing lie of myth. According to Girard, the institutionalization of these three cultural domains and the differentiation among the members of society that they bring about are "a tenacious mystification, an effacement of bloody tracks, and *an expulsion of the expulsion itself.*"[80]

This rise of human culture through a new kind of attention and through a capacity for language also correlates with the formation of mimetic desire, which in this understanding of hominization is a more sophisticated inclination toward acquiring objects than are animal instincts and appetites. The evolution from animal instincts to human desire takes place as a result of the combination of the process of symbolization, which begins with the shared recognition of the cadaver of a common victim, and the effects of mimesis on animal instincts. In Girard's words, "human desire consists of the grafting of mimesis on to instinctual patterns and the over-activation, aggravation, and disorganization of the latter."[81] Later, he clarifies that the aggravation and disorganization of instinctual patterns are identical with the symbolization that effects

---

[77] For a more extensive treatment of these three poles of human culture, see Palaver, *René Girard's Mimetic Theology*, 153–93.
[78] Girard, *Things Hidden*, 32.
[79] Ibid., 118–19.
[80] Ibid., 50; emphasis added.
[81] Ibid., 95.

human consciousness: "For there to be desire according to our definition, the effects of mimesis must interfere, not directly with animal instincts and appetites, but in a terrain that has already been fundamentally modified by the process of hominization: in other words, the mimetic effects and a wholesale reprocessing of symbols must develop in unison."[82] It seems that Girard sees the new kind of shared, prolonged attention on the dead victim as extending animal needs and appetites beyond the threshold at which the force of instinct can control them. The three poles of culture, particularly prohibitions and rituals, develop to take over where instinctual patterns no longer suffice. The gradual development of these cultural institutions corresponds to the continued effect of acquisitive mimesis upon desires that seek satisfaction from increasingly symbolic objects.

Thus, desire within the early forms of culture is much closer to animal instincts/appetites than it is to the modern form of (metaphysical) desire that Girard thematizes in *DDN* and which we will consider again in the following section. As was the case with animal needs and appetites, Girard does not see human needs and appetites as *generated* by acquisitive mimesis, but they are significantly shaped by it such that they are "aggravated" and "disorganized" into *desires* for more than the simple satisfaction of alimentary and sexual needs and appetites. For example, the human need/appetite for food is not generated by mimesis; it is a biological necessity. However, the particular objects desired, and the means by which, and the contexts in which, they are consumed become increasingly shaped by acquisitive mimesis and the cultural institutions that have developed to reduce and divert its effects. Such is the case with the modern form of desire as well, but the degree of symbolization within modern desire distinguishes it significantly from this earlier form of desire. The objects of modern desire are transfigured to such a degree that they appear to be superabundantly "real" and to possess a value far greater than the objects of the earlier form of desire appeared to possess.

I will now turn to give a summary sketch of Girard's view of the development of desire into its modern form. The Judeo-Christian Scriptures and their unveiling of the workings of mimetic rivalry leading to victimage play the most significant role in this development. As was the case with the sketch I just provided of Girard's view of the rise of human culture, the sketch that follows oversimplifies Girard's own account, but it will help us clarify Girard's understanding of his key terms.

2.3.4 The Judeo-Christian Scriptures and the Emergence of Metaphysical Desire[83]

The effects of the three basic cultural institutions in minimizing rivalry gradually diminish over time, as the fear and tranquility produced by the earlier mimetic crisis and the founding murder, respectively, fade from the collective cultural memory.

---

[82] Ibid., 283–4.
[83] Chapter 3 of Scott Cowdell's book (*René Girard and Secular Modernity*), which is entitled "Scripture and Secularization," gives a much more detailed account than I am able to provide here of Girard's understanding of the role of the Judeo-Christian Scriptures in the development of modern culture. See Cowdell, *René Girard and Secular Modernity*, 83–115.

As the weakening of the cultural institutions brings about an increase in rivalry, the movement toward crisis begins again, and, eventually, some socially acceptable form of the victimage mechanism is enacted. Each new instance of victimage produces a new period of tranquility, a deepening of attention and symbolization, and a renewal and intensification of the cultural institutions put in place to prevent another mimetic crisis. As these institutions develop through the repetition of this cycle, they effect an increasingly greater degree of symbolization of objects and a greater degree of societal differentiation, which further minimize rivalry by inserting social distance between potential rivals.[84] It appears, however, that no matter how developed the cultural institutions established to minimize rivalry become, the victimage mechanism continues to be necessary as the means for restoring a degree of unity, reconciliation, and tranquility when mimetic crises arise. The effects of acquisitive mimesis on human desires escalate as the cultural institutions develop such that these institutions are only ever partially successful in minimizing rivalry and preventing the return of a crisis; the victimage mechanism appears to be the only possible means of guaranteeing this success.

The Judeo-Christian Scriptures, according to Girard, interrupt the cycle of rivalry leading to victimage and the ongoing development of more or less violent cultural institutions intended to minimize rivalry. They do so by revealing violent victimage to be a contingent, unnecessary, and humanly enacted (and re-enacted) mechanism. The Old Testament narratives assert the wrongfulness of this victimage by clearly identifying the human culprits (rather than deities) who have enacted it: Cain is labeled as a murderer, the story of Joseph retells a founding cultural myth from the perspective of the victim,[85] and the prophetic books make explicit the underlying purpose of prohibitions, "which is the maintenance of harmonious relationships within the community."[86] The Gospels further this revelation by fully developing the theme of the *skandalon*, that is, the object-turned-obstacle that provokes rivalry and eventually leads to the violent and unnecessary crucifixion of an innocent victim.[87] They make fully visible, for the first time, the rivalrous effects of acquisitive mimesis and the victimage that has resulted from those effects in the past and that will continue to follow from them in the future if humanity remains blind to the violent cycle that it has enacted throughout history. Although the effects of this revelation have been slowed by a portion of the Christian tradition that has mistakenly misread Christian revelation through the old sacrificial lens, Christ's revelation of the human and contingent nature

---

[84] Girard, *Things Hidden*, 50.
[85] Ibid., 147, 153.
[86] Ibid., 154–5. This is obviously a highly truncated and insufficient account of Girard's understanding of the Hebrew scriptures and their impact on the development of human culture and history. For two lengthier treatments of Girard's reading of the Old Testament, which present his interpretations of the stories of Adam and Eve, Cain and Abel, Abraham and Isaac, Joseph and his brothers, the Ten Commandments, the prophets, the psalms, and the story of Job, see Wolfgang Palaver's chapter 5, entitled "Biblical Revelation and Christianity," in *René Girard's Mimetic Theology*, especially pp. 200–12 and Cowdell's *René Girard and Secular Modernity*, 84–95.
[87] Girard, *Things Hidden*, 416–31. Again, see Palaver, *René Girard's Mimetic Theology*, 212–21 and Cowdell, *René Girard and Secular Modernity*, 95–106 for a fuller account of Girard's reading of the New Testament and its impact on human culture.

of victimage has still profoundly influenced human history by gradually undermining the effectiveness of victimage as a means of temporarily resolving mimetic crises.[88]

This brief account of the role that the Judeo-Christian Scriptures play in interrupting and unveiling the cycle of victimage that has shaped human history provides an insightful description of the effects of Judeo-Christian revelation upon human history and raises certain questions that Girard does not treat, since they seem to fall outside the domain of his own intellectual curiosity. One question that is significant from a theological perspective is: How do the Judeo-Christian texts undermine the effectiveness of the victimage mechanism? For Girard it appears to be sufficient to show that these texts are continually attempting to expose the victimage mechanism as a humanly enacted violence undertaken as the apparently sole means for maintaining peace. He asserts that any attempt to respond to this revelation by passing the blame for victimage off onto some particular group of others is always based on a misreading of Scripture and only maintains the victimage mechanism by reenacting it in a slightly new variation.[89] But, how is it that the Judeo-Christian revelation of humanity's responsibility for the ongoing history of victimage slowly renders the victimage mechanism ineffective?[90] Girard does not explore this question of how in *Things Hidden*. He simply asserts that Christian revelation does have this effect, and he offers a particular "non-sacrificial reading" of the Gospel and a "sacrificial reading" of a portion of the Christian tradition that support his assertion.[91]

Yet, this question "how?" is significant for gaining an adequate understanding of Girard's assertion that the Judeo-Christian Scriptures play a role in the development of desire in its modern, metaphysical form. Desire, most properly speaking according to Girard, "is what happens to human relationships when there is no longer any resolution through the victim, and consequently no form of polarization that is genuinely unanimous and can trigger such a resolution. But human relationships are mimetic nonetheless."[92] Jean Michel Oughourlian, one of Girard's conversation partners in *Things Hidden*, notes that, according to this view, desire (in its modern form) creates an (interdividual) psychological domain in which to work out the mimetic crisis. It partially takes the place of the sociological-cultural domain in which the victimage mechanism functioned, but which has been gradually subverted by Judeo-Christian revelation:

> Given that there exists a world—our own—in which the mechanisms of culture are exposed to the slow but inexorable subversion of a Judeo-Christian element

---

[88] Girard, *Things Hidden*, 288.
[89] Ibid., 174.
[90] Another way of asking this question would be, how did Christ's revelation of humanity's responsibility for its history of violence so impact those who became witnesses of his resurrection that this revelation came to be contained within the New Testament texts? I will respond to this question directly in the next chapter when I consider James Alison's understanding of the disciples' experiences of Jesus' death and resurrection. See Chapter 3, Sections 3.2.3 and 3.2.4.
[91] Girard's non-sacrificial reading of the Gospel is the topic of Book II, chapter 2 and his sacrificial reading of historical Christianity, that of Book II, chapter 3 in *Things Hidden*.
[92] Girard, *Things Hidden*, 288.

tempered by the sacrificial interpretation, the mimetic crisis must be lived out in this modified modern version, by each individual in his relationships with others.[93]

Thus, understanding how Judeo-Christian revelation undermines the victimage mechanism is a necessary step in understanding how the undermining of this mechanism transforms desire into its modern form. Girard does not give direct attention to the connection between these two phenomena. However, it seems that he sees the disclosure of the victimage mechanism as immediately rendering it less effective as a means of bringing about cohesion among the members of a group. The exposure of the violent and contingent act undermines its previous capacity to unite individuals around a common "victim" because it reveals the group's identification of the victim to be wholly arbitrary. If members of the group begin to have increasing insight into how they have generated and maintained group cohesion through arbitrary and avoidable violence (rather than through divinely ordained violence as they had previously imagined it), then they begin to question the legitimacy of their participation in the mechanisms producing cohesion and in the group itself. It is not clear, in *Things Hidden*, whether Girard believes that there is some fundamental conviction within individuals that arbitrary and, therefore, "illegitimate" violence and victimization are to be avoided, or whether, instead, he sees Judeo-Christian revelation as possessing both revelatory and transformative power, which not only exposes the arbitrariness of the victimage mechanism, but also invites and empowers individuals to refuse to cooperate in violence. The latter seems more likely, but Girard treats scripture as a text that is like other cultural anthropological texts rather than as a privileged means of God's self-revelation to humanity. Scriptural texts, which convey "biblical myths," represent the inversion and the undoing of all other cultural myths, which serve to conceal founding violence.[94] Because Girard treats scripture in this way, the transformative power of Judeo-Christian revelation is not given explicit attention. As a result, the question of how the Judeo-Christian Scriptures undermine the effectiveness of the victimage mechanism is left unconsidered for the most part.

A more explicitly theological account of Judeo-Christian revelation is necessary to undertake such a consideration. James Alison's work will provide the means for considering this question more explicitly in the following chapters of this study. Adequately understanding the shift from the full and effective operation of the victimage mechanism to the formation of metaphysical desire, to which Oughourlian referred above, also requires this more explicitly theological perspective.

To be fair to Girard, this perspective is simply not his own.[95] He is content with being descriptive. And his description of the role that Judeo-Christian revelation plays in the emergence of metaphysical desire illuminates the deep influence that the Judeo-Christian Scriptures have had on modern societies and the modern "individual." With

---

[93] Ibid., 288–9.
[94] Ibid., 141–58.
[95] I will make the case more fully in the final section of this chapter (in conversation with some theologians who have argued to the contrary) that Girard has chosen to avoid these explicitly theological questions in order to maintain a more intensive focus on anthropological ones.

the exposure of the arbitrariness of the victimage mechanism, the growing rivalry surrounding a particular disputed object can no longer generate sufficient unanimity concerning the identification of a "legitimate" victim. In this context, when cultural prohibitions, rituals, myths, and increasing social differentiation can no longer keep rivalry to a certain manageable threshold in modern societies, the victimage mechanism becomes partially internalized. It begins to operate within the network of interpersonal relationships that forms each individual, rather than being fully enacted upon a commonly identified "culprit." The number of scapegoats multiplies because each subgroup or individual within a particular society believes themselves to have identified the real "culprit" responsible for the social crisis and upheaval. As rivalry surrounding a disputed object builds, the various desiring subjects must find a way to keep it hidden from open view. Thus, they attempt to hide their desire for the object from one another. Desire is rerouted, so to speak, into Dostoyevsky's underground, where it develops—or disintegrates—into desire for the (mis)perceived "more substantial" being of others.

The conditions are set for the emergence of the dynamics of metaphysical desire, which Girard described in *DDN*. The building rivalry increases the object's value in the eyes of the subjects. This perceived value of the object gets transferred to the model who designates it as valuable to the subject and who, therefore, appears to desire it more authentically than the subject himself.[96] In *Things Hidden*, Girard adds a helpful description of the metaphysical form of desire by distinguishing it from appetites/needs:

> This process of transfiguration does not correspond to anything real, and yet it transforms the object into something that appears superabundantly real. Thus it could be described as metaphysical in character. We might well decide to use the word 'desire' only in circumstances where the misunderstood mechanism of mimetic rivalry has imbued what was previously just an appetite or a need with the metaphysical dimension.[97]

He goes on to say, "The 'metaphysical' threshold or, if we put it a different way, the point at which we reach desire properly speaking, is the threshold of the unreal."[98] Thus, to a much greater extent than the earlier and more "primitive" form of desire, desire in its modern, metaphysical form is by its very nature "unreal." It is fabricated by rivalry that no longer has a means of resolution through victimage. Yet, it is not fabricated out of nothing; it is fabricated out of real needs and appetites that have been "whipped up" (within the "generator of desire" that is reciprocal mediation) into desires for the unreal objects of prestige and a sense of autonomy.[99] Desire in its modern, metaphysical form, which is the paradigmatic form of desire for Girard at this point in his thinking, is the aggravation and exaggeration of human needs and appetites into the realm of

---

[96] Girard, *Things Hidden*, 295–6.
[97] Ibid., 296.
[98] Ibid., 297.
[99] See Section 2.2.1, p. 51 above.

unreality. That is, desire in its modern form is insatiable by its very nature because it seeks satisfaction in "objects" that are nothing more than the subject's misperception of his or her own relationships to others.

2.3.5 Conversion—Freedom from the Metaphysical Form of Desire

Even this skeletal account of Girard's view of the rise of human culture and modernity presented in *Things Hidden* shows that, for Girard, the metaphysical form of desire is a modern phenomenon that has been effected by the historical impacts of (1) the victimage mechanism on acquisitive mimesis and (2) Judeo-Christian revelation on mimetic desire. Through this reading of history, Girard distinguishes, though not always explicitly, this modern form of mimetic desire from mimesis (broadly speaking), acquisitive mimesis, and mimetic desire prior to modernity, each of which is an increasingly specialized category within a more generic one—with mimesis being the most generic and metaphysical desire being the most specific. Girard's reading elaborates the central role that the Judeo-Christian Scriptures play in the historical development of metaphysical desire. Girard's perspective in *Things Hidden* appears to be that, by gradually undermining the effectiveness of the victimage mechanism, Judeo-Christian revelation opened the path for the development of desire into its modern, metaphysical form. Yet Girard does not see the effects of this revelation as ultimately ending with the emergence of metaphysical desire. As we saw in our treatment of *DDN*, Girard asserts that the ultimate meaning and end of the novels he has studied and of desire are not death, but conversion.[100] As we will see more clearly in the next section dealing with Girard's mature thought, Girard believes that Judeo-Christian revelation does effect conversion from rivalrous desire.

With a clearer understanding of Girard's distinctions between acquisitive mimesis, mimetic desire, and the metaphysical form of mimetic desire in place, we can now clarify the particular domain within which conversion operates. The primary context in which talk of "conversion" is meaningful for Girard is metaphysical desire. In the modern world, it is from metaphysical desire that conversion brings about freedom. Conversion, in Girard's primary usage, indicates freedom from dependence upon the misperception of the "being" of particular others as significantly more or less real (i.e., more or less autonomous or self-sufficient) than one's own.

Thus, Girard understands conversion as primarily a modern phenomenon. Even though at this point in his thinking Girard has come to a greater appreciation of the central role that Judeo-Christian revelation has played (and continues to play) in the overcoming of the victimage mechanism and the dynamics of conversion, in *Things Hidden*, he continues to turn to Proust as his paradigmatic figure for illustrating those dynamics. Girard describes the early Proust, as portrayed in the novel *Jean Santeuil*, by saying that Proust "imagines that ... self-sufficiency does exist somewhere, and that sooner or later he will be able to possess it. He dreams continually of the moment of this conquest and represents it to himself as if it had already taken place." In contrast,

---

[100] Girard, *DDN*, 294.

"[t]he late Proust knows that narcissism has no existence *in itself*" and he comes to see the need to "demystify" his own desires and not just those of others.[101] In Girard's understanding, then, conversion most properly speaking effects freedom from the metaphysical form of desire, which is the modern form of rivalrous desire.

This understanding of conversion is negative rather than positive in that it identifies what conversion is a freedom (or a turning away) *from*, but it does not identify what conversion is a freedom *for*. The lack of a positive understanding of freedom is partially, I suggest, the result of the lack of clarity in Girard's understanding of mimetic desire at this point in his thinking. While he has made a distinction between mimetic desire and the metaphysical form of it peculiar to modernity, he has not yet been fully able to conceive of mimetic desire or of acquisitive mimesis as operating outside of some form, modern or otherwise, of a rivalrous mode. Conversion effects freedom from metaphysical desire, but does conversion also effect freedom from mimetic desire altogether? Or, to ask the question another way, is mimetic desire inherently and inescapably rivalrous, even if we can see that it is not inherently metaphysical? Girard's answer seems to be "no," even at this stage, but he has not yet worked out conceptually how this can be understood.

When distinguishing psychosis from rationality, Girard makes it clear that it is not possible to escape from mimetic desire altogether:

> [For] behaving normally is not a matter of escaping from mimetic desire (no one can do that) but of not giving into it to the extent of losing sight of the object entirely and only being concerned with the model. Being rational – functioning properly – is a matter of having objects and being busy with them; being mad is a matter of letting oneself be taken over completely by the mimetic models, and so fulfilling the calling of desire.[102]

Thus, mimetic desire is inescapable; according to Girard, it is fundamental to, and constitutive of, being human. Yet, it also seems, based on Girard's treatment, that historically speaking mimetic desire has most often been oriented toward luring the subject into some form of rivalry; in the modern world, "fulfilling the calling of desire" means giving in to metaphysical madness. If mimetic desire is both fundamental to the human person and yet also historically oriented toward rivalry, then it is difficult to articulate what Girard means by conversion. Girard asserts clearly that conversion effects freedom from metaphysical desire. Given his claim that mimetic desire is inescapable, it would seem that conversion does not effect freedom from mimetic desire as a whole. However, Girard has not yet articulated whether the operation of mimetic desire as such can be distinguished from some earlier rivalrous (or rivalry-oriented) form of it, even though he is able to and does distinguish it from its modern metaphysical form. As a result, he is not able to come to a clear conclusion about the effects of conversion on mimetic desire and acquisitive mimesis as such. Without such a conclusion and without the capacity to imagine mimetic desire in something other

---

[101] Girard, *Things Hidden*, 397–8.
[102] Ibid., 311.

than a rivalrous mode, Girard is not able to say much positively about the freedom effected by conversion.

In the next section of this chapter, in which I will treat Girard's more mature thought found in two of his later works, I will show that Girard becomes more able to conceive of mimetic desire in a non-rivalrous mode later in his career and, as a result, is able to distinguish in certain places between mimetic desire as such and the rivalrous mode of mimetic desire according to which it has operated most visibly throughout history.

2.4 Girard's Mature Thought: Mimetic Desire in a Gospel Perspective?

Toward the end of *Evolution and Conversion*, Girard acknowledges that his understanding of culture and desire has continued to develop since his writing of *Things Hidden*: "*Things Hidden* was still written from the perspective of anthropology and, therefore, Christianity seems like a kind of 'supplement', rather than converting everything to its perspective. Today I would write from the point of view of the Gospels."[103] In this section, I will suggest that two of his more recent books, *I See Satan* (1999) and *Evolution and Conversion* (2004), demonstrate that, in the later part of his career, Girard has partially fulfilled this intention to write about mimetic desire from the perspective of the Gospels.

While Girard does come to see mimetic desire as "intrinsically good" due to his effort to more fully adopt, and conform his thinking to, a Gospel perspective, he does not become fully able to distinguish mimetic desire (as the network of connectivity within which subjects come to be subjects) from a rivalrous mode of mimetic desire that tends toward some form of violence and victimage. Several apparently contradictory assertions about mimetic desire in these more mature works will reveal that Girard shifts back and forth between his literary-cultural perspective and the perspective that he derives from the Gospels. This constant shifting suggests that Girard has yet to construct a clear theoretical account of what he refers to as "a Gospel anthropology."[104] Instead, he has a "novelistic" and cultural anthropology that is still in the process of being "converted" to a Gospel perspective.

I contend that, while keeping with his understanding of his own intellectual task as "an interpreter of texts,"[105] and while enabling many insights about human culture, desire, and the "mimetic mechanism," Girard's reluctance to travel far into the realm of Christian theology, even when interpreting the Judeo-Christian Scriptures,[106] directly correlates with his inability to conceptualize adequately the anthropology that he believes to be fully disclosed in the Gospel narratives.

---

[103] Girard, *Evolution and Conversion*, 215.
[104] *I See Satan*, 191. Girard also openly acknowledges that giving such a theoretical account is not his primary aim, nor is it within his own "logical ability," that is, his own intellectual capacity (*Evolution and Conversion*, 144–9).
[105] *Evolution and Conversion*, 144.
[106] *I See Satan*, 191.

After considering some of Girard's apparently contradictory assertions regarding mimetic desire in exploring *I See Satan* and *Evolution and Conversion*, I will identify and articulate the nature of the transition that he is undergoing in moving from a literary-cultural perspective (as developed in *DDN* and *Things Hidden*) to a Gospel perspective. I will then draw out two related conceptual difficulties in his anthropology revealed by these contradictions. Finally, I will consider briefly Girard's limited exploration into the domain of theology and the conceptual difficulties that result from his reluctance to, or disinterest in, taking this exploration farther. I will engage with the work of Kevin Mongrain, Grant Kaplan, and Wolfgang Palaver in this conversation about the theological character of Girard's writing.

2.4.1 Mimetic Desire and Human Freedom

In these two more recent works, Girard seems to alternate between what he calls a Gospel perspective, in which he is able to distinguish between mimetic desire as such and a rivalrous mode of it, and a literary-cultural perspective, in which he uses the term "mimetic desire" to refer to mimetic rivalry leading to victimage. More careful attention to the presence of Jesus as one who exists outside the network of mimetic rivalry through a perfect and peaceful imitation of his Father allows Girard to assert explicitly the fundamental or intrinsic goodness of mimetic desire. Thus, it seems that Jesus demonstrates a new kind of imitation (and a new kind of model) that enables Girard to make an explicit conceptual distinction between mimetic desire and mimetic rivalry. Despite these assertions, however, Girard still at times reverts to identifying mimetic desire and the mimetic mechanism with the dynamics of rivalry leading to violence.

We saw that in *Things Hidden* Girard does not explicitly clarify how he understands the relationship between mimetic desire as such and conversion. Conversion means freedom from metaphysical desire, but whether it means freedom from mimetic desire altogether is never clearly stated. In *I See Satan* and *Evolution and Conversion*, Girard still lacks clarity on this point, despite his explicit assertions regarding the intrinsic goodness of mimetic desire.

Toward the beginning of both *I See Satan* and *Evolution and Conversion* and consistent with his transition to what he calls a Gospel perspective, Girard asserts that mimetic desire is the mechanism through which humans are able to exercise their freedom:

> Even if the mimetic nature of human desire is responsible for most of the violent acts that distress us, we should not conclude that mimetic desire is bad in itself. If our desires were not mimetic, they would be forever fixed on predetermined objects; they would be a particular form of instinct. Human beings could no more change their desire than cows their appetite for grass. Without mimetic desire there would be neither freedom nor humanity. Mimetic desire is intrinsically good.[107]

---

[107] Girard, *I See Satan*, 15. Girard makes the same assertion, accompanied by the same confused argumentation in *Evolution and Conversion*, 58. And Girard repeats his affirmation of the inherent goodness of mimetic desire, this time as the basis of all learning in *Evolution and Conversion*, 76.

Here Girard seems to confuse himself as to what precisely is the ground for the possibility of human freedom. The statement above makes it sound as if it is the "mimetic" part of "mimetic desire" that distinguishes humans from animals and makes possible human freedom. But fundamental to Girard's account of hominization in *Things Hidden* is the claim that animals and humans are both mimetic, especially with regard to acquisitive behavior. What distinguishes humans from animals is not mimesis, but "desire."

Whereas the acquisitive mimesis of animals is governed by instinct, the acquisitive mimesis of humans operates primarily within the domain of desire. Animal behavior is governed by the dynamics of an "instinctual" mimesis rather than by mimetic desire. Animals learn what particular objects are worth striving for by instinctually imitating the acquisitive behaviors of the nearest, most dominant model while also instinctually submitting to the established dominance patterns of their particular group. Because instinct governs their imitation, animals are not free to choose their models. Humans, on the other hand, are distinct from animals because we are free to desire according to the models of our own choosing, even if we aren't fully aware of this freedom due to the system of rivalry in which we are inevitably first socialized, at least partially. Desire takes the place of instinct and becomes the mechanism through which persons can freely shape themselves.

Therefore, despite Girard's partially confused argumentation, his assertion above does articulate his explicit recognition that mimetic *desire* is the distinctive capacity of human beings and it is intrinsically good because it is the means by which we are able to exercise our freedom to desire what (and to become who) we choose by choosing whom we imitate. This basic assertion constitutes the beginning of the development of a Gospel anthropology within the conceptual framework of mimetic theory.

However, the further development of such an anthropology is impeded by Girard's lingering identification of mimetic desire with a rivalrous mode of that desire, including its modern metaphysical form. This lingering way of thinking conflicts with the Gospel perspective that he is beginning to articulate. Toward the end of *Evolution and Conversion*, Girard defines freedom in opposition to the mimetic mechanism without distinguishing the mimetic mechanism from mimetic desire: "Desire is always mimetic, but some human beings resist desire and being carried away by mimetic violence.... To talk about freedom means to talk about man's ability to resist the mimetic mechanism."[108] Here Girard seems to identify desire with the mimetic mechanism as a force that must be resisted for freedom to be possible. If we take this statement at face value, it appears (contrary to his understanding) that Girard is claiming that mimetic desire is always rivalrous and, therefore, freedom is only possible as an alternative to mimetic desire.

In his next chapter when talking about our contemporary situation, Girard makes an even more explicit assertion of the intrinsically rivalrous nature of mimetic desire and human relations, saying, "Human relations are essentially relations of imitation, of rivalry."[109] Here imitation and rivalry are presented as synonyms; the possibility of freedom again appears to exist only outside of mimetic desire.

---

[108] Girard, *Evolution and Conversion*, 222.
[109] Ibid., 238.

Rather than understanding Girard to be presenting an internally incoherent view of mimetic desire and freedom, I suggest that it is more accurate to see Girard as in the midst of a transition in his use of his chosen terms. These latter assertions about resisting mimetic desire to attain freedom reflect Girard's perspective in *DDN* and *Things Hidden*, in which mimetic desire always referred to rivalrous desire and, therefore, the only way to talk about freedom was to speak of it negatively as freedom from rivalrous desire. Although Girard has begun to acknowledge explicitly that mimetic desire is intrinsically good and that it is not identical with its rivalrous mode, he has not yet developed a consistent conceptual language for maintaining this distinction. At the end of this chapter, I will argue that a systematic theological perspective is necessary for developing a theoretical vocabulary adequate for this task.

2.4.2 The Christian Character of Conversion

While Girard has not yet developed a Christian language for distinguishing the intrinsic goodness of mimetic desire from its frequently rivalrous mode of operation, he does seem to have come to a consistently Christian understanding of conversion in these two more recent texts. Unlike in *DDN* and *Things Hidden*, in which conversion was seen primarily as a modern phenomenon for which Girard identified Proust and *The Past Recaptured* as a paradigmatic illustration, in these more mature works Girard turns to the New Testament depictions of the conversions of Peter and Paul to illustrate the dynamics of conversion. With this transition, conversion comes to be seen more explicitly as a universal, rather than a primarily modern, phenomenon. In the story of Paul's conversion and in the encounter between Jesus and Peter in the courtyard in Luke's Gospel, Girard hears Jesus asking the same question, with his voice or with a look: "Why do you persecute me?"[110] This question expresses the basic form of conversion for Girard:

> Christian conversion is always this question that Christ himself asks. Because of the simple fact that we live in a world whose structure is based on mimetic processes and victim mechanisms, from which we all profit without knowing it, we are all accessories to the Crucifixion, persecutors of Christ.[111]

Conversion, then, begins with an encounter in which one is confronted by Christ, who, by asking the question "Why do you persecute me?", brings about a recognition that one has always been a persecutor without knowing it.

Thus, by focusing on the conversions of Peter and Paul, Girard starts to see how the process of conversion that he depicted in *DDN* is initiated. It begins through an encounter with Christ, who, coming in the form of a victim, invites one to recognize

---

[110] Girard, *I See Satan*, 191, and *Evolution and Conversion*, 198. Cf. Palaver, *René Girard's Mimetic Theory*, 230.
[111] Girard, *I See Satan*, 191.

oneself as persecutor. This recognition leads, in turn, to the possibility of "recapturing the past" and subsequently discovering one's freedom to choose one's models in the present.

Girard begins to see that this constructed identity as an unknowing persecutor is the inevitable result of the subject's rejection and denial of his more fundamental identity as an imitator. An encounter with Christ enables a positive (non-rivalrous) imitation of Jesus, who perfectly imitates his Father.[112] Girard clarifies that what is imitated by those persons who imitate Jesus is not his personal habits or specific social behaviors, but rather "his own *desire*, the spirit that directs him toward the goal on which his intention is fixed: to resemble God the Father as much as possible."[113] Imitating the desire of Jesus requires a willingness to relinquish the false sense of the autonomy of the subject's own desire, which has led him or her to persecute those who threaten to expose his or her reliance on imitation. Jesus "threatens" to do precisely this as he repeatedly makes clear that he desires nothing but that which the Father desires for him. In other words, Jesus openly acknowledges the imitative nature of his own desire, and he freely chooses God the Father as the sole model who will shape his desire. Here Girard sees that Jesus' open acknowledgment of his own imitation immediately threatens those who wrongly believe that their identity depends upon an active covering up of their own imitation. Imitating Jesus consists of an imitation of his choosing to imitate the desire of God the Father. Girard describes the saints as "links in the chain" of this positive imitation of Jesus' imitation of the Father.[114]

When talking about conversion from this Gospel perspective, Girard again begins to describe persons as always operating within the domain of mimetic desire. However, now he distinguishes between mimetic desire that operates in the "satanic fashion" of accusing one's neighbor, and mimetic desire that operates in imitation of Jesus and, therefore, strives to love and forgive one's neighbor.[115] Thus, when Girard is describing conversion and imitation of Christ, his transition to a Gospel perspective appears to be further underway than it does when he is elaborating upon the "mimetic mechanism" understood as the cycle of mimetic rivalry leading to scapegoating. Here it becomes clearer once again that Girard understands human beings as always formed in and by mimetic desire, but not as forever bound to a rivalrous and victimizing mode of mimetic desire. Girard, then, has come to recognize much more explicitly that mimetic desire is not inherently rivalrous since the conversion effected by Christ is not a freedom from mimetic desire altogether. It is a freedom to openly imitate the desire of Jesus who imitates the Father.

2.4.3 The Converted Subject as the Norm of Subjectivity

Girard recognizes that imitating Jesus coincides with consciously acknowledging a previous aspiration to autonomy that "[had] always made us bow down before

---

[112] Girard, *Evolution and Conversion*, 222.
[113] Girard, *I See Satan*, 13; Girard's emphasis.
[114] Girard, *Evolution and Conversion*, 222.
[115] Ibid., 225, 262.

individuals" ensnarled in rivalries into which they drew us.[116] This recognition in *I See Satan* recalls Girard's language for describing conversion in *DDN*, in which freedom from mimetic rivalry leads to a recognition of the imitative nature of desire. Thus, from the beginning of his career to his more recent work, Girard sees conversion as involving a conscious acknowledgment of the mimetic structure of the individual's desire, which has always persisted "underneath" one's misguided efforts to attain complete independence and autonomy from the desires of others.

It is not until later in his career, however, that Girard, in *Evolution and Conversion*, explicitly recognizes the "converted subject" as the one who finds herself enabled to accept herself as an imitator, and, in doing so, becomes the norm of authentic subjectivity. In admitting the need for a critique of the subject, Girard ultimately affirms the authenticity of the converted subject: "[T]here should be some critique of the subject: it does not have to be a total negation of the idea of subjectivity, but it should be addressed as the question of the converted subject who is capable of seeing himself as part of the mimetic process."[117] Thus, the converted subject, as someone capable of seeing herself as an imitator, becomes the norm by which all subjectivity is known and judged. Girard does not elaborate on this point, but I would suggest that, for Girard, authentic or converted subjectivity is determined by the extent to which the subject consciously recognizes and accepts her own constitution in and by mimetic desire and, therefore, the extent to which she has been shaped by mimetic rivalry and contributed to various forms of victimage. In becoming free to accept herself as an imitator, the converted subject also becomes free to play a much more conscious and deliberate role in shaping herself by choosing the models from whom she will receive her desires and the various worlds of possibilities (or selves) that those desires will open up for her.

From this description of converted subjectivity, we can suggest what might constitute "unconverted subjectivity" for Girard. The unconverted subject is someone who is not yet aware of and, therefore, does not yet fully possess her ability to consciously acknowledge and accept her own nature as an imitator. She has been misguided by the rivalrous models around her to believe that the only desire worth pursuing is one that arises spontaneously from herself. As a result, she begins her quest for an autonomous self that does not exist. Because the unconverted subject refuses to see herself as an imitator, she continually tries to hide any experience of herself as such from herself and others. She is not free to imitate the models of her own choosing because she denies all reliance on models whatsoever. Instead, the only "choice" available to her, as far as she is able to judge, is to imitate those persons who appear to be the most autonomous (i.e., independent from the desires of others) while, in imitation of her models, denying that she is imitating anyone at all.

Here Girard reveals an opening within his perspective for being able to assert some degree of continuity in the subject before and after conversion. The subject most properly speaking is that part of the individual that is able to take a stand and cannot avoid doing so, either of acknowledgment and acceptance or of denial and rejection,

[116] Girard, *I See Satan*, 14–15.
[117] Girard, *Evolution and Conversion*, 151.

toward his or her constitution in and through mimetic desire. The continuity of the subject from a Girardian perspective (though not explicitly asserted by Girard himself) lies in the constancy and inescapability of the individual's exercise of this capacity.

This capacity to take a stand in relation to one's constitution in mimetic desire is the basis for a related capacity that further defines and holds together the individual's subjectivity—the capacity either to actively take up the process of searching for and choosing his models, or to relinquish this conscious choosing, as the result of a previous denial of his constitution in mimetic desire, in favor of a half-conscious search for a model that might confer autonomy. The converted subject is the norm of subjectivity for Girard because the converted subject is able to actualize or consciously enact his subjectivity by recognizing and accepting what he actually is—an imitating subject necessarily dependent on others as models. This acceptance allows the subject to actualize the relative freedom that corresponds to the kind of creature he is. It requires leaving behind his former pursuit of an absolute autonomy.

Girard's acknowledgment of the significance of the converted subject, with his related capacities to (1) accept his own imitative nature and (2) choose the models from whom he will receive the self/selves (i.e., the worlds of possibilities) that will constitute his identity, helps to make visible the continuity and the unity of the individual as a subject. Although Girard does not seem to be interested in explicitly asserting this continuity and unity of the individual subject, such an assertion is necessary for Girard's talk of conversion to be meaningful. For "conversion" to have meaning, we must be able to identify something that is "converted" from one form or mode of existing to another. It cannot be desire that is converted because desire, for Girard, is the whole network or field in which subjects arise and are constituted as such. In a Girardian perspective, the subjects, who possess a fundamental capacity to choose their mode of relating to their constitution in and by mimetic desire, are converted from one particular mode of standing in relation to their constitution in desire (one of denial and rejection) to another mode (one of acknowledgment and acceptance).

2.4.4 A Gospel or "Revealed" Anthropology in Place of Theology

The lack of an assertion from Girard of the continuity and unity of the individual subject is closely related to the lack of greater conceptual clarity in Girard's thinking concerning the distinction between mimetic desire as such and mimetic rivalry leading to victimage. A recognition of the continuity of the mimetically desiring subject requires a clear conceptualization of the subject's constitution in and by mimetic desire as conceptually prior to the subject's formation in a rivalrous (or a positive) mode of mimetic desire.[118] Conversely, a clear conceptualization of the distinction between mimetic desire and its rivalrous mode of operation will lead to greater clarity as to what remains constant within the subject before and after conversion. Although Girard

---

[118] I first recognized the need for a theology incorporating mimetic theory to more explicitly postulate an understanding of human subjectivity that is conceptually "prior" to mimetic desire in an earlier essay. See John P. Edwards, "The Self Prior to Mimetic Desire: Rahner and Alison on Original Sin and Conversion," *Horizons* 35.1 (Spring 2008): 7–31.

became more aware of and began to address these two related conceptual difficulties, later in his career, he had not yet addressed them systematically enough, and so they remained conceptual unclarities even within his more recent works. I believe that a theological perspective is necessary for adequately understanding and resolving these conceptual difficulties.[119] Girard openly acknowledged that he intentionally refrained from entering into theological discourse. Instead, he moved within the field of what he called a "Gospel anthropology,"[120] or what I have previously argued might best be understood as a "revealed psychology."[121] In saying that he has refrained from doing theology in favor of exploring a Gospel anthropology, Girard seems to mean that he put aside questions of what the Gospels might reveal about who God is and what God's intention for humanity might be. Instead, Girard was almost exclusively concerned with understanding what the Gospel portrayals of the person and life of Jesus of Nazareth reveal (i.e., re-present)[122] to us about the dynamics of human relations as they actually are—always mimetic and often rivalrous and victim producing. He saw any direct investigation into questions about God and God's intention for humanity and human history (i.e., questions about teleology) as potential and often actual obstacles to a thorough investigation into the Gospels' clear and comprehensive unveiling of the psychological and sociological dynamics of mimetic rivalry leading to a group enactment of victimage.

In a previous essay arguing that Girard's work is best understood as a "revealed psychology," I drew in part on Eugene Webb's classification of Girard within the French psychoanalytic tradition to assert that "Girard's thematization of a 'mimetic psychology' is possible only as a result of the meaning unveiled in the texts of Scripture. It is in this sense that I would describe Girard's psychology as 'revealed.'"[123] I go on to suggest that it would be most helpful "to identify Girard's relationship to theology as a psychologically and sociologically coherent understanding of a portion of the [content of Christian faith]"—namely, what most Christian theologians have called original sin.[124] In other words, Girard's use of the adjective "Gospel" and my use of "revealed" are both intended to recognize explicitly that mimetic theory is a fruit of the meaning made available through the texts of Scripture and by an intelligence operating "behind" the texts in and through those writing them. As "revealed" in this sense, mimetic theory, at least in Girard's development, is aimed primarily at providing a sophisticated psychosocial, or anthropological, reading of a significant portion of that meaning.

---

[119] More specifically, a systematic theological perspective that locates, distinguishes, and relates the categories of nature, sin, and grace within the conceptual domain of mimetic theory would provide an adequate theoretical language for maintaining the distinction between mimetic desire as such and its rivalrous (as well as its positive) mode(s), and for asserting the continuity of the individual before and after conversion without reinforcing a misguided belief in the myth of the "autonomous self."

[120] Girard, *I See Satan*, 191.

[121] Edwards, "From a 'Revealed' Psychology to Theological Inquiry," 124.

[122] Girard, *I See Satan*, 137; see especially footnote 1. Here Girard writes, "From an anthropological standpoint I would define Christian revelation as the true representation of what had never been completely represented or what had been falsely represented: the mimetic convergence of all against one."

[123] Edwards, "From a 'Revealed' Psychology to Theological Inquiry," 124. Cf. Webb, *The Self Between*.

[124] Ibid., 126.

Girard consciously avoided any substantial reflection on the explicitly theological questions of why and how the profound meaning that he believed to be contained in the Judeo-Christian Scriptures was made knowable to human beings in such a way that eventually led to the creation and wide influence of these texts. Instead, he simply asserted that a particular kind of conversion was necessary for it to have become possible, and then he largely focused on the content of what is revealed about the psychological and sociological dynamics of relationships within and among people and communities. In my earlier treatment of Girard's work, I employed the classical theological distinction between *fides quae* and *fides qua* (i.e., between the content and process of Christian faith) to demonstrate that Girard's writing remains almost exclusively within the realm of deeply insightful psychological and sociological reflection on a portion of the *content* of Christian faith, avoiding, for the most part, reflection on the more fundamental and methodological questions about the *process* and nature of faith, conversion, and theology.[125] Even within his sustained reflection on a portion of the *content* of Christian faith, Girard's work operates largely as a certain kind of social psychology and sociology (e.g., French psychoanalytic or Lacanian), rather than theology.

However, despite Girard's choice to think "anthropologically" (i.e., psychosocially) rather than theologically with the Gospel texts, he came right up to the edge of theological discourse when he talked about the resurrection. In describing the resurrection as "the spectacular sign of the entrance into the world of a power superior to violent contagion,"[126] a power that is the Spirit of God, Girard was at least implying the beginnings of an understanding of who God is and what God intends for humanity. But Girard went no further theologically. Girard said only that this power enlightens the disciples and discloses to them their participation in the mechanism of rivalry and victimage that brought about the execution of their master and friend.[127] The disclosure of their participation in Jesus' crucifixion turns the disciples into a dissident minority that breaks the unanimity of the crowd by confessing its own guilt and proclaiming the innocence of the victim for the first time in history. Girard did not attempt to think about what the effectiveness of the power consists in, or the kind of God who is enacting it, or the final end toward which that God might intend it to be directed, or how the fulfillment of such an end is related to the historical effects of its entrance into the world. These theological and teleological questions were beyond Girard's direct interest in the Gospel texts.

Girard also stated that he did not see his own anthropological pursuits as opposed to the exploration of any number of theological questions; however, he did see a significant benefit from putting aside theological considerations in favor of exploring more directly his anthropological concerns: "The anthropological widening of the Incarnation in no way eclipses theology; it shows its relevance by putting the abstract idea of original sin into more concrete form, as James Alison has powerfully

---

[125] Ibid., 125–8.
[126] Girard, *I See Satan*, 189.
[127] Ibid., 189–90.

observed."[128] Thus, the primary fruit of this anthropological approach, in Girard's eyes, is its ability to concretely depict the dynamics of sin operating within human history, including an account of their anthropological origin and the *possibility* of their being overcome.

At least one contemporary Christian theologian suggests that it is more accurate and helpful to investigate Girard's work beginning with the assumption that he is a certain kind of Christian theologian, namely, a theologian of spiritual transformation in the tradition of early Christian monasticism.[129] Kevin Mongrain, first using the work of Hans Urs von Balthasar and then drawing on the early Christian monastic tradition inspired by Evagrius of Ponticus and developed by his most prolific student, John Cassian, argues that we do a disservice to Girard if we don't start from the premise that Girard is a fundamentally Christian thinker who should be seen as reading the biblical narrative and salvation history from the point of view of a theologian of the spiritual or contemplative type, or what has been called "a theologian of the heart."[130] Mongrain's argument includes a summary account of the development in Girard's thought that aligns with what I have shown in this chapter.[131]

While I partially agree with Mongrain's assessment of Girard as a kind of "contemplative, apocalyptic theologian"[132] in that Girard firmly believed that a specific kind of spiritual transformation is necessary to allow Christian theology to advocate for a "true gnosis" rather than some form of "false gnosis" that puts "God under human gaze, arrogantly reducing the personal Mystery of God to a mere object that can be narrated or defined from some master perspective acquired independently of prayer."[133] I hesitate in classifying Girard as a theologian on the terms that Mongrain has put forth. I believe that it is true, as Mongrain argues, that Girard was writing from the perspective of a committed Christian thinker even in his early works. As I have tried to show, the vast majority of Girard's writing assumed and proceeded from the meaning made available through Judeo-Christian revelation and was dedicated to elaborating a portion of that meaning. However, I believe it is more appropriate to classify Girard's work as a "revealed psychology" or a "revealed anthropology" than as "theology" (or even contemplative or spiritual theology). As Mongrain affirms, "[in Girard's work] God receives insufficient attention. Instead what we get in Girard is a complex but one-sided story of humanity's creation and maintenance of a self-concealing 'mechanism' of sin, with little attention paid to the nature and identity of the God who redeems."[134] Girard's focus remained on developing a psychologically and

---

[128] Ibid., 190.

[129] Mongrain, "Theologians of Spiritual Transformation," 81–111.

[130] See, for example, *Evagrius Ponticus: The Praktikos & Chapters on Prayer*, trans. John Eudes Bamberger, O.C.S.O. (Collegeville, MN: The Liturgical Press and Cistercian Publications Inc., 1972).

[131] Mongrain argues that Girard's early writings suggest (though not intentionally) that mimesis (and, therefore, human beings) is inherently rivalrous, but later he makes a much clearer distinction between mimesis as an "anthropological given" and mimetic rivalry (Ibid., 83). I would disagree with Mongrain's reading slightly here in that I think he sees Girard's development toward a "Gospel perspective" to be somewhat more complete than what I attempted to demonstrate above.

[132] Ibid., 87.

[133] Ibid., 88.

[134] Ibid., 93.

sociologically sophisticated description of the dynamics of original sin. And while, in his later writings, particularly *I See Satan*, Girard acknowledged that conversion as he understood it gave Christian believers the freedom to imitate Christ and the saints as models of positive mimesis, I would be hesitant to characterize Girard as a "theologian of the cloistered heart," not because it is "unreasonable to read him as thinking within the basic theological ambit of the monastic tradition's insistence that the mind's understanding of God must be both the product and expression of a contrite, prayerful heart,"[135] but because he did not direct his energy toward writing in this way or advocating spiritual practices that would foster the conversion (or true gnosis) that I believe he was seeking.

Wolfgang Palaver, perhaps the most respected Girard scholar in the world today, summarizes Girard's "primary objective" by saying that it "exists much more in an anthropological apologetics of biblical thought… [that is,] in displaying the plausibility of biblical revelation without having to revert to any rash theological presuppositions."[136] Palaver's view suggests that Girard operates within what I might call a kind of "negative" (in the sense of "apophatic") theology of grace. As Palaver says, Girard's "discreet approach toward overarching theological inquiries *does not imply any systematic denial of grace.*"[137] In other words, Girard's insistence on maintaining his anthropological focus in reading the New Testament supports and protects an authentic Christian theology of grace. As Girard advanced in his own thinking partly in dialogue with Christian theologians, he became more explicit that part of the objective of his anthropological approach was to shed light on the deep anthropological insight contained in the biblical narrative and to support the development of a Christian theology of grace that coheres with that anthropological insight. Yet, even as this theological objective came more into view, it still remained secondary, and he himself avoided engaging in any explicit development of a theology of grace.

I'm not so interested here in arguing that Girard's work should never be approached as a theology of spiritual transformation, as Mongrain suggests.[138] Rather, both the work of Mongrain and that of Palaver support the view that I am asserting here, namely, that throughout the course of Girard's writing, even while recognizing his increasing openness to engage with particular theological categories, such as grace, the person of Jesus, conversion, and the communion of saints, Girard focused primarily on elaborating the psychological and sociological dynamics of mimetic desire, most often in its rivalrous form, as they are revealed in particular biblical passages and as he saw them operating within an increasing number of texts and contexts, both secular and religious.

Palaver's characterization of Girard's primary objective as "an anthropological apologetics of biblical thought" provides strong support for Grant Kaplan's project in *René Girard, Unlikely Apologist*, which is an extensive and impressive application

---

[135] Ibid., 100.
[136] Palaver, *René Girard's Mimetic Theology*, 228.
[137] Ibid.; emphasis added.
[138] It seems more appropriate to leave this particular question to be discussed by scholars of Christian monasticism and contemplative theology.

of Girard's thought and mimetic theory to contemporary Christian apologetics and to particular themes within fundamental theology.[139] Kaplan agrees with Mongrain's assessment that Girard's repeated claims to be engaged in a scientific study of the Bible rather than in theology have thrown at least some Christian theologians "off Girard's theological scent."[140] Then Kaplan builds on Palaver's comparison of Girard with Kant in which Palaver asserts that, unlike Kant's project of articulating "religion within the limits of reason alone," Girard's development of mimetic theory accepted from the beginning the graced fact of the resurrection.[141] In addition, Girard placed his development of mimetic theory within that horizon of understanding from the beginning. Indeed, he recognized more and more explicitly over the course of his career that mimetic theory is not possible outside of that horizon.[142] Affirming Palaver's assessment, Kaplan adds, "The concavity of a world without grace ... enables Girard to illustrate how grace transforms the sinful shape of things when it enters into the story." He goes on to say, "Beyond offering heuristic devices to help make Christian dogmatic claims intelligible, mimetic theory lays bare the processes of religious conversion."[143] Kaplan uses this placement of mimetic theory as already within "the horizon of conversion" to articulate the driving question of his effort to demonstrate the contribution that mimetic theory can make to a contemporary Christian fundamental theology, namely, "Is mimetic theory a mode of discourse for the *already* converted, in order to help make explicit their faith commitments, or is it a mode of discourse that aims to bring about conversion?"[144]

Based on the depiction in this chapter of the development in Girard's thought, I suggest a slightly different relationship between mimetic theory in Girard's usage and the dynamic of Christian conversion. In my view, mimetic theory as Girard develops it has the *potential* to help Christian theologians illustrate *how* grace transforms the sinful dynamics of mimetic rivalry leading to scapegoating violence, that is, the processes of religious conversion. Girard's articulation of mimetic theory assumes and asserts the necessity of religious conversion for coming to perceive clearly the dynamics of mimetic desire. In Girard's articulation, mimetic theory has the *capacity* to illuminate the dynamic process of such a transformation effected by grace, but Girard did not go far down the road of using mimetic theory to show us how this transformation happens. Rather, Girard simply asserted that, based on his anthropological reading and elaboration of mimetic rivalry within the biblical narrative, a religious conversion must have occurred in the lives and self-understandings of Jesus' disciples for the meaning revealed through that narrative to be available in the first place.[145] However,

---

[139] Indeed, Kaplan rightly makes use of this particular treatment of Girard by Palaver in his own introduction (Kaplan, *René Girard, Unlikely Apologist*, 11).

[140] Kaplan, *René Girard, Unlikely Apologist*, 4–5; cf. Mongrain, "Theologians of Spiritual Transformation," 84–85.

[141] Kaplan, *René Girard, Unlikely Apologist*, 12–13; cf. Palaver, *René Girard's Mimetic Theology*, 230.

[142] As Kaplan says, mimetic theory "already works within the horizon of conversion, or grace" (13).

[143] Ibid.

[144] Ibid., 13–14; italics in original.

[145] I first made this assertion previously. See Edwards, "From a 'Revealed' Psychology to Theological Inquiry," 125.

Kaplan, along with many of the Girardian theologians who he engages throughout his project, including Raymund Schwager and James Alison, goes much farther than Girard did toward using Girard's mimetic theory to illuminate the "how" or the process of religious conversion.

My contention in this present work is twofold. First, while Girard's bracketing of specifically theological questions in favor of his anthropological (or psychological and sociological) reading of a portion of the content of Christian faith did allow him to sharpen his primary objective of elucidating the dynamics of mimetic rivalry leading to victimage, a full account of the "Gospel anthropology" that Girard attempted to construct must be accompanied by a theological, and therefore teleological, perspective that strives to *understand*, rather than simply observe and depict, the dynamics of mimetic rivalry in the light of Christian faith. That is to say, the Gospel or "revealed" anthropology that Girard is seeking must ultimately be a *theological* anthropology because it is only through the light of faith received by the disciples that the dynamics of mimetic rivalry were made visible and began to be undone. The Spirit reveals to the disciples *not only the fact* that they were unknowingly entangled in these dynamics of rivalry, *but also the fact* that the God of their friend and master Jesus has desired from the beginning something very different for them and for all of humanity. In other words, both their own sinfulness *and* God's desire for their full freedom are among the facts revealed to the disciples in their encounter with the crucified and risen Christ. The Spirit gradually leads the Christian community to understand that God has had a creative intention for humanity since the beginning of history and draws us to inquire further into what this intention is. Only by trying to make sense of the whole of this "data" (which includes the revelation of divine intentionality toward human beings and human history) can we begin to approximate a full account of the Gospel anthropology that Girard sought. To phrase this first part of my contention in the context of Mongrain's claim, affirmed by Kaplan, that many theologians have been "thrown off Girard's theological scent" by Girard's repeated claims to be engaged in anthropology instead of theology,[146] I would add that Girard himself was partially thrown off his own theological scent by those claims as well.

Second, and as a corrective to Girard's unintended self-misdirection, Alison's theological application and appropriation of Girard at the level of theological method should be understood as an ongoing and explicit investigation into the nature of religious conversion and religious knowing using mimetic theory. As I will show in the chapters that follow, the primary objective of Alison's theological project has been to use mimetic theory to inquire into the nature and the process of conversion experienced by the disciples upon encountering the crucified and risen Christ, and then through this inquiry to develop a clearer theological understanding of the nature of Christian conversion, and its relationship to Christian knowing and theological reflection. Although Alison does not explicitly assert this primary objective, my exploration of his theological corpus will demonstrate that this is the case. It will subsequently

---

[146] Kaplan, *René Girard, Unlikely Apologist*, 4–5; cf. Mongrain, "Theologians of Spiritual Transformation," 84–85.

show that any contributions that Alison makes to what Kaplan refers to as "particular theological questions" or "making reasonable revealed objects of faith"[147] are a result of (and thus secondary to) the fruit of Alison's primary objective in using mimetic theory to illuminate the more fundamental theological questions of Christian conversion and Christian knowing. As I put it previously, the most fundamental question that Alison's theology asks is:

> [I]f Girard's description of original sin as an enslavement in rivalry that includes its own occlusion is accurate, then what must have happened to and within the disciples when they met the crucified and risen Christ for them to have been led to see their own enslavement for the first time? That is, he enquires into the nature and dynamic of conversion to Christ as the condition for the possibility of Christian knowing. In other words, he investigates the *fides qua* precisely as the condition for the possibility of knowing the *fides quae*.[148]

In taking this approach, Alison provides the missing piece to Girard's attempt to develop a "Gospel" or "revealed" anthropology. For such a Gospel anthropology to be true to its own source, one must think theologically, and more specifically, teleologically and methodologically, about the meaning revealed in and through the Judeo-Christian Scriptures. The conceptual difficulties in Girard's articulation of mimetic theory are evidence of the need for this fundamental theological inquiry as a complement to Girard's own anthropological approach.[149] Only by reflecting upon what the God of Jesus Christ might intend for humanity and how that intention is related (or not) to humanity's entanglement in the victimage mechanism will one be able to accurately distinguish between mimetic desire and its rivalrous and positive modes of operation.

In the next two chapters, I will investigate James Alison's theological method. In doing so, I will lay the foundation for addressing the conceptual difficulties in Girard's effort to develop a Gospel anthropology. By integrating Girard's mimetic theory into an explicitly and unhesitatingly fundamental theological perspective, Alison has been articulating for the last twenty-seven years a theological anthropology informed by mimetic theory as a happy by-product, so to speak, of his sustained primary objective of developing a theological method that takes seriously Girard's deepening investigation into the dynamics of mimetic desire.

---

[147] Kaplan, *René Girard, Unlikely Apologist*, 5–6.
[148] Edwards, "From a 'Revealed' Psychology to Theological Inquiry," 127.
[149] Kaplan's *René Girard, Unlikely Apologist* also demonstrates the need for more attention to fundamental theological questions from a Girardian perspective and his work goes a long way toward contributing to this lacuna.

Part Two

An "Inductive" Theological Method and a *Theological* Anthropology Informed by Mimetic Theory

3

From "Conversion" to Theological Reflection: Receiving a "Revealed" Perspective through the Forgiveness of Sins

To give his people knowledge of salvation by the forgiveness of their sins.

(Lk. 1:77)

James Alison's personal and intellectual engagement with René Girard's writings, initiated and sustained by his experiences of being "read" and addressed by the Spirit of Christ via those writings beginning in 1985,[1] led Alison to see the disciples' experiences of meeting the risen Jesus as the pivotal moment in their ongoing processes of conversion and as the central paradigm for a Christian understanding of the dynamic of conversion to Christ. This foundational insight into the relational dynamic of conversion opened up for Alison a path of theological inquiry distinct in its aim from Girard's anthropological inquiry. However, while distinct from Girard's pursuit, Alison's project depends significantly upon the anthropological, that is, psychological and sociological, insights of Girard's understanding of mimetic desire, scapegoating, and conversion.

Whereas Girard chose to focus his inquiry into the New Testament texts using the new anthropological perspective that these texts have made knowable, Alison's insight into the disciples' encounter with the risen Jesus leads him to consider in detail the relational context and the divine intentionality that could have made it possible for this new understanding of self, God, and others to penetrate into the minds of the disciples (as well as his own mind), and gradually undo so much of what they had believed to be true about themselves. Alison's inquiry makes use of Girard's thought in order to ask "what must have happened to and in the disciples upon meeting the crucified and risen Christ that led them to see their enslavement" in rivalry for the first time and to

---

[1] We saw at the outset of this study that Alison describes his first experience of reading Girard as one of being "read like an open book" ("Girard's Breakthrough," 848–9). In a longer essay, Alison describes this same experience as one of being "ambushed" and "read" by the Spirit of Christ via Girard's *Things Hidden*. See Alison, "On Learning to Say 'Jesus Is Lord': A 'Girardian' Confession," in *Faith beyond Resentment*, 149.

begin to perceive that enslavement as something other than God's intention for them and for the rest of humanity?[2]

This theological mode of inquiry allows Alison to give a fuller account than Girard was able to give of the whole "data" made known to the disciples in the resurrection—data that necessarily include the revelation to human persons of a clearer understanding of God's desire for all of humanity. Thus, Alison's theological approach makes it evident that the efforts of believers to understand what is revealed in Christ about God's intentionality for humanity and all of creation cannot be separated from human efforts to uncover the "mimetic anthropology" that Girard believes to be re-presented most clearly in the texts of the New Testament.

Alison views the disciples' experiences of the resurrection as a moment of forgiveness that enabled them to see fully for the first time the "intelligence operative in the mind of Christ," which Alison refers to most frequently as "the intelligence of the victim."[3] This understanding of the New Testament accounts of the resurrection appearances leads him to see a reciprocal relationship between conversion and theology. Although Alison does not provide a systematic account of his own theological method, I will argue that his reading of the disciples' experiences of meeting the risen Jesus provides the hermeneutic key for understanding his view of theology and his own theological performance.

Alison's reading of the disciples' resurrection experiences and his partial expressions of his view of theology and conversion cohere to represent theology as a participation in God's address to humanity by means of the self-reflexive articulation of the intelligence operative in the mind of Christ. God's address is expressed most fully in the living presence of the crucified Christ. One both receives and participates in that address through an experience of being forgiven, which converts the recipient into a witness of the crucified and risen Christ, and causes his or her intelligence to be gradually "subverted from within" by the intelligence of the victim. Theology is the witness' participation in this "subversion from within."[4] In this sense, theology is a fruit of conversion. The reciprocal nature of the relationship between theology and conversion becomes apparent as the witnesses' theological expressions become an occasion for new or renewed experiences of conversion in the witnesses' readers or hearers.

Although these reciprocal movements, first from conversion to theological reflection and then from theological expression to new experiences of conversion, may not necessarily occur separately in time, for the sake of developing Alison's view of the

---

[2] Edwards, "From a 'Revealed' Psychology to Theological Inquiry," 127.

[3] "The intelligence of the victim" is Alison's preferred way of talking about Jesus' clear vision of who God is and of the mechanism of violence that has trapped and ensnared humanity leading human groups to seek peace through the creation of victims. I will elaborate Alison's meaning and use of this phrase in the opening section of this chapter in which I present Alison's epistemology. For Alison's own explanation of the phrase, see especially *The Joy of Being Wrong*, 77–83.

[4] As I indicated briefly in the introductory chapter, this phrase "subversion from within" is Alison's preferred way of talking about how the intelligence operative in the mind of the subject undergoing conversion is gradually exposed, undone, and replaced by the clearer perspective operating in the mind of Christ. I will give it significant treatment at the end of this chapter after I have done the work of clarifying Alison's understanding of the disciples' experience of conversion initiated by their encounters with the crucified and risen Christ.

relationship between theology and conversion, I will address them separately here. The present chapter will develop Alison's implicit understanding of the movement from conversion to theological reflection; that is, it will present theology as a fruit of conversion. And the next chapter will develop his view of the movement from theological expression to the potential conversion experiences of others; that is, it will present theology as an occasion for conversion.

3.1 Alison's Epistemology—An Overview

To follow Alison's reading of the disciples' experiences of Jesus' crucifixion and their experiences of the resurrection, it will be important to begin with an account of his (Girardian) epistemology. I will make use of a distinction that Alison does not use, but that will bring clarity to the interrelationships among his major epistemological terms: intelligence, perception, memory, and imagination. The distinction is between two realms or dimensions of human knowing. I will refer to the first as the background of human knowing, or to what Michael Polanyi identifies as "the tacit dimension."[5] By this, I mean all that which is not available as an object of awareness, attention, and reflection, but which instead makes conscious awareness, attention, and reflection possible. In describing Jesus' efforts to make the intelligence of the victim accessible to the disciples, Alison himself points to the necessity of identifying this background and tacit realm of knowledge without making the distinction explicit:

> [T]here was nothing arcane or occult about the intelligence of the victim: Jesus had been trying to make it plain as day. The drama was that Jesus was revealing... [s]omething... which goes beyond the roots of what makes us aware.[6]

And he goes on to say,

> The problem was for them [the disciples], and is for us, that the intelligence that was in Jesus was an intelligence at the level of what makes us conscious, what makes us aware... a background to understanding... the filter... our programming.[7]

Thus, Alison points to this background, tacit dimension of knowledge in describing the intelligence of the victim. The "roots," "programming," "filter," or "background" to knowing makes conscious awareness, attentiveness, and reflection possible. However, instead of describing this background and tacit dimension of knowing at length, Alison, following Girard, talks about the antecedence of the rivalrous social

---

[5] Michael Polyani, *The Tacit Dimension* (Chicago: University of Chicago Press, 1966).
[6] Alison, *Knowing Jesus*, 40.
[7] Ibid., 41. And describing the difficulty for the disciples in receiving the intelligence of the victim in *The Joy of Being Wrong*, Alison writes, "The beginning of the perception of the intelligence of the victim is already an alteration in what constitutes human consciousness" (*The Joy of Being Wrong*, 81).

other, which includes the whole interpersonal and cultural network of people, values, institutions, environment, etc., that constitute the framework of one's perception and knowing. In a Girardian view, this antecedent social other makes up the tacit or background dimension of knowing.

This background, tacit dimension is distinguished from a foreground and explicit dimension of knowledge in which the human subject participates in the process of directing his or her awareness, attention, and reflection toward particular objects. This distinction between background and foreground "realms," between tacit and explicit "dimensions" of knowledge, will allow me to articulate more clearly Alison's epistemology, beginning with his use of the word "intelligence." Intelligence in Alison's usage pertains to both the background and the foreground of human knowing: that which makes awareness, attentiveness, and reflection possible, and that which, as it gives persons their subjective awareness, is appropriated by them as the explicit, fundamental understandings of self, other, and the world that guide them in choosing how to navigate the at least partially hostile terrain of human relationships.

Alison's use of the word "intelligence" is never abstract—that is, he never refers to intelligence as such. Instead, when he talks about intelligence it is always in the context of the intelligence of the victim, that is, the intelligence operative in the mind of Christ, or in the context of the intelligence operative in the minds of the disciples. From the consistency of Alison's use of this term in one of these two contexts, I suggest that for Alison, intelligence is always "operative," or "narratival," in two senses.

In the first sense, referring to its movement in the background, intelligence is operative in that it feels as though it is moving toward an end. It has a degree of subjectivity, directionality, or intentionality that is prior to the subjects that it shapes and influences.[8] This sense of intelligence as having a direction and an intention that is prior to subjects suggests that it has a momentum; persons experience unthematically this prior intelligence as operative, as moving toward an end that is not under their direct influence, and as feeling like a narrative that has as its protagonist someone other than themselves.

Secondly, this intelligence operates in the foreground of knowing in that, as it shapes persons, it is gradually appropriated by them and becomes the understanding of self, others, and God out of which those individuals operate in the world. It becomes the fundamental understanding that makes up, and enables subjects to tell, the undergirding narrative of their own experienced identity. The basic human capacity for perceiving the world and telling a story of one's place within it involves the subject's participation in, and operation out of, the background intelligence that

---

[8] We saw in the last chapter that Girard's understanding of desire attributes to it a degree of subjectivity. There is a way in which Girard sees desire as being the true subject since it is always the desire of the other that precedes and originates a "self" within persons. I described Girard's view of desire as the pool of connectivity from which human subjectivity arises and which holds human persons together. Alison's description of intelligence as "operative" suggests that he understands intelligence as correlative with desire. Each mode of desire carries with it, and operates according to, a particular intelligence. Thus, the intelligence according to which a particular mode of desire operates, together with that desire, "possesses" and gives subjectivity to individuals. A sense of this comes through in Alison's treatment of the "intelligence of the victim" in *The Joy of Being Wrong*, especially pp. 79–81.

makes perceiving and storytelling possible. That is, this participation makes possible a foreground intelligence that consists of the person's foundational understandings of self, others, and God from which he or she makes decisions about how to navigate, or reconnoiter, the potentially hostile terrain of human relationships.

Thus, for Alison, intelligence, like desire, seems to both possess and be possessed by individuals and groups. The intelligence according to which desire operates has a pseudo subjectivity of its own since it is not generated by the subject, but instead is received, along with desire, from a preceding other. Desire and the intelligence according to which desire operates gradually inscribe subjectivity, or self-reflexive awareness, into the individual. Thus, intelligence in Alison's usage is operative in that it has an objective that is determined by its source, which, for Alison, is either the vivaciousness of God or the satanic lie that violence is necessary for creating peace. Then intelligence becomes operative within the persons it "possesses" in that it becomes the conscious or unconscious basis upon which they navigate the cultural-social (relational) world around them. In this second sense, intelligence shapes the subject's foundational understanding in the world and his or her experienced identity.

Finally, in Alison's usage, "intelligence" does not exclusively or even primarily designate the activity of the intellect. Rather, intelligence is that which makes awareness possible in all of its "valences" or aspects—emotional/affective, spiritual/immaterial, intellectual/cognitive. Intelligence involves the activity of all these valences of awareness, which are inextricably intermeshed with one another.[9] The reason for distinguishing them notionally is that persons often attend to just one of these valences of experience at a time. I will suggest later in this chapter that, as a result of this tendency, it is beneficial for our understanding of Alison's view of the disciples' experience of the resurrection to consider each of these valences separately.

Yet part of Alison's strategy (and this is a fruit of Girard's influence) is to maintain the interconnectedness of these valences of human experience. As a result, he often refers to them interchangeably, or he groups two or three of them together toward a particular end. By highlighting this interconnectedness, Alison strives to depict the unity of the foreground, explicit dimension of human knowing to emphasize its distinction from the deep background structures of desire and intelligence that make the foreground dimension possible. This strategy also serves a fundamental aim of his theology, which I will develop in the rest of this work, namely, to argue that true understanding can never be a purely intellectual activity.

With this description of Alison's use of "intelligence," which draws out the distinction between that which subjects are able to consciously attend to and that which makes human awareness possible, I can now identify what constitutes knowledge in this framework. True knowledge is always the fruit of a process of subversion of a false

---

[9] I use the word "valence" here very loosely (and I am not at all tied to this particular word, except that I need to use some word) to indicate something like varying dimensions or aspects of human experience. But I prefer to speak of "valences" rather than "dimensions" or "aspects" because I think that the latter two words tend to communicate a stronger impression of distinctness among them and I believe that this impression obscures Alison's basic meaning. In Alison's view these "valences" of experience are not separate from each other, but, as I say here, always inextricably intermeshed.

intelligence by a higher, or true, intelligence. False intelligence consists of a series of deceptions masquerading as insight. In the background, these deceptions are accepted implicitly as part of the cultural milieu in which the subject finds him or herself. In the foreground, these deceptions function as a fundamental understanding of self, others, God, and the world grounded in the illusion of a discrete and self-originating subject.[10]

True intelligence, on the other hand, is most fully operative in the mind of Christ, and Alison refers to it most frequently as the "intelligence of the victim."[11] We will see later in this chapter, as well as in the next, that false intelligence in Alison's Girardian framework might aptly be referred to in several ways, including the "intelligence of the persecutor," the "intelligence of the lie," or even the "intelligence of death." True knowing, then, always involves the exposure and subversion by true intelligence of a subject's operation according to a false, deceptive intelligence. The subject comes to know this subversion in the form of a narrative about the subject's coming to remember rightly who he or she had been, and to perceive and imagine clearly who he or she is being enabled to become. We will see toward the end of this chapter that, in Alison's perspective, it helps to read the New Testament accounts of the resurrection appearances through this lens.

"Memory," "perception," and "imagination" are terms that Alison sometimes uses distinctly and sometimes rather interchangeably to depict the transformation that results from the subject's experience of the process of subversion. It is in this realm of the subject's memory, perception, and imagination of "reality" that subversion (or conversion) takes place. I will consider several descriptive passages from his second book, *Raising Abel*, to show how Alison uses these terms. Speaking of memory as it is being reshaped by the intelligence of the victim, Alison writes:

> If we practice the *memory* of the self-giving of the forgiving victim ... , then we are empowered to have our memory unbound from its deceit, we can see and accept and remain free from our mendacious self-construction of the past, our lie is revealed to us as something capable of being forgiven, which *also and simultaneously* allows us to imagine a future which has no end. I suggest to you that the instruction "Do this in memory of me" and the exhortation "Fix your mind on the things that are above ... where Christ is seated at the right hand of God" are exactly the same instruction: the loving self-giving of the past and the future promise of receiving a full self-giving *are the same thing*. ... That is forgiveness of sins and the healing of memories is the same thing: what unbinds our past is what opens up our future.[12]

Here Alison explicitly links our capacity for remembering the past and imagining a future. The healing of our memory and the recovery and growth of our capacity for imagining a future "full of hope" (Jer. 29:11) occur simultaneously and are even presented as being identical. Alison goes on to identify this capacity for right

---

[10] I will delineate the series of deceptions that make up such a false intelligence toward the end of this chapter. See Sections 3.2.5.5 and 3.2.5.6.
[11] In Chapter 4, I will also refer to this intelligence as the "intelligence of forgiveness incarnate."
[12] Alison, *Raising Abel*, 115; Alison's emphasis.

remembering of the past and right imagining of the future with the capacity for right perception of the present:

> This revelation [of God brought about by Jesus] makes it possible for our memory, and through it, our life-story and our person, to be called into existence in such a way that the memory and the past does not form a threatening present, but rather a present which is in a process of constant enrichment by what is being given it, and where the future is precisely the continuation of an ever greater and ever richer reception of life.[13]

For Alison, the same underlying dynamic—namely, the awareness (or lack thereof) of one's own relationship to victims—shapes the human perception of past, present, and future. Thus, the human capacity for memory, perception, and imagination is one and the same. In Alison's usage, all of these terms refer to a basic human capacity (that can be more or less fully received) to "see" and, therefore, relate to "reality" as it is made discoverable through the reception of forgiveness from the crucified and risen Christ.

In his identification of memory, perception, and imagination, Alison allows for a degree of distinction derived from the temporal and narrative quality of human knowing and being. In this regard, Alison sometimes distinguishes among memory, perception, and imagination by using "memory" to refer to one's knowing of one's past, "perception" to refer to one's knowing of one's present, and "imagination" to refer to one's knowing of one's future.

Despite these distinctions, Alison emphasizes the inseparability and even interchangeability of the terms in referring to the subject's basic capacity for perceiving or knowing reality. Speaking of the conversion that made possible the advent of Hebrew monotheism, Alison contrasts the singular capacity for knowing or perceiving with the background structures of intelligence and desire:

> What the advent of Hebrew monotheism looked like could, and can, only be detected in the radical reversal of desire which it produces. It is not that a new 'It' begins to open up *before* our gaze, a gaze brought into being by the relationships that have taught us what we can see and desire. Instead, 'I Am bringing everything to be' [Exodus 3:14] starts to emerge, as it were, from *behind* our capacity for gaze ... by producing profound alterations of the patterns of desire which enable us to be 'selves' at all, such that we find ourselves ceasing to be self-grasping 'I's' who share in the creation of 'its' by rivalry, defense, paranoia and projection.... It is not *what* we see, but our capacity for gaze itself that is undergoing transformation.[14]

This emphasis on the relational patterns of desire "behind" (i.e., constitutive of) the human capacity for knowing and perceiving characterizes Alison's Girardian

---

[13] Ibid., 116.
[14] James Alison, *Broken Hearts and New Creations* (New York: Continuum/London: DLT, 2010), 114–15; Alison's emphasis.

epistemology.[15] Alison's frequent identification or linking of the terms "memory," "perception," and "imagination" brings this background structure of knowing to the fore of his readers' attention. In his view, this is what is required to consider the dynamics of conversion and simultaneously invite his readers into the possibility of being encountered by the Spirit of Christ as well.

3.2 The Disciples' Experience of Meeting the Risen Jesus as the Beginning of "Conversion"

Alison's reading of the disciples' experience of meeting the crucified and risen Jesus functions as the source and fundamental criterion of his theological reflection throughout the whole of his corpus thus far. This should not be a surprising claim to anyone who has read Alison's first three books, since, in each one, Alison's first or second order of business involves investigating the disciples' experience of the resurrection or summarizing and expanding upon his previous investigation of it.

In the first chapter of *Knowing Jesus* (1993), his first substantive theological work, Alison develops his first and longest treatment of the disciples' resurrection experience.[16] This treatment is the foundation for the rest of the book, which is directed toward an educated but non-academic audience and which develops an understanding of Christ, the church, and the ground of human knowing. In *Raising Abel* (1996), after briefly introducing the book's eschatological theme and overviewing mimetic theory, Alison returns to his previous reading of the disciples' experience of the passion and resurrection to frame his approach to developing an understanding of what he calls "the eschatological imagination."[17]

Alison takes a slightly different tack in *The Joy of Being Wrong*, which was written as his doctoral dissertation in 1994 (prior to his writing of *Raising Abel*) and eventually published in 1998. In this longer and more academic work, after opening with an extended treatment of Girard's "theory," Alison uses the second chapter to develop a theological anthropology using mimetic psychology supported by the more developed psychological perspective of one of Girard's colleagues, J.-M. Oughourlian, and in conversation with the theological perspectives of Joseph Ratzinger, Walter Kasper, and John Milbank, among others. Not until chapter 3 does Alison turn to the question of soteriology. After explicating his view of revelation, he returns to his earlier exploration of the disciples' experience of the resurrection in *Knowing Jesus*, which he summarizes at length.[18] This delay, so to speak, in his treatment of the resurrection in this text is due to the demands of the work as a dissertation and does not reflect any shift in its foundational importance for his theological method. He describes the anthropology

---

[15] I think it could be argued that this emphasis is the essential element of any "Girardian" epistemology. See *Evolution and Conversion*, 172–3.
[16] Alison, *Knowing Jesus*, 3–30.
[17] Alison, *Raising Abel*, 25–30.
[18] Alison, *The Joy of Being Wrong*, 70–7.

that he develops in chapter 2 of that work as "an anthropology of conversion," and he gives this anthropology its descriptive force through his presentation of the disciples' experience of the resurrection in chapter 3.

More recently, in the text for an adult Christian theology course entitled *Jesus the Forgiving Victim: Listening for the Unheard Voice*, Alison devotes the first session to summarizing Girard's psychology, as it is helpful for coming to a deeper understanding of Christian theology.[19] Then, in the second session, Alison demonstrates the centrality of the disciples' experience of the risen Jesus to his theological method. Here he gives a close reading of Luke's account of Jesus' appearance to the two disciples on the road to Emmaus. His reading of this story serves as the central narrative around which the course is structured.

Together these four texts demonstrate that Alison's treatment of the disciples' experience of the crucified and risen Jesus consistently provides the foundation for his engagement in theological inquiry. Alison's consistency in beginning his theological work with a reading of the disciples' experience of the resurrection is far more than a stylistic technique. Instead, the disciples' experience of the risen Jesus, as Alison has come to understand it through the influence of Girard, provides the lens through which he structures his approach to the rest of Scripture and his theological understandings of all the mysteries of Christian faith. For Alison, the disciples' experience of conversion through their encounter with the risen Jesus is the origin of, and the criterion for, all authentic theological reflection and expression.

Although *Knowing Jesus* strives to bring out the "inner coherence between key [Christian] doctrines,"[20] as do his two longer and more systematic books, *Raising Abel* and *The Joy Being Wrong*, Alison's writings do not set out to provide systematic definitions of his key terms, nor are they directed primarily toward an academic audience. Rather, one of Alison's primary goals is to draw his readers into a deeper awareness of, and attentiveness to, the experience of conversion to Christ as it was first undergone by the apostolic witnesses.

3.2.1 Girard's Influence on Alison's View of the Disciples' Resurrection Experiences

To understand the motivating context for Alison's interest in investigating anew the New Testament accounts of the resurrection appearances, it will be helpful to give some attention to the initial influence of Girard's work on Alison's curiosity about the disciples' experiences of conversion. Within the context of Girard's influence, the accounts of the resurrection appearances become for Alison not primarily narratives about something that happened to Jesus of which the disciples were mere observers, but rather narratives about something that the Father did within the life of Jesus to make possible a revelatory happening within the disciples as they found themselves

---

[19] *Jesus the Forgiving Victim: Listening for the Unheard Voice* (Glenview, IL: Doers Publishing, 2013) is a four-volume text and video introduction to Christian faith for adults. The video series is produced by the Raven Foundation.
[20] From the author's introduction, *Knowing Jesus*, xii.

in the living presence of the friend and teacher they had abandoned to crucifixion.[21] Understanding this context will also allow for a clearer consideration in the next chapter of the Alison's view of the relationship between mimetic theory and Christian revelation.

Although Alison first came across Girard's work in early 1985 when he found a copy of the original French edition of *Things Hidden*, the insight that led Alison to his first substantial written theological reflections employing Girard's thought (in *Knowing Jesus*) began to develop several years later while Alison was reflecting on Girard's first book, *Deceit, Desire and the Novel*.[22] Alison says that while reading this text he was struck by the development of Girard's argument regarding the conversions undergone by the protagonists of the novels he was investigating and by the novelists themselves. In particular, Girard's description of the strong contrast between the "old self" (prior to conversion) and the "new self" (after conversion) engaged Alison.[23] Girard's description of this contrast helped Alison to begin to make sense of his own experience of conversion and eventually suggested to him "a way of reading the gospels in light of the Resurrection."[24] That is, Girard's characterizations of the sharp contrast between the "before" and "after" of conversion as portrayed by his novelists, along with Girard's argument about the experience that must have occurred to make that portrayal possible, fostered in Alison a new curiosity about the New Testament accounts of the resurrection and what gave rise to them: the experience of the disciples in meeting the risen Jesus. Alison intuited that the structure of the conversion experiences of Girard's selected novelists and their protagonists was similar in essence to the structure of the experiences of the disciples upon meeting the risen Jesus and, therefore, the New Testament accounts of those experiences might have significant similarities to the depictions of conversion which Girard believed to be at the center of the novels he investigated. Alison believed that if his insight was sound, then he could use Girard's reading of the conversions in the novels to illuminate and deepen his own understanding of the New Testament resurrection accounts and the experiences of the disciples that made those accounts possible.

Knowing Jesus, originally written as a series of lectures presented at Blackfriars, Oxford, in 1991, is partially Alison's pursuit of the intellectual curiosity sparked by his

---

[21] Alison describes this view of the resurrection when he disagrees with Eric Gans' confinement of the decisive moment of Christian revelation to Christ's appearance to Paul. In response to Gans, Alison says, "The Christian revelation was not, as Gans rightly suggests, a revelatory experience undergone by Jesus. However, neither was it a single, Pauline moment of insight. Rather it was the resurrection [of Jesus] from the dead made available to a large number of people, including, finally, Paul" (*The Joy of Being Wrong*, 70–1).

[22] While Alison did publish one short article in Portuguese engaging Girard's thought before writing *Knowing Jesus*, this earlier article ("A AIDS como lugar da revelação: René Girard e uma teologia pastoral") had a much narrower focus; it considered what Girard might contribute to the development of a pastoral theology arising out of the aids epidemic in Brazil.

[23] Girard reasons that the unity of the conclusions in the novels he has investigated, which consists in the "conversion" of the hero, is only possible because the novelists themselves have each experienced the same process of conversion, which has made it possible for them to depict that conversion within their novels. See the beginning of the last chapter in Sections 2.2 and 2.2.1.

[24] This quotation comes from a Skype interview I conducted with James Alison on May 23, 2011.

reading of *Deceit, Desire and the Novel*.[25] As I have noted, it begins with an exploration of the disciples' experiences of meeting the risen Jesus.[26] Although not stated explicitly in the text, the influence of *Deceit, Desire and the Novel* upon Alison's investigation is evident in the "before" and "after" depictions of the disciples that shape Alison's reading of their experience of the resurrection. One of the things that Alison has learned from Girard, even at this early stage in his career, is the necessity of an experience of "conversion" for coming to a true perception of reality through the discovery of one's own participation in various forms of rivalry and violence.[27] Alison's investigation in *Knowing Jesus* reflects his assent to this basic insight of Girard's, and it shows how this assent has begun to shape his understanding of Scripture and the nature of theological reflection.

Alison provides an early indication of his basic theological method when he frames the question of "knowing Jesus," not as a question of *what* Christians claim to know *about* Jesus, but as that which Alison sees as the prior question of *how* Christians, beginning with the disciples and continuing to the present, have come to know Jesus, in the sense of *believing in* him as the crucified and risen Lord.[28] Alison's exploration of the disciples' experience of meeting the risen Jesus is, in the first place, his attempt to answer this question of how.[29]

Although Alison explicitly names this experience as a conversion only two or three times in this text, the parallels between Girard's description of the conversions of his novelists and Alison's constructive excavation of the disciples' experience from the New Testament accounts of the resurrection appearances are so great that we can assert that, for Alison, the disciples' experience of meeting the risen Jesus is the pivotal moment within an experience of conversion as Girard's work has led Alison to understand it. It seems that Girard's sustained hypothesis about the conversions of his novelists helped Alison to realize that the conversions that the disciples underwent upon meeting the risen Jesus constituted the beginning of a new, life-altering insight into who they were, who Jesus is, and who God is. Furthermore, the underlying assertion that frames Alison's approach to the question of Christian "knowing" is that this conversion of the

---

[25] Alison's reflection on the cover of the first edition of the book fills in a little more of his motivation for writing those essays. He indicates that the intellectual curiosity sparked by reading Girard provided him the tools that allowed him to interpret, in light of the Gospel, his experience of being "generously received" by the patients of an AIDS hospital in Brazil. So, it was the impact of Girard's thought upon Alison's imagination that helped him make sense of his present life experiences and then led to his writing of the essays that were eventually published as *Knowing Jesus*.

[26] The first chapter is devoted to this exploration (*Knowing Jesus*, 3–30).

[27] Girard first comes to see the necessity of conversion for perceiving reality when he recognizes the unity of the conclusions of the novels he investigates. He recognizes that the novelists' personal experiences of conversion from rivalrous mimesis enabled them to disclose the rivalrous form of the mimetic structure in their novels, which culminate with the conversion of their heroes. See Section 2.2. in the last chapter. Girard eventually comes to see this assertion of the necessity of conversion for clear knowing as a fundamental epistemological principle and he states it as such in *Evolution and Conversion*, 172–3.

[28] Alison, *Knowing Jesus*, 3–8.

[29] We can recall from the end of the last chapter that this question of "how" is one that Girard knowingly leaves unconsidered when he insists upon confining his inquiry into the Gospel texts to the realm of "anthropology." See Section 2.4.4.

disciples constituted the removal of a blindness that had been preventing them from having a clear and accurate knowledge of themselves, Jesus, and God.[30] The removal of this blindness was necessary for a true perception of Jesus, as well as of themselves and of God, to become possible.

As I indicated in the last chapter, Alison does not just follow Girard; he goes farther. Instead of simply looking for evidence that the disciples undergo an experience of conversion as Girard understands it, he asks what that experience consisted of and offers a compelling hypothesis concerning how their experience of conversion begins and unfolds. Alison asserts that it is ultimately an experience of being forgiven that enables the removal of blindness and the subsequent transformation that Girard identifies as conversion. All of their knowing and preaching *about* Jesus were made possible and shaped by their reception of forgiveness *from*, and the healing of their relationship *with*, the risen Jesus, who approached them as a forgiving victim.

Girard's depiction of conversion led Alison to reconsider the disciples' experiences of meeting the risen Jesus. The fruit of this rereading for Alison is a new understanding of conversion to Christ—one that sees conversion as the effect of being forgiven and as the condition for the possibility of any clear perspective and true understanding of self, Jesus, and God. This view of the disciples' experience of conversion through their reception of forgiveness from the crucified and risen Jesus shapes both Alison's understanding and performance of theology from the beginning of his theological career. I now turn to investigate and develop his view of the disciples' experiences of Jesus' death and resurrection.

3.2.2 Alison's Method for Exploring the Disciples' Experience of Jesus' Death and Resurrection

To explore the "density" of this experience of meeting the risen Jesus,[31] Alison begins by reconstructing the relational context of Jesus and his disciples preceding the resurrection because this context is the condition for the possibility of their being able to experience the risen Jesus at all. While many people were observers and even participants in Jesus' crucifixion, only Jesus' friends and followers became the first witnesses of his resurrection.[32] As Alison writes, the resurrection

> was not the sort of happening that could be witnessed casually.... The very fact of witnessing it at all meant a degree of involvement in a complex set of human relationships, which culminated in their being able to witness it. That was true of all the disciples to whom Jesus appeared. Jesus' appearances to them took place

---

[30] Alison, *Raising Abel*, 22.//
[31] Alison uses the word "density" to indicate that the disciples' experiences of meeting the crucified and risen Jesus are extremely complex and require a significant amount of unpacking. See *Knowing Jesus*, 23 and *The Joy of Being Wrong*, 71.
[32] Alison sees the Apostle Paul as the one exception to this description of the first witnesses of the risen Jesus. Prior to meeting the risen Jesus on the road to Damascus, Paul's only relationship to Jesus was that of persecuting the followers of the "Way" (*Knowing Jesus*, 21–2).

within the framework of their friendship with him, their hopes concerning him, their feeling of guilt at having abandoned him.[33]

In other words, the disciples' capacity to become witnesses of the risen Jesus, whatever that experience consisted of, was possible only as an outgrowth and, as Alison says, the "culmination" of the ways in which their identities had already begun to be shaped by their growing friendships with Jesus during his life and their failure in being faithful to those friendships in the face of his public persecution and death.[34] Alison sees the latter circumstances as the most immediate context for their experience of the resurrection, since the disciples' experience of their friendships with Jesus after his death was a devastating conclusion to what they had hoped would lead to the fulfillment of Jesus' promises of the kingdom of God.

As he considers the disciples' likely experience of their friendship with Jesus after his death, Alison describes his method as an attempt to be attentive to the ordinary human responses of disorientation, grief, fear, and guilt that would have resulted for any psychologically "healthy" individual in such circumstances:

> I'm not trying to give an imaginary psychological description of the disciples. I'm trying rather to bring out the ordinary human responses to Jesus' death that were present. That is to say, whose absence would have been remarkable, and the sign of deeply psychologically deranged personalities. These responses are either present or hinted at in the New Testament texts. The reason for this is to illustrate something of the network of relationships into which Jesus began to appear, starting on that Sunday morning. The resurrection was first perceived from within those complexes of relationships that had been left severed and dangling on the Friday before, and had been developed over the years leading up to that.[35]

Here Alison states up front that in his attempt to explore the disciples' experiences of the resurrection, he is not going to look primarily to New Testament scholarship or historical/cultural studies. Instead, Alison is going to employ a method that will imagine and attend to the psychologically "ordinary" human responses to the circumstances surrounding Jesus' death. Alison sees this imaginative (but not "imaginary") approach as necessary for understanding the relational, psychological context in which Jesus' appearances to the disciples likely took place. Having an imaginative sense of this context will help readers better understand the disciples' experience of encountering (or, rather, being encountered by) the risen Jesus.

---

[33] Alison, *Knowing Jesus*, 8.
[34] Alison does not give an account of the New Testament passages noting those disciples who remained with Jesus until the end. Such an account would need to allow room for some form of failure in faithfulness to their friendships with Jesus other than abandonment. Within Alison's framework, this failure might be best identified as a fundamental (but unrecognized) belief in the ultimacy of death that becomes an invisible obstacle to belief in the living God. I will argue this more fully below in Sections 3.2.3 and 3.2.5.2.
[35] Alison, *Knowing Jesus*, 11.

Alison's imaginative reconstruction of these "ordinary human responses to Jesus' death" and the "network of relationships" that likely developed among the disciples as a result also sets the groundwork for Alison to pursue his intuition that Girard's psychological description of the "before" and "after" of conversion would provide a helpful tool in drawing out the shifts in perspective that take place within the disciples upon meeting the risen Jesus.[36] We will see below that a combination of Alison's attention to the "ordinary" psychological responses of the disciples and his application of Girard's psychological insights leads Alison to see that the disciples' experience of meeting the risen Jesus is at its core an experience of receiving forgiveness.

Alison recognizes that investigating such a unique and paradigmatic experience as the resurrection presents difficulties especially within our culture, which is hypersensitive to the variety of factors that contribute to the uniqueness of each person's experience. Without imagining that it is possible to grasp fully the experience of the disciples, Alison attempts to draw out their likely experience of Jesus' death in broad strokes.

3.2.3 An Imaginative Reconstruction of the Disciples' Post-crucifixion Experience

Alison begins his reconstruction of the disciples' post-crucifixion experience by suggesting that Jesus' death must have felt to them like a real end to their relationship with him. Because Jesus was no longer there, they had to work alone through their feelings, memories, hopes, and expectations about what Jesus would bring about as the Messiah.[37] Thus, Jesus' death likely first left the disciples shocked and extremely disoriented. They had completely reordered their lives according to their growing belief in Jesus; they had chosen to leave everything behind and follow him.

Despite whatever pronouncements Jesus had made during his life about his impending death and the disciples' abandonment of him, when faced with the actuality of his death, the disciples could not help but respond to it like it was an end to all they had believed and hoped about him. In the days after Jesus' death, the disciples were overcome with disappointment.[38] They had not believed that Jesus would die without having brought the kingdom of God to its fulfillment. This was a man who had called

---

[36] We saw in the last chapter that Eugene Webb classifies Girard's work as essentially "psychological" in the sense of the French psychoanalytic tradition. And Webb sees this classification as consistent with Girard's own acknowledgment that mimesis (not violence) plays a "primordial role" in his perspective. See Eugene Webb, *The Self Between: From Freud to the New Social Psychology of France* (Seattle: University of Washington Press, 1993), 210; cf. Girard, *Violent Origins: Walter Burkert, Rene Girard, and Jonathan Z. Smith on Ritual Killing and Cultural Formation* (Stanford, CA: Stanford University Press, 1987), ed. Hamerton-Kelly, 123.

Webb's thesis finds further confirmation in a more recent statement in which Girard identifies *Deceit, Desire, and the Novel* (Baltimore: Johns Hopkins University Press, 1976) and *A Theatre of Envy: William Shakespeare* (New York/Oxford: Oxford University Press, 1991) as the works most representative of his thinking, since in these texts Girard draws out the dynamics of metaphysical desire and his "interdividual" psychology as he sees them depicted by his selected modern novelists. See *Evolution and Conversion*, 27. Cf. Kirwan, *Girard and Theology*, 14.

[37] Alison, *Knowing Jesus*, 9.
[38] Alison, *The Joy of Being Wrong*, 73.

God "Father" and who had spoken and acted with such interior authority that he seemed to be different from anyone they had ever known. However, his death appeared to suggest that the kingdom of God he preached would not come; this must have filled the disciples with grief and even brought them close to despair. Alison suggests that with Jesus' death, the perspectives of the Jewish and Roman authorities on Jesus must have become more persuasive for the disciples:

> [I]t is extremely unlikely that, when he died, [the disciples] didn't come to accept something of those authorities' point of view about Jesus. Death is final and puts to an end the voice of the dissident, making those who killed him ... seem ... reasonable people.... The disciples on their way to Emmaus were sunk in the grief of those for whom Jesus' death was the triumph of the point of view of his persecutors. This viewpoint worked like this: this Jesus was a sinner, and in killing him, God's will was being done, since he had broken God's law. His death included hanging on a tree which meant, according to Deuteronomy (Deut. 21:23; cf. Gal. 3:13), that he died under the curse of God.[39]

It seems likely that the disciples would have at least been inclined to wonder whether the authorities had been right about Jesus all along. The apparently undeniable triumph of the perspective of the persecutors must have caused them to doubt what had led them to place such trust in Jesus in the first place.

In addition to, and in tension with, their extreme disorientation, disappointment, and grief, the disciples must have felt significant fear and guilt. Alison notes that they would have had reason to fear that the public humiliation and shame of Jesus' execution as a criminal could spread to incriminate the disciples, who were foreigners linked to the one who had been executed.[40] The accounts of the disciples in the locked room suggest that an atmosphere of fear surrounded them.[41] Finally, the disciples must have felt significant guilt, a "sense of moral failure," for having betrayed or abandoned their friend when his public humiliation and crucifixion were imminent.[42]

Alison summarizes his psychological description of the disciples after the crucifixion by saying, "What we have then, in the apostolic circle, is a group of disillusioned, frightened, guilty, mournful, semi-traitors."[43] Into this network of disorientation, disappointment, grief, fear, and guilt, the living presence of Jesus irrupted Easter morning and in the days following.

---

[39] Alison, *Raising Abel*, 26–7.
[40] Alison, *The Joy of Being Wrong*, 73. Alison cites Acts 1:6 as evidence that the disciples may well have thought themselves to be part of a politico-messianic movement. This would have greatly increased their fear of political retaliation after Jesus' execution.
[41] Alison, *Knowing Jesus*, 10; cf. John 20:19-31.
[42] Alison, *Knowing Jesus*, 9; *The Joy of Being Wrong*, 73. And those who did stay may well have also felt guilt about not having stood up to the crowd and risked their own lives in defending Jesus' innocence.
[43] Alison, *The Joy of Being Wrong*, 73.

Alison's narrative about this network of relationships suggests that, despite the disciples' growing friendships with Jesus throughout his public ministry, the disciples still held (or were held by) a foundational belief in the ultimacy of death. Alison writes,

> Jesus was able to move *toward* death without being moved *by* death (cf. Heb. 12:2, … for the joy that was set before him, he bore the cross, despising the shame …) … This was not, of course something that the disciples could begin to understand while they were accompanying him, since death was for them, as it normally is for all of us until we begin to understand the Gospel, the definitive stumbling block.[44]

The disciples' disorientation, grief, fear, and guilt demonstrate that, in Alison's words, death remained for them, as it is for most of us, "the definitive stumbling block." Their fear of death kept them from standing up for Jesus in the face of his persecution, and their belief in the ultimacy of death, rather than in the kingdom of God that Jesus preached, determined their perspectives on themselves, Jesus, others, and God both prior to and after Jesus' death. Thus, Jesus' death appeared to them to be the definitive end of everything he had preached and lived for. Yet, this fear of death arising from their belief in death's ultimacy was so fundamental that they would not become directly aware of its operation within themselves until they found themselves being freed from it through an offer of forgiveness from the crucified and risen Jesus, who would make undeniably clear to them for the first time that death was not ultimate.

3.2.4 The Resurrection Narratives as the Key to Alison's View of the Whole of Scripture

In *Knowing Jesus*, addressing believing Christians in a relatively conversational style, Alison assumes that his readers accept the veracity of the resurrection narratives and, therefore, he does not entertain the question of whether the resurrection was an objectively observable event.[45] Instead, Alison opens his investigation of the resurrection appearances in *Knowing Jesus* by posing two questions: "[H]ow did the resurrection irrupt into that network of tangled, sorry relationships [among the disciples] that were jarring painfully [after Jesus' death]? [And] of what, insofar as we can describe a unique and a normative experience, was the resurrection experience made up?"[46]

These questions make it clear that Alison intends to consider the resurrection as it was experienced by the disciples since it is first and foremost to their experience that the New Testament accounts of the resurrection appearances bear witness. What we have in these accounts, from Alison's perspective, are testimonies of the disciples' experiences of transformation as they found themselves in the presence of the risen Jesus. Yet those experiences are recorded from the perspectives of early "Christian"

---

[44] Alison, *Raising Abel*, 41.
[45] I will consider Alison's perspective on the historical or objective observability of the resurrection at the end of this section when I relate Alison's approach to some standard methods of biblical scholarship.
[46] Alison, *Knowing Jesus*, 13.

communities who were undergoing a similar transformation as they happened to find themselves meeting the living presence of the crucified Jesus through the oral tradition that grew out of the first disciples' testimonies of their resurrection experiences.[47] Alison writes, "the texts themselves are the witness, put into writing, of the irruption into the midst of a group of humans of a completely new phenomenon ... It is equally clear that if Jesus had *not* been raised, then there would have been no such texts."[48] While Alison is making a claim from the perspective of faith in the risen Christ, which someone from outside such a perspective may not accept as self-evident, this assertion reveals how Alison views the resurrection narratives. The resurrection accounts, as well as the New Testament texts as a whole, are the written record of the apostolic group's witness of an irruption of something completely new into their midst. But these accounts are recorded by others who claim to have become witnesses to this "something new" through the apostolic group's participation in it and ongoing testimony about it. In other words, we have an account of the experience of the disciples upon meeting the risen Jesus understood through the experiences of those who were enabled to encounter (in some sense) the risen Jesus through their reception of the testimonies of the first witnesses.[49] These texts are the fruit of an encounter. More accurately, they are the fruit of a series of encounters that began with, and unfolded from, this first encounter between the risen Jesus and his first disciples.

I believe that this view of the resurrection narratives—as the fruit of a series of encounters between the risen Jesus and his disciples, which began with Jesus' appearances to those disciples who had followed him during his earthly life and were extended to include others through the witnessing of these first disciples—is the view implied in Alison's notion of theology as a form of witness to the risen Christ. I will develop this line of thought in the next chapter. For now, I have summarized Alison's understanding of the resurrection narratives for two more immediate reasons: first, to suggest how this understanding has led him to a view of the Scriptures as a whole, and, second, to set the context for presenting Alison's interpretation of the disciples' experiences of encountering the risen Jesus.

To the first objective: Alison's view of the resurrection narratives becomes the source of his view of the whole of Scripture, both Old and New Testaments. For Alison, not only the accounts of the resurrection appearances, but also the Gospels as a whole, are the fruit of an interpretive encounter with the crucified and risen Jesus. In his

---

[47] I am aware that some biblical scholarship indicates that the resurrection narratives are influenced by anti-Docetic polemics. See, for example, Richard Burridge's *What Are the Gospels? A Comparison with Graeco-Roman Biography* (Cambridge: Cambridge University Press, 1992), James D. G. Dunn's *Jesus Remembered* (Grand Rapids, MI: Eerdmans Publishing, 2003), and Raymond Brown's *An Introduction to New Testament Christology* (Mahwah, NJ: Paulist Press, 1994). However, here I am presenting Alison's view of the resurrection narratives.

[48] Alison, *The Joy of Being Wrong*, 71; Alison's emphasis.

[49] This view of the resurrection narratives as the fruit of an encounter made possible by a reception of the testimonies of the first witnesses is strongly supported by Richard Bauckham's presentation of the origin of the Gospels in *Jesus and the Eyewitnesses: The Gospels as Eyewitness Testimony* (Grand Rapids, MI: Eerdmans, 2006). Here he argues persuasively in favor of seeing the Gospel texts as "much closer to the form in which the eyewitnesses told their stories or passed on their traditions than is commonly envisaged in current scholarship" (p. 6). I will explore Bauckham's view in more detail at the end of this section.

more recent text for an introductory course on Christian faith, Alison presents his biblical hermeneutic by looking at Luke's account of Jesus' appearance to the disciples on the road to Emmaus. Placing Luke's narrative in the context of competing strains of biblical interpretation after the destruction of the Temple, Alison sees in this story one instance of the early Christian response to a central hermeneutical question within ancient Jewish communities—through whose eyes do you read the texts of Scripture? Who is the Rabbi whose interpretation of the Scripture you follow? In Alison's view, the story of Jesus' appearance on the road to Emmaus is saying in part that "Christians" are claiming to read the Hebrew Scriptures through the eyes of Jesus, who is a crucified and living Rabbi.[50] Alison summarizes his view of this narrative for a non-academic audience by saying:

> In other words, we read through the eyes of one who is present amongst us and who causes us to undergo a complete change of belonging to our world so that we find him interrupting us, speaking to us from out of the periphery of our vision, from just off the screen of what we can understand, including us in a story which is his story, the one of which he is the protagonist. What we … find is that his story gradually makes much better sense of our story, as we thought we knew it. We find ourselves being taken somewhere else, drawn into a bigger framework. And this requires something outside us. *This is not just a text. It is a text and meal with a third person* [the crucified and risen Jesus, our Rabbi].[51]

For Alison, Scripture is not merely a text; rather, it is the fruit and the occasion of an interpretive encounter between God and humanity. The texts of the Hebrew Scriptures give witness to a history of interpretive encounters between God and the Hebrew people and thus become an instrument in the hands of skilled rabbis for inviting God's people in the present into new or renewed encounters with God. The New Testament accounts of the resurrection appearances to the disciples give witness to a definitive instance of such an interpretive encounter, which becomes available to be experienced by others through the disciples' efforts to articulate a new understanding of themselves and the Hebrew Scriptures. Thus, the texts of the New Testament are written records of testimonies to the movement of God toward humanity in history. They are occasions of effective speech from God through the person of the crucified and risen Christ to those who are being invited to leave behind a fraudulent and violent way of being human and are being called together to form a new kind of human community. The texts are, thus, a text and a meal with a third person; that is, they act as occasions of being called out (ἐκκλησία) and gathered by the risen Christ[52] and they involve us in Christ's ongoing project of "reconciling the world to himself" (2 Corinthians 5:19).

Alison's approach to Scripture draws to the fore the multiple layers of interpretive and transformative encounters that are behind the New Testament texts and of which

---

[50] *Jesus the Forgiving Victim*, 28.
[51] Ibid., 46; emphasis added.
[52] Ibid.

the texts themselves are one form of evidence. The texts bear witness to the impact of this series of encounters upon the witnesses, and in bearing witness to it, they become instruments for making a similar encounter available to others.

In light of this approach, it seems most accurate to characterize Alison's hermeneutic as kerygmatic and ecclesial. His hermeneutic is essentially kerygmatic in that he sees the Gospels as a fruit of the disciples' encounter with the risen Christ, which serves as the occasion for others to be invited into a new and ongoing encounter with Christ. That is, the texts of Scripture are an essential component in the communication of God toward humanity, which seeks to transform persons into participants in God's act of communication. His hermeneutic is simultaneously ecclesial because such an encounter with the risen Christ effects a transformation that leads persons into a new way of belonging together. The interpretive encounters with Christ as a forgiving victim proceed from and move toward the community that is called forth by the risen victim himself. As written witnesses of these encounters, the New Testament texts also give witness to, and act as an instrument of, the formation of this community.

Because Alison reads the texts of Scripture with this kerygmatic and ecclesial hermeneutic, he also asserts that the spirit with which one reads the texts is a necessary condition for one's understanding of them. He writes that the texts bear witness to God's historical act of communication toward us "[only] if we read them in the same spirit as that which allowed them to be written."[53] In another essay, he describes that spirit by saying: "[the Scriptures] can only really be read by people who are themselves undergoing that discovery of their own involvement in the lie. That is to say that they can only really be understood by people who *find themselves being 'read'* by the text in question."[54] And this "being read by the texts" is only possible to the degree that "we are willing to allow ourselves to be uncovered as frauds."[55] This point is central to Alison's view of biblical scholarship: to understand the texts, one must approach them as the fruit and potential instrument of a revelatory spirit that, through a non-rivalrous and forgiving mode of presence, exposes one's tendencies to hide from oneself and others one's own rivalrous and, therefore, violent mode of relating. Persons will have access to the meaning being communicated through the texts only if they find themselves possessed by this spirit before approaching the texts or while reading them.[56]

---

[53] Alison, "What Sorts of Difference Does René Girard Make to How We Read the Bible?," in *Broken Hearts and New Creations*, 238.

[54] Alison, "The Priestly Pattern of Creation and a Fraudulent Reading of St. Paul," in *Broken Hearts and New Creations*, 212; Alison's emphasis.

[55] Ibid.

[56] In the next chapter, I will argue that for Alison it does not need to be one or the other (receiving the right spirit before or while reading the texts). The reason is that, while texts are an important form of witness, they are not the only form. One could encounter the crucified and risen Christ outside of any reading of texts, Scriptural or otherwise. Such an encounter may open one to have that encounter deepened through reading Scripture or other texts later. One might even have such an encounter outside of any explicitly Christian context (as Girard did initially). We will see in the next chapter that Alison develops a notion of the christoformity of grace as an alternate to Rahner's notion of the anonymous Christian. What he means is that grace or conversion always has the form of Christ, whom he identifies as the forgiving victim. The important question to keep in mind as we explore his reading of the disciples' experience is: What is its essential "form" which others can experience within other contexts?

It is important to keep in mind that Alison sees in the resurrection narratives the fruit, and the evidence, of a transformative encounter with the crucified and risen Jesus. In Alison's view, anything else expressed within these texts, polemical or otherwise, is secondary to their giving witness in writing to a series of profound experiences of transformation via the living presence of the crucified Jesus. This is his kerygmatic hermeneutic for reading the New Testament resurrection narratives and the New Testament as a whole. He does not dismiss other methods of biblical exegesis (whether they be historical-critical, literary, sociological, contextual, etc.), since each of these hermeneutical approaches could (and should) be used in conjunction with the fundamental premise that the texts of Scripture are the fruit of a series of transformative encounters unfolding from the encounter between the risen Jesus and his first disciples. To the extent that these methods could be useful in helping to fill out the shape of the initial encounter or its historical unfolding, they would support Alison's ecclesial and kerygmatic approach.

Because of this approach, Alison refrains from viewing the resurrection narratives as literal, historical accounts of the resurrection; doing so would be to fundamentally misunderstand the nature of the Gospel texts. Because they are testimonies, the resurrection narratives communicate personal, historical experience from the perspective of those who witnessed, in the sense of having participated in, the experience of meeting the risen Jesus.

Richard Bauckham's study *Jesus and the Eyewitnesses: The Gospels as Eyewitness Testimony* (2006) offers support for Alison's view of the resurrection narratives as testimonies by offering a historical account of the likely relationship between many of the eyewitnesses of Jesus' life, death, resurrection and the gospel writers. Bauckham summarizes the effect of this view upon one's reading of the Gospels by saying,

> Understanding the Gospels as testimony, we can recognize [the] theological meaning of the history [which is included in the Gospel narratives] not as an arbitrary imposition on the objective facts, but as the way the witnesses perceived the history, in an inextricable coinherence of observable event and perceptible meaning. Testimony is the category that enables us to read the Gospels in a properly historical and a properly theological way. It is where history and theology meet.[57]

Thus, as testimony, the resurrection narratives communicate the historical event and the perceived theological meaning together as an inseparable whole that constitutes

---

This question of whether, in Alison's view, the spirit necessary for understanding Scripture must come from reading Scripture itself or from some other source prior to being able to read Scripture at all will be a central question of this and the next chapter that argue that for Alison theological reflection (as well as the texts of Scripture) is both the fruit and the occasion of conversion. The question also parallels the driving question of Grant Kaplan's work as we saw at the end of the last chapter, "Is mimetic theory a mode of discourse for the *already* converted, in order to help make explicit their faith commitments, or is it a mode of discourse that aims to bring about conversion?" (Kaplan, *René Girard, Unlikely Apologist*, 13–14).

[57] Bauckham, *Jesus and the Eyewitnesses*, 5–6.

the witness' account of the resurrection. From the perspective of faith in Christ, the Gospel texts are testimonies precisely in this sense.

The Gospels texts as a whole, and the resurrection narratives in particular, are *not* reports of objective, disinterested observers who are describing the chronology of the events that they observed from the periphery. In Alison's and Bauckham's view, the Gospels are not attempting to report a chronologically accurate account of events. This is not to say, however, that the objective observability of the resurrection (by the disciples or anyone else who happened to be present) is invalid as a historical question that might interest some people, nor that the gospel texts should never be used in support of an investigation into such a question. What Alison would say, however, is that the Gospel texts alone are not equipped to answer such questions because of the kind of texts that they are. Therefore, to subject them to these questions in the hope that they will provide an answer is to fundamentally misunderstand them.

3.2.5 The Conversion of the Disciples upon Meeting the Risen Jesus

Bauckham's nuanced and historically grounded argument demonstrating the continuing influence of living eyewitnesses to Jesus' life, death, and resurrection throughout the period when the Gospels were written lends significant support to Alison's use of the resurrection narratives as trustworthy accounts of the disciples' experiences of encountering the risen Jesus.[58] Bauckham argues that testimonies from living eyewitnesses passed on to their disciples and throughout the early Christian communities, from the time of the resurrection throughout the following ninety or so years in which the Pauline and Gospel materials were written, would have held primary authority within those communities. In addition, these living testimonies (living in the sense that they were actively being shared and confirmed by the living eyewitnesses) would have been of primary importance to the Gospel writers themselves.[59] Finally, the collection of other testimonies that the Gospels writers drew from in writing their narratives would have been preserved as coming from particular eyewitnesses (though

---

[58] Bauckham writes, "Part of my intention in this book is to present evidence, much of it not hitherto noticed at all, that makes the 'the personal link of the Jesus tradition with particular tradents,' throughout the period of transmission of the tradition down to the writing of the Gospels... at least historically very probable" (p. 7). The interior quote comes from V. Taylor's *The Formation of the Gospel Tradition* (2nd ed.; London: Macmillan, 1935), 41–2. Bauckham concludes his introduction by saying, "So, in imagining how the traditions reached the Gospel writers, not oral tradition but eyewitness testimony should be our principal model" (8).

Buackham recognizes that in asserting the primary influence of eyewitness testimony on the writing of the Gospels he is moving against the bulk of contemporary biblical scholarship, namely those that follow the method of form criticism that began in Germany in the early 1900s, those that follow the Scandinavian alternative to form criticism based on a study of oral transmission in rabbinic Judaism developed by Birger Gerhardsson (1961), and those that follow a kind of middle way based on a modified understanding of the process of oral transmission first presented by Kenneth Bailey (1995), and including N. T. Wright (1996) and James D. G. Dunn (2003). Bauckham addresses each of these methods and their shortcomings in making a persuasive case in favor of the direct influence of eyewitness testimonies on the writing of the Gospels.

[59] Bauckham, *Jesus and the Eyewitnesses*, 257–60.

no longer living), rather than gathered into some anonymous pool of narratives through the process of oral transmission.[60]

Bauckham's three assertions suggest that the Gospel accounts of the resurrection appearances are the result of eyewitness testimonies being shared by the eyewitnesses themselves, received by a series of others, and then put into writing by persons who were attempting to preserve the eyewitnesses accounts as such while the eyewitnesses themselves, or their immediate followers, were still alive to corroborate the narratives.[61] Bauckham's understanding of the Gospel narratives as the preservation of eyewitness testimony supports Alison's use of the accounts of the resurrection appearances as windows into the disciples' experience of meeting the crucified and risen Jesus. If we view the Gospel writers as consciously engaged in an effort to preserve the eyewitness testimonies precisely as testimonies, then Alison's effort to gain insight into the disciples' experience through the Gospel narratives is coherent.

Alison's kerygmatic and ecclesial biblical hermeneutic adds to Bauckham's view by providing a persuasive account of *why* people in the first century decided to preserve these testimonies, first orally and then in writing: they had become occasions of effective encounter with the crucified and risen Jesus. Those who passed on and preserved these oral and written testimonies were being converted into witnesses of the forgiving victim. Transformed by the experience of hearing and/or writing these testimonies, they themselves felt compelled to act as witnesses to the crucified and risen Christ. In the next chapter, I will develop Alison's implicit view of how this experience of being transformed and "converted" into witnesses of the crucified and risen Christ spread from the first disciples through the history of Christian witnesses. For now, though, I am suggesting that Bauckham's historical and cultural argument concerning the origins of the Gospel texts and my interpretation of Alison's kerygmatic and ecclesial approach toward that same history cohere, and each one strengthens the other.

Having provided some support for Alison's approach to the resurrection narratives with reference to Bauckham's study, I now turn to present Alison's view of the disciples' experience of meeting the risen Jesus. It is important to recall that Alison's use of his epistemological terms—intelligence, perception, memory, and imagination—is intentionally open to the whole of human experience and not restricted to describing the activity of the intellect. Thus, Alison's reading of the disciples' experience of the resurrection includes the various "valences" of human experience that I mentioned above—emotional/affective, spiritual/immaterial, intellectual/cognitive. While we often use these valences for attending to human experience as a kind of lens that allows us to process a portion of experience at a time, they are actually intermeshed. However, it will be helpful to focus on each one of these valences to offer a fuller depiction of Alison's account of the disciples' experiences of meeting the risen Christ. This will allow me to begin to draw out Alison's insight into the reciprocal relationship between the dynamic of conversion to Christ and theological reflection. The interplay

---

[60] Ibid., 260–3.
[61] Bauckham goes so far as to argue that the Fourth Gospel, the Gospel of John, was likely written by an eyewitness, John, the "beloved disciple." See pp. 358–411.

among these valences of experience constitutes the "space" within which the dynamic process of conversion and transformation resulting from an encounter with the risen Christ takes place.

This investigation into Alison's reading of the disciples' experience of the resurrection and the process of conversion that it effected will support the claim at the end of the last chapter regarding the difference in Alison's and Girard's treatment of the New Testament. Whereas Girard's reading of Scripture is grounded in an assertion that nothing short of a religious conversion must have occurred in the lives of the disciples for them to come to see and proclaim the view of God and human beings contained in the Gospel texts, Alison employs mimetic theory to attend carefully to the disciples' experience and to observe and articulate the dynamic process of religious conversion contained within it. We will see that Alison reflects on the process of conversion that "lies behind" the Gospel witness in much more depth than Girard. Alison's extended attentiveness to the disciples' experience of the resurrection provides the foundation for his underlying theological perspective, which has led him to develop a theological anthropology through the lens of Girard's mimetic theory.

3.2.5.1 *The Emotional/Affective "Valence" of the Disciples' Experience of the Resurrection*

Alison's reconstruction of the disciples' experience after Jesus' crucifixion is first an emotional/affective and relational account. That is, Alison is interested in imagining the felt emotional experience of the disciples in response to their perception of the shifts in their relationships with Jesus and with one another in the face of Jesus' public humiliation and death. Alison himself describes his method of exploring the disciples' experiences as "psychological," and he clarifies his use of this term by saying that he will try to "bring out the ordinary human responses to Jesus' death that were present [within the disciples]...[which] are either present or hinted at in the New Testament texts."[62] Alison applies this same approach in his exploration of the disciples' experiences of the resurrection, attempting to bring their "ordinary" emotional and relational experience to the fore.

Alison suggests that initially this emotional valence of the disciples' experience would have consisted of extreme shock and confusion. In *Raising Abel*, he makes this point by emphasizing the degree to which their imaginations were bound by their unexamined belief in the ultimacy of death:

> Now try to imagine the kind of shock which befalls those who are entirely bound in by death and whose vision of God has not been freed from shading into death when someone who was killed under the system of death, apparently punished by God, and certainly considered to have been the purveyor of a falsified vision of God, suddenly appears again, beyond death.[63]

---

[62] Alison, *Knowing Jesus*, 11.
[63] Alison, *Raising Abel*, 42.

If the disciples were shocked by Jesus' death, then they must have been considerably more shocked by his resurrection. Death by crucifixion was a familiar experience in the world of the Roman Empire,[64] but the disciples had no expectations and no categories for making sense of finding themselves in the living presence of someone "whom they had known before, whom they knew to have died, who came back into their midst."[65]

According to Alison, this initial experience of shock was likely as exhilarating as it was terrifying. The disciples must have immediately sensed that the friend and teacher whom they loved was not completely lost, but alive; yet they also must have been acutely aware of the fear for their own lives that had prevented them from being present or speaking out more boldly in support of the beloved friend whom they knew to be innocent. How could Jesus not be deeply hurt and angry in response to their fears? And how could he fail to hold them accountable?

According to Alison, the disciples' initial experience of shock, excitement, and terror quickly opened up into an experience of forgiveness because the disciples very quickly discerned that Jesus felt no anger or resentment toward them. Alison writes:

> The resurrection is forgiveness: not a decree of forgiveness, but the presence of gratuity as a person. The simple fact of Jesus' appearance to his disciples, as soon as they had recovered from their consternation at the presence of what was quite outside their experience, was the presence of forgiveness. Their sorrow, and guilt, and confusion, could be loosed within them, because the focus of their sorrow and guilt and confusion had come back from right outside it, and was not affected by it. There was no element in the presence of the risen Jesus of any reciprocating by Jesus of what had been done to him.[66]

Here Alison emphasizes the centrality of forgiveness to the disciples' experience of the crucified and risen Jesus in such a way that highlights the fundamentally relational character of that experience. And he also initially defines forgiveness as a lack of reciprocity (i.e., vengeance). Alison brings to the fore the way in which the disciples' relationships with Jesus during his public ministry and leading up to and including his crucifixion provide the context in which it is possible for the disciples to experience the resurrection as the presence of forgiveness to them. This experience of forgiveness is mediated by a reversal of their expectations, which, despite their deepening friendships with Jesus through his public ministry, are shaped by customarily violent social others.

Within this emotional/affective valence of the disciples' awareness of their experience, I see in Alison's reading three central, interconnected aspects: gratuity, a lack of reciprocity (i.e., vengeance), and familiarity. Alison first describes the forgiveness made available to the disciples through the resurrection as "the presence

---

[64] For a historical look at the practice of crucifixion in the Roman Empire, see Martin Hengel's *Crucifixion: In the Ancient World and the Folly of the Message of the Cross*, trans. John Bowden (Philadelphia, PA: Fortress Press, 1977).

[65] Alison, *The Joy of Being Wrong*, 71.

[66] Alison, *Knowing Jesus*, 16. Alison reads this experience of forgiveness as a personal presence back into the story of Cain and Abel in Genesis. See *Raising Abel*, 134.

of gratuity as a person." He characterizes this foundational aspect of their experience of the resurrection as an encounter with Jesus' presence as "utterly other," that is, as completely outside the realm of anything they had ever experienced or could possibly have expected.[67] The presence of Jesus irrupted into their midst despite the disciples' complete unpreparedness to find him alive and approaching them. According to Alison, the otherness and unexpectedness of Jesus' presence likely prevented the disciples from having an impression that Jesus' presence was dependent upon anything they had done; thus, his presence to them was completely gratuitous, that is, freely given and unmerited.[68]

The disciples' experience of Jesus' presence as gratuitous was supported by the non-reciprocating (i.e., non-vengeful) nature of his presence. In the midst of their shock and confusion upon finding themselves in the presence of Jesus and with their lingering guilt following Jesus' death, the disciples may have expected some form of retribution or at least extreme disappointment from Jesus. As Alison says, their expectations would have been formed, not according to a gratuitous other, but rather according to the "customary," vengeful other.[69] But the presence of the risen Jesus offered no signs of reciprocity or retribution. Alison points to the risen Jesus' first words to the disciples in the various resurrection accounts as evidence of the disciples' experience of the lack of any element of reciprocity in Jesus for the violence done to him.[70]

Finally, the disciples' experience of Jesus' presence as gratuitous and non-vengeful was intertwined with their experience of his presence as familiar. Alison writes that the risen Jesus " ... without ceasing to be other, was the presence of recognizable, familiar love for them."[71] Thus, despite the otherness, the disciples come to the recognition that "It is the Lord" (John 21:7). The recognizability of Jesus' presence and love confirmed that there was no hint of vengeance in him and allowed for them to begin to experience forgiveness. As I quoted Alison above, the disciples' "sorrow, and guilt, and confusion, could be loosed within them, because the focus of their sorrow and guilt and confusion had come back from right outside it, and was not affected by it."[72]

The same Jesus whom they had loved, failed, and lost was being given back to them freely, lovingly, and from outside the realm of anything they could have merited or controlled.

3.2.5.2 *The Spiritual/Immaterial "Valence" of the Disciples' Experience of the Resurrection*

We could think of Alison's description of the emotional valence of the disciples' experience of receiving forgiveness gratuitously from someone they had grown

---

[67] Alison, *Knowing Jesus*, 14.
[68] Alison, *The Joy of Being Wrong*, 74.
[69] In Alison's Girardian perspective, the "customary" others that we encounter within the existing social order operate largely according to a system of retribution and desert (*Knowing Jesus*, 16).
[70] Alison, *The Joy of Being Wrong*, 74–5. Cf. in Luke 24:38, Jesus says, "Why are you troubled?" In Matthew 28:10, "Do not be afraid." And in John 20:19, 21, 26, "Peace be with you."
[71] Alison, *Knowing Jesus*, 15. See also *The Joy of Being Wrong*, 74.
[72] Alison, *Knowing Jesus*, 16.

to love and trust as a kind of first, or most immediately attended to, layer of their experience of encountering the risen Jesus. But with time, the disciples are able to attend to their experience of the risen Christ more deeply, not in a way that negates their more immediate awareness of it, but in a way that builds upon it. By talking about their growing attention to a "spiritual" or "immaterial" valence of their experience, I want to trace briefly what Alison sees as their experience of a fundamental shift in and transformation of their "capacity for gaze."[73] This transformation at the deepest "level" is what the New Testament often refers to as *metanoia*, and this is what I am referring to most specifically with the word "conversion." It is a transformation that causes a major shift or even reversal in all of the other valences of experience, and it occurs at the "boundary" between the background and foreground dimensions of knowing, such that the "operative intelligence" that previously constituted the background dimension becomes exposed and gradually subverted by a higher intelligence.

This experience of conversion for the disciples consists fundamentally of a process of transformation in which the disciples become aware of, and gradually leave behind, their belief in the ultimacy of death and are converted into witnesses of the life made fully available to them for the first time through the living presence of the crucified Christ. In Alison's Girardian perspective, this transformation cannot be reduced to a purely personal or interior sphere since it consists in becoming aware of, and being freed from, a fundamental belief in the ultimacy of death—a background intelligence that has been received unknowingly through the individual's formation in and through culture. Thus, in labeling the disciples' experience of transformation or conversion as part of the spiritual valence of their experience, I am pointing out that what is transformed, from Alison's perspective, is their awareness of their relationship to the cultural/social other and the unacknowledged but widespread belief in the ultimacy of death, which has led them and others to participate in violence out of fear of death.

While Alison does not make this spiritual valence of experience explicit as such in his treatment of the resurrection appearances, he does point to it when he uses the Johannine language of "belief," which he connects to the Girardian language of "possession."[74] In *Raising Abel*, for example, he approaches this experience by interpreting John 14:1 and 14:29 in terms of Jesus' relationships with his disciples during his life and leading to his death and resurrection:

> Jesus' role has been to choose and sustain some people in whose presence he can act out, [and] make humanly comprehensible, what it is to be a human whose

---

[73] Alison, *Broken Hearts and New Creations*, 114–115. See Section 3.1 above.

[74] In Girardian circles, "possession" is a semi-technical term that refers to the fundamental influence of the other in shaping the identity of the self. In Alison's usage here, one can be "possessed" by the spirit of someone who is locked into a fear of death and a rivalrous mode of relating to others, or one can be "possessed" by the Spirit of the risen Christ whose gaze is always fixed on the vivaciousness of God.

In explaining his use of the phrase "the intelligence of the victim," Alison speaks of it possessing the disciples: "[By intelligence of the victim], I mean the exploratory and creative human understanding concerning God and humanity which Jesus showed in his life leading to his death and which was made manifest to the apostolic group by his resurrection. And as they became possessed of this intelligence the disciples began to reread the process leading up to Jesus' death. " See *The Joy of Being Wrong*, 80.

mind is entirely possessed by the aliveness of God. It is their believing in Jesus, and thus their following what happens in what he is about to carry out, which will permit these witnesses to have their minds and imaginations possessed in the same way.... He wants his witnesses to understand that what is about to happen to him is not accidental, but is part of what will allow them to come to understand the deathlessness of the Father. That is: he is going to his death *to create a belief.*[75]

Thus, for Alison, Jesus invited the disciples into a relationship with him to lead them, through his death and resurrection, into a belief in the deathlessness of God, or, as he says a few pages later, into a "*belief* in the utter vivaciousness of God."[76] Here the language of "belief" and "possession" refers to a fundamental dimension of experience of which the disciples are not yet aware as existing and operating within them. During Jesus' life, the disciples are largely unaware of their lack of belief in the living God. To put it another way, they are not aware of their fundamental belief in the ultimacy of death, which leads them to believe that death either silences or appeases "God."[77]

Alison quotes a passage from the Letter to the Hebrews as a succinct description of the ultimate fear of death (within humanity), which Christ destroys through his own death:

> Forasmuch then as the children are partakers of flesh and blood, he also himself likewise took part of the same; that through death he might destroy him that had the power of death, that is, the devil; and deliver them who through fear of death were all of their lifetime subject to bondage. (Heb. 2:14-15)[78]

Here Alison sees articulated the divine intention leading to incarnation: to "deliver them who through fear of death were all of their lifetime subject to bondage." The means of this delivery from fear of death is a going to death. Humanity is unaware of its fundamental belief in (and fear of) the power of death and, therefore, requires someone who, because his gaze is fixed on the utter vivaciousness of God, can go to death willingly to reveal humanity's fear of death to itself, while simultaneously making a show (or spectacle) of death.

Thus, interpreting the visible marks of death on the body of the risen Jesus in Luke's and John's accounts, Alison describes the disciples' encounter with the crucified and risen Jesus as simultaneously revealing to them their fundamental belief in the ultimacy of death and Jesus' clear vision of the emptiness of death for God. Alison argues that, by including mention of the visible marks of the crucifixion, Luke and John are telling us that the risen Lord was in fact dead, but that

---

[75] Alison, *Raising Abel*, 61; Alison's emphasis. Cf. John 14:1, "... believe in God, believe also in me." And John 14:29, "I tell you this now before it happens, so that when it happens, you may believe."
[76] Alison, *Raising Abel*, 64; Alison's emphasis.
[77] In *Wrestling with God and Men* (Madison, WI: University of Wisconsin Press, 2005), Steven Greenberg, an orthodox Jewish rabbi, argues that the holiness code of the Temple in ancient Jerusalem was essentially a way of avoiding death by ritually appeasing God.
[78] Alison, *Raising Abel*, 29.

death is nothing but a vacant form for God, something whose reality has been entirely emptied out, which can only be detected in the form of the traces in the human life story of someone who has overcome death.[79]

The risen Jesus, through the forgiving mode of his presence to the disciples, reveals death to be "an empty shell" and, therefore, nothing to be feared.[80] In becoming witnesses to the crucified and risen Christ, the disciples begin to believe that, while death happens, God's relationship to persons is not hindered by it.

In receiving forgiveness from the risen Jesus, the disciples simultaneously affirmed that the same Jesus whom they grew to love during his life and whom they abandoned to death was alive and was, and had always been, living in a mode that was unafraid of death because he knew death to have no bearing on his relationship with God. As Alison writes, "So the risen presence is of the dead-and-risen one as gratuitous forgiveness revealing love beyond death."[81] The disciples' reception of this forgiveness made possible an experience of the love of God embodied in the person of the crucified and risen Christ, which, in turn, enabled them to discover and repent of their own belief in the ultimacy of death, which had led to their unfaithfulness to Jesus during his passion and death. Thus, for Alison, the reception of forgiveness from the living presence of the crucified Jesus effects a conversion within the disciples on the level of their foundational belief about death and life and God's relationship to each of them. The disciples are converted from believers in the ultimacy of death, operating in a basic mode of rivalrous self-preservation, into witnesses of the living presence of the dead and risen Christ. Through their witnessing, they invite others to encounter this same Christ and undergo a transformation. Alison identifies the disciples' belief in the ultimacy of death as the source of their inability to understand what Jesus, during his earthly life, was revealing to them about God:

> It was not that they merely did not understand, and after the resurrection, with the coming of the Holy Spirit, they did understand. The nonunderstanding itself was related to death. Their understanding of what Jesus was about was marked by the normal human limit of understanding which is that death is a definitive reality, and therefore their relationship to Jesus and what he was teaching was something circumscribed by the normal parameters of human life and death.[82]

It is important to qualify Alison's frequent descriptions of God's "utter vivaciousness," God's complete non-involvement in death, and God's seeing death as a "vacant form" and "an empty shell." By describing God in these ways, Alison is not suggesting that

---

[79] Ibid.
[80] Alison, *Raising Abel*, 29.
[81] Alison, *The Joy of Being Wrong*, 76.
[82] Ibid., 139. For a further elaboration of this belief in the ultimacy of death as a limit of human understanding, see my "Being Freed from the Illusion of the Enemy: James Alison on Contemplative Prayer and Eucharistic Liturgy," in *Who Is My Enemy? Religious Hope in a Time of Fear. Selected Papers from the Theology Institute* 42 (Villanova, PA: Villanova University Press, 2011), especially 5–7.

death is not a created part of the biological cycle of all living creatures. Instead, Alison is referring primarily to two widespread and overlapping human experiences of death, namely, death as the most extreme form of social exclusion and violence, and death as an expression of divine judgment. Alison describes these common, even universal, experiences of death as fundamental misperceptions that have come to act as "the normal limit of human understanding."

With his use of the language of God's vivaciousness and non-involvement in death, Alison is asserting that God's self-revelation in Christ is an attempt to reveal to human persons the non-necessity and non-divinity of death experienced and perceived as a form of exclusion from human belonging and from God's providence. This assertion includes two claims. First, Alison is saying that God is in no way involved in the deadly human mechanism of exclusion and victimization. God does not desire, and never has desired, the exclusion and victimization of any portion of creation, which often result in death. Death is not an enactment or a sign of divine judgment against persons. This revelation is a reversal of the commonly held, but often tacit, belief that God desires the punishment of evildoers in such a way that supports and even demands the human enactment of exclusion and violence against those deemed to have violated God's law.

Second, these descriptions of God express the fundamental Christian belief that God's offer of loving relationship to persons is in no way hindered by death, regardless of whether death is the result of some form of human exclusion. In this sense, death is a "vacant form" and an "empty shell" in God's view because it has no bearing on God's power to love persons and, thereby, hold them in being. As we saw above in Alison's treatment of the passage from Hebrews, God chose to enter into human history as one of us in order to lead persons to see and come to believe in the non-definitiveness of death. In the person of the Son, God undergoes death both as the end of biological life and as an extreme form of exclusion and victimization to make it possible for persons to see that neither aspect of death is a sign of divine judgment; and neither presents an obstacle to God's capacity to give God's self and God's life to persons.

3.2.5.3 The Intellectual/Cognitive "Valence" of the Disciples' Experience of the Resurrection

As we have seen, the disciples' experience of receiving forgiveness from the crucified and risen Jesus effects a spiritual transformation on the level of their most fundamental beliefs about death. Such a transformation constitutes the beginning of a shift in the sociological and cultural patterns that have shaped their foundational beliefs. We have also glimpsed how changes in the relational and spiritual valences of the disciples' experience, resulting from the presence of the risen Jesus, had an impact upon their intellectual/cognitive understandings. I will expand upon these glimpses to show that their reception of forgiveness from the risen Jesus also begins to change their understanding of who God is and what God's desire for humanity's salvation entails. In other words, it leads them to engage in theological reflection.

We can get a sense of the origins of how the disciples' experience of conversion leads them to re-imagine God from one of Alison's reflections on the disciples' experience of the marks of Jesus' death, which helped them to recognize him, and to which Luke and John each attest.[83] Alison states the significance of the testimony of the visible marks of Jesus' death by saying that they

> [mean] that when Jesus rose, it was not a simple continuation of his life (as if he were simply a few days older), with his wounds cured by God, but rather that he was given back to the disciples as simultaneously dead and alive. In the risen Lord there is no chronological distance between the death and the life; rather the complete "otherness" of the resurrection life is that it is not on the same level as either human life or human death, and is thus able to give back both simultaneously.[84]

The disciples' perception of the "otherness" of this life could not have been limited to any one valence of their experience, but must have suffused and overflowed the whole of their capacity for perception, memory, and imagination. But they were gradually able to intellectually articulate their experience of this resurrection life. They engaged in theological reflection as they came to recognize that the crucified and risen Jesus was alive in a way that was beyond any experience of life or death that they had known. The disciples must also have realized that it was this "other level" of being alive that enabled their friend, teacher, and the one they allowed to die to be given back to them gratuitously and without any hint of vengeance. In being given back the whole of Jesus' human life and death, not as a condemnation against them but as an invitation into a whole new way of being, the disciples experienced the resurrection as an offer of forgiveness that they could not have imagined possible for "God" as they had previously understood "God," or even for Jesus as they had thought they had known him.

This imaginative reconstruction of some of the disciples' likely theological reflections in the wake of the irruption of the crucified and risen Christ into their lives sets the stage for detecting and developing Alison's conception of theological reflection as authentically possible only as the outgrowth of an experience of conversion that undoes an identity derived from a false intelligence. To more clearly articulate the movement from conversion to theological reflection in Alison's reading of the disciples' experiences of meeting the crucified and risen Christ, I will return to my treatment of one of Alison's central terms, "operative intelligence," and to his primary description of conversion as a "subversion from within." Here I will stay closer to Alison's own contextualization and usage of these phrases, which engage the whole person and include all of the "valences" of the disciples' experience.

---

[83] Cf. Luke 24:36–49 and John 20:19–29.

[84] Alison, *The Joy of Being Wrong*, 76; see also *Knowing Jesus*, 18–19. The French sacramental theologian, Louis Marie Chauvet, makes a very similar argument about the marks of death on the body of the risen Jesus. In his shorter book *Sacraments*, he writes, "[The resurrection] cannot be reduced to a simple return to his previous state; his risen body bears the marks of the wounds of his death, therefore, all the scars of his concrete historical life." *The Sacraments: The Word of God at the Mercy of the Body* (Collegeville, MN: Liturgical Press, 2001), 156.

3.2.5.4 Intelligence Operative in the Mind of Christ

We saw in my earlier treatment of "intelligence" at the beginning of this chapter that Alison describes "conversion" as the subversion from within of the false intelligence operative in the minds of the disciples by the intelligence operative in the mind of Christ, which Alison most frequently describes as the "intelligence of the victim." To better explain the nature of this subversion and the theological reflection that it makes possible, I will consider the intelligence of the victim that is operative in the mind of Christ, the intelligence of the lie operative in the minds of the disciples prior to the resurrection, and Alison's assertion that the former subverts the latter.

Alison uses the Pauline language of the "mind of Christ" (and Paul's exhortations that those who have come to believe in Christ should take on the mind of Christ) to link this phrase with his own use of the phrase "the intelligence of the victim." This is Alison's descriptor for the knowledge that Jesus possessed while alive on earth and that is made fully available to the disciples for the first time through the resurrection. In his letter to the Philippians, Paul says, "Let the same mind be in you that was in Christ Jesus."[85] Alison sees in this Pauline invitation a confirmation of Alison's own view that "conversion" to Christ leads to a subversion from within of the intelligence operative in the minds of the disciples by the intelligence operative in the mind of Christ. By linking his phrase "the intelligence of the victim" with Paul's words, he is suggesting that the understanding of conversion and theological reflection that he is articulating coheres with the experiences of the first disciples, including Paul.[86]

The intelligence operative in the mind of Christ is the fullest and most humanly accessible source of "the knowledge of salvation."[87] The mind of Christ, unlike the minds of other persons, is entirely "fixed on the things that are above."[88] Alison uses this second Pauline metaphor to identify the source of Christ's intelligence, which comes from the fixedness of his gaze upon the Father, who is "above." From Alison's Girardian perspective, Jesus' "fixedness" on the Father throughout his life is the source of Jesus' identity or his self-perception. Jesus lived with an interior conviction that his identity arose from his reception of God's loving regard toward him and that this regard was not hindered by human rejection and violence, or even death. This conviction allowed Jesus to move toward his death out of love for human beings despite the human fear of death that he had learned through his development and socialization as a human being. Alison writes,

> Jesus' understanding was not marked by [death]: he was thus able creatively to imagine the possibility of a self-giving into the hands of violent men as not only a

---

[85] Philippians 2:5. And in 1Corinthians 2:16, Paul says, "'For who has known the mind of the Lord so as to instruct him?' But we have the mind of Christ."

[86] Brian Robinette makes this point as well, showing that Alison's "intelligence of the victim" is the same intelligence that Paul is referring to with the language "the mind of Christ." After quoting Philippians 2:5–8, he asserts, "[t]he 'mind of Christ' is one freed from rivalry with God, translucent to the divine Other, whose Otherness is received as total Gift rather than an obstacle to the project of becoming a self." See *Grammars of Resurrection*, 297.

[87] Luke 1:77.

[88] Alison, *Raising Abel*, 15–23, and 35–41. Cf. Colossians 3:2.

salvific revelation of the sort of love the Father is, trusting himself into his Father's hands, but also as an educational exercise for those as yet unable to understand the nondefinitive nature of death.[89]

This reception of his identity from the reciprocal gaze between Jesus and the Father became the source of both Jesus' non-rivalrous, non-appropriating, peaceful pattern of desire toward others, and his understanding of God, self, and the rest of the created world. Alison describes the content of Jesus' understanding, or intelligence, which he received from the fixedness of his gaze on the "things that are above," as "the utter vivaciousness of God." In other words, the intelligence operative in the mind of Christ consists of a clear perception of God as fully alive and without any desire for death for humanity—indeed, even without any perception of death as an ultimate form of violence and exclusion.

Alison gives an account of his understanding of God's utter vivaciousness through an exegesis of the New Testament passages in which Jesus debates with the Sadducees about their denial of the resurrection.[90] Alison points out that in Luke's account, after Jesus responds to the Sadducees' use of a levirate law in Deuteronomy as support for their denial of the resurrection, Jesus concludes by quoting Exodus, "I am the God of Abraham, and the God of Isaac, and the God of Jacob."[91] Alison gives his understanding of Luke's testimony about Jesus by saying: "The reply has no apparent bearing on the resurrection of the dead, but rather is about who God is. God has nothing to do with death nor with the dead, but instead declares to Moses that he is the God of three people who were apparently dead at the time." According to Alison, Jesus is telling the Sadducees that they do not understand the power of God and is indicating "the sort of power which characterizes God, something of the quality of who God is. This 'power,' this quality which God always is, is that of being completely and entirely alive, living without any reference to death."[92]

As Jesus' operative intelligence, this clear understanding of God allows Jesus to move through life and through his relationships without being constrained by a fear

---

[89] Alison, *The Joy of Being Wrong*, 139.
[90] Alison, *Raising Abel*, 37–9; and *The Joy of Being Wrong*, 116–19. Cf. Mark 12:18-27; Matthew 22:23-33; Luke 20:27-38.
[91] Alison, *Raising Abel*, 38; *The Joy of Being Wrong*, 116. Cf. Luke 20:37 which is a quotation of Exodus 3:6, 15, 16.
[92] Alison, *Raising Abel*, 38. I should reiterate my earlier point at the end of the last section regarding an important qualification concerning Alison's frequent descriptions of God's "utter vivaciousness," God's lack of "any reference to death," or in other places "God's complete non-involvement in death." By describing God in these ways, Alison is not primarily speaking of death as an inevitable part of the biological cycle of all living creatures. Rather, he is referring to death as it has often been experienced by humans throughout history, namely, death as the most extreme form of social exclusion and violence. By describing God as "utterly vivacious" and lacking any reference to death, Alison is making two assertions about God. First, he is saying that God is in no way involved as an active agent in the deadly human mechanism of exclusion and victimization. According to Alison, Jesus' death and resurrection reveal that God does not desire (and never has desired) the exclusion and victimization of any portion of creation, which often results in death. Second, he is saying that death as a biological reality nor as a form of human exclusion has any bearing on God's love toward human beings and all of creation.

of death, despite his experience of this fear as a human being.[93] Jesus' intelligence allows him to see that his identity comes from the Father and that the Father's love is not affected by death. As long as Jesus receives his identity from the Father, he has no reason to acquiesce to the human temptation to live out of a fear of death. Jesus teaches this understanding of God during his life, but he knows that his view of God cannot be perceived by persons whose perception is structured by death. The content of his teaching is made available to his disciples only in the resurrection, which reveals that God's love is such that it is "unaffected by death, and that for that love death [is] no necessary separation, for love [can] carry on being reciprocal even through death."[94]

Because Jesus' mind is fixed on God, he has not only a clear perception and true understanding of God, but also a clear perception of the Sadducees as part of a humanity conditioned by sin. Thus, the Sadducees' understanding is not simply influenced by their experience of a fear of death; rather, it is bound by a belief in the ultimacy of death, which acts as the controlling principle of their operative intelligence. Alison's treatment of these accounts of Jesus' debate with the Sadducees describes his understanding of the "intelligence" operative in the minds of persons who have not yet come to know the vivaciousness of God through the forgiveness of their sins. Although the intelligence of the Sadducees and that of the disciples might have been distinct due to the difference between each group's relationship with Jesus during his life and the relative openness of each to his teaching and preaching, they were similar in that each was circumscribed by a fundamental, unperceived belief in the ultimacy of death. The Sadducees demonstrate this belief in their debate with Jesus about the resurrection; and the disciples, in their various responses to Jesus' persecution and execution. I will now turn to consider Alison's view of the intelligence operative in the minds of the disciples prior to Jesus' resurrection.

3.2.5.5 Intelligence Operative in the Minds of the Disciples

In Alison's view, the intelligence operative in the minds of the disciples is perceptible only via the intelligence operative in the mind of Christ; it does not perceive its own operation. This occlusion from its own view allows it to remain operative. Through what Alison calls a "subversion from within" the intelligence that has been operative in the minds of the disciples becomes perceivable and open to reflection. Thus, any explicit exploration of the intelligence in the minds of the disciples is always a presentation of an understanding that has developed in hindsight—as the intelligence being described was becoming increasingly less operative.

While the intelligence operative in the minds of the disciples begins to be perceivable only as they receive the intelligence operative in the mind of Christ via

---

[93] Jesus' experience of the fear of death is most clearly attested to in the accounts of the "agony in the garden." See Matthew 26:36-46; Mark 14:32-42; Luke 22:39-46.
[94] Alison, *The Joy of Being Wrong*, 116. Here, again we should qualify Alison's description of God as "unaffected by death" as asserting the non-ultimacy of death due to the power of God's desire to hold persons in being beyond the end of their biological lives.

the resurrection, their intelligence has been influenced by their relationships with Jesus prior to his crucifixion. For Alison, the disciples' relationships with Jesus during his life and death were the necessary preconditions for their experiences of meeting the crucified and risen Jesus.[95] Alison sees the disciples' relationship to Jesus during his life and death as a period of formation in which they are building the relational "framework" that would prepare them to become witnesses of the revelation of the deathlessness of God in and through their experiences of Jesus' resurrection from the dead. The disciples' growing trust in the love that was in Jesus and in the kingdom of God that he preached and enacted made it possible for them to experience Jesus' resurrection as an offer of forgiveness lacking any hint of vengeance or retribution. Alison is implying that the disciples' relationships with Jesus during his life influenced their preexisting, tacit belief in the ultimacy of death. Although their relationships with Jesus during his earthly life did not undo this belief, they at least caused the disciples to begin to become consciously aware of their existing perceptions of God's relationship to violence and death. This period of growing trust in Jesus opened the disciples to receiving faith in the crucified and risen Christ and to discovering the utter vivaciousness of the God whose love held him in being beyond his crucifixion and death. This opening up of the disciples to faith began to occur even while they continued to operate substantially according to what we might call the "intelligence of the lie," or "the intelligence of death."

We saw a statement of Alison's understanding of this "intelligence of death" above in my description of the spiritual valence of the disciples' experience of the resurrection. I concluded that section with a quotation from *The Joy of Being Wrong* in which Alison identifies the cause of this intelligence's previous occlusion as a false belief in the definitiveness of death.[96] Despite the disciples' friendships with Jesus, their operative intelligence prior to encountering the crucified and risen Christ, like that of all persons who have not come to perceive the vivaciousness of God, had as its limit a belief in the ultimacy of death. That belief circumscribed their understanding of God, themselves, and others. We also saw above that this boundary of the disciples' operative intelligence was most visible in their experience of, and response to, Jesus' crucifixion.[97] The extreme disorientation, shock, guilt, and fear that led the disciples to remain together in a locked room are the clearest evidence of the belief in death that served as the limit of their pre-resurrection understandings of God, self, and others.

When Alison describes this boundary of death as "the normal human limit" of understanding, we should recall his description of his method of exploring the disciples' experience of the crucifixion as a drawing out of their "ordinary human responses to Jesus' death that were present."[98] For Alison, then, "ordinary" or "normal"

---

[95] Alison, *Knowing Jesus*, 8. I quoted this passage at length earlier in this chapter. See Section 3.2.2.
[96] Alison, *The Joy of Being Wrong*, 139.
[97] See Section 3.2.3 above, "An imaginative reconstruction of the Disciples' post-Crucifixion experience."
[98] Alison, *Knowing Jesus*, 11. Cf. Section 3.2.2 above.

human responses, desires, understandings, and beliefs are such to the extent that they are circumscribed by the misperception of death as definitive.[99]

In using the adjectives "ordinary" and "normal" to describe a humanity structured by death, Alison resists using a description such as "sinful" humanity. This resistance does not reflect a desire to downplay the effect of sin on humanity and its intelligence; rather, it reflects Alison's desire to protect against a common misunderstanding of sin within Christian theology—one that establishes sin as the foundational and controlling concept in a Christian view of the human person. When such a misunderstanding of humanity prevails, the notion of sin becomes the "theological equivalent of a pillar of salt; something which is no longer on its way out of anything."[100]

Alison argues that a Christian view of the human person, and subsequently of sin, is definitively revealed by God and fully discovered by human persons only in the offer and reception of forgiveness from the crucified and risen Jesus. As a result, he defines sin in terms of the historical conditions through which it becomes humanly perceivable. From this vantage point, sin is that which is being forgiven, or "that which can be forgiven."[101] That of which the disciples find themselves being forgiven in meeting the risen Jesus is a pattern of believing, desiring, thinking, and responding to others—that is, a way of being human in all of its dimensions—that is structured by a previously unnoticed and unquestioned belief in death as ultimate. This way of being human is best identified, in Alison's view, as "forgivable," rather than "sinful."

Labeling the intelligence that operates within this forgivable way of being human as an "intelligence of the lie" (or "the intelligence of death") highlights its inherently deceptive quality. When describing the operation of this intelligence, Alison accepts Girard's description of mimetic rivalry leading to victimage. The intelligence operative in the minds of the disciples is the intelligence of rivalry and victimage. It is an intelligence of the lie because its operation depends upon the disciples' belief in a series of three false premises, culminating in a belief in the ultimacy of death.

As we saw earlier, the first false premise is that individual subjects generate and possess desires. This premise is given credence by playing on persons' imitated desire to have a unique identity, which might be expressed through the originality and spontaneity of their own desires. The premise is accepted by persons through the operation of imitative desire itself, since the desire to possess a unique identity is learned by imitating the desire of others. However, acceptance of this premise blinds persons to the imitative operation of desire that induced them into accepting the premise in the first place. Thus, the imitated desire to possess a unique and independent identity—one that is largely independent from the influence of others—inclines persons to be formed according to the collectively held (mis)perception that

---

[99] Speaking about the human discovery of original sin through the resurrection just before the passage quoted above, Alison describes the "sinful" or "normal" condition of humanity as "shot through with death": "The resurrection reveals that human beings are already shot through with death in a way that no amount of struggle can avoid. It is not that we are sick, but that we are dead. Life is not something fought for, but something given." *The Joy of Being Wrong*, 138.

[100] Alison, *The Joy of Being Wrong*, 263; Cf. Genesis 19:26.

[101] Alison, "An Atonement Update," 65. Alison comes to this definition of sin in the process of recovering the priestly understanding of atonement as a liturgy in which God is the protagonist moving toward humanity and offering forgiveness.

each person is the spontaneous and original source of his or her desires, which both express and constitute the individual's unique identity.

In the Girardian narrative, this collectively held and perpetuated perception gives rise to conflict and rivalry among individuals moving in similar or overlapping social spheres. Since persons are not in fact capable of originating their own desires and, therefore, their own identities, they tacitly seek out and imitate the desires of those who appear to be the most independent and original. In this way, they maintain their (mis) perception of the spontaneity and originality of their own desires. As the Girardian story goes, the unknowing or inattentive imitation of the desires of particular others, serving as the misguided means of having "original" desires, generates conflict and rivalry among those moving within the same sphere of imitation, since persons are trying to demonstrate their originality to themselves and to others by engaging in imitation.

The escalation of the rivalry within the group leads to the discovery and operation of a second premise: namely, that the only effective way of mitigating the rivalry and regaining some semblance of peace and cohesion within the group is through the group's common identification, exclusion, and killing of a culprit who can be convincingly accused of instigating the growing rivalry. We hear this premise articulated quite clearly by the high priest, Caiaphas, as he persuades the rest of the Pharisees to identify Jesus as such a culprit:

> You do not understand that it is better for you to have one man die for the people than to have the whole nation destroyed. (John 11:50)

The identification of someone whom all (due to their own self-deceit) can be easily persuaded to identify and punish as a culprit creates a sense of cohesion over and against a common enemy, thus overcoming the previous dynamic of growing rivalry.

A third false premise arises from the experience of renewed group cohesion that results from putting the identified culprit to death. The group experiences this newfound cohesion or "peace" as a divine validation of their violent actions, and of death as the ultimately effective means of maintaining peace. In other words, persons are led to misperceive death as ultimate since it seems that even God, or the divine, cannot provide a nonviolent or deathless path to peace. Therefore, God appears beholden to death, and appears to desire and advocate violence as the path to peace. In naming what is believed to be ultimate, this third premise forms the boundary of the disciples' understanding and operates as the controlling principle of their intelligence.

These three cumulative (but false) premises—(1) individuals are the source of their own desires, (2) the only mechanism for reestablishing or maintaining social cohesion and peace is the violent exclusion of someone deemed to be responsible for instigating rivalry, and (3) death is ultimate—shape the disciples' relationships with themselves, others, and God. Although I have presented them here in a sequential fashion to show their interrelation, they are learned as a whole since they are always already operating interrelatedly in the culture in which persons are formed.

Persons who operate according to the intelligence that comprises these three premises—that is, the intelligence of the lie—including the disciples prior to their experience of the resurrection, are unaware of its operation and, therefore, unable to reflect upon it. It acts as a background or tacit intelligence. This "intelligence of death" (which names it according to its controlling or highest premise) is also appropriately called an "intelligence of the lie" not only because it consists of a fundamental misperception of desire, the social order, and the divine, but also because it hides itself from persons' explicit awareness.

Alison's understanding of the disciples' experience of conversion hinges on an account of how the intelligence operative in the mind of Christ infiltrates and exposes this false, deceptive intelligence. We will see that, in this account, Alison points to the interrelation between God's initiative in effecting conversion and the human person's cooperation with God by correlating the terms "revelation" and "discovery." A subversion of the intelligence operative in the minds of the disciples requires an interruption of this intelligence by another intelligence that "reveals" itself by opening the disciples to a process of "discovery"—a process that their present intelligence resists.

3.2.5.6 Subversion from Within

The phrase "subversion from within" is Alison's way of describing the transformation of the human person through the exposure and undoing of a false and tacit intelligence by a higher and illuminating intelligence. In the presence of the crucified and risen (i.e., the dead-and-alive) Christ, the intelligence operative in the mind of Christ—the intelligence of the victim—becomes fully discoverable by the disciples for the first time. As the disciples recognize the risen Christ and receive "forgiveness of their sins" (Luke 1:77), that is, as they are forgiven of, and overcome their blindness to, a way of being human that is structured according to death, they become open to receiving "the mind that was in Christ Jesus" (Phil. 2:5). In Alison's treatment, the transformation of the intelligence of the disciples consists of an exposure of the intelligence of the lie or the intelligence of death by the intelligence of the victim, which, through its capacity to expose the lie, demonstrates itself to be of a higher order.

Given this view of the disciples' transformation as a dynamic that interrupts and acts upon the whole person, I can now consider more carefully what Alison means by describing this transformation as a "subversion from within." In doing so, I will also draw out his view of how their experience of being converted to the crucified and risen Christ necessarily included the beginning of their engagement in theological reflection.

The intelligence in the mind of Christ (the intelligence of the victim) works to expose the intelligence of the lie operative in the disciples by enabling Jesus to submit himself fully and knowingly to the workings of the intelligence of the lie in such a way as to make the intelligence operative in him discoverable by the disciples. Jesus' crucifixion appears to reassert and confirm for the disciples the validity of their partially acknowledged perceptions of God, despite the ways that Jesus' relationship with them during his life had led them to begin to become aware of and question those perceptions. In the forgiving presence of the crucified and risen Jesus, the disciples, after moving beyond their shock and disorientation to recognize that "It is the Lord" (John 21:7), could perceive directly for the first time their operation according to a hidden belief in the ultimacy of death. This insight was accompanied by the beginning of an awareness of the power of a "higher" understanding, present in Jesus, that was enabling them to see what had been imperceptible.

Alison gives one of his most helpful elaborations of the meaning of his phrase "subversion from within" in the first chapter of *Raising Abel*, where he presents his understanding of the principle of analogy by distinguishing it from two contrasting views of the relationship between the "divine story" and the "human story."[102] The first view that he describes denies the principle of analogy by claiming that the human story, or human nature, is wholly sinful and, therefore, must be covered up or supplanted by the divine story of God in Christ if the redemption of humanity is to be made possible. Alison describes such a view in terms of its corresponding understanding of the resurrection, such that this perspective "imagines the resurrection to be the overcoming of death, but not its assumption."[103] The second view downplays the necessity of redemption and the degree to which self-deception leading to violence shapes human culture. It perceives the human story and the divine story as having a strong resonance. These two stories are depicted as similar rather than analogous. Alison summarizes the corresponding understanding of the resurrection by saying, "In short ... the element of violence is ... present in human life, but not so present as to make the risen life something radically different from what we already know and live."[104] Alison then uses the phrase "subversion from within" as his attempt to make sense of the principle of analogy that he distinguishes from the two preceding views:

> It seems to me that the presence of the crucified and risen victim suggests that in fact the divine story is related to the human story, but *as its subversion from within*. That is to say that human violence, the dominion of death, is so powerful that we can't tell the divine story at all [on our own]. However God, by becoming human, created a real human story which is the celestial subversion from within of our violent history and as such we can find points of contact with it, because it is the turning inside out of our story, the construction of a story that is not that of a violent lynching, but of a peaceful un-lynching, so to speak. For the divine story to be at all comprehensible to us we need it to start from, and make sense of, the story that we do know how to tell, but only insofar as it enables us to begin to tell a story that must always include the human overcoming of that story.[105]

With the phrase "subversion from within," Alison suggests that the relationship between the divine and human stories is more complex than either of the two previous views acknowledge. In encountering the crucified and risen Christ, persons are invited into a process of discovering the "divine story," which neither supplants the human

---

[102] Alison, *Raising Abel*, 31–1.
[103] Ibid., 31.
[104] Ibid., 32.
[105] Alison, *Raising Abel*, 32; Alison's emphasis.

story of violence and victimization (which would be another form of projection onto God of human violence), nor simply affirms it (which would amount to either diminishing or denying the history of human violence). Instead, it makes it possible for humans to overcome the story of human violence and victimization by being transformed into imitators of Jesus' peaceful reception of an identity from the Father. This transformation of persons into imitators of Jesus' peaceful mimesis takes place as a "subversion from *within*," or a "turning inside out," of the "ordinary" human way of relating to one another.

But, what does this "subversion from within" look like? How is it experienced by those persons who find themselves being offered forgiveness when they expected to be met with vengeance? Alison's answer in brief is that subversion from within is experienced as an interior collapse of one's habitual patterns for creating identities through comparisons with, and exclusions of, various others.

He vividly illustrates this experience of interior collapse in one of his more methodologically explicit essays, "Theology amidst the Stones and Dust." Here he reads three biblical and/or historical narratives and tells one personal story as examples of the kind of collapse that occurs as the beginning of the subversion made possible by the forgiveness of sins.[106] They are (1) the story of Elijah and the still small voice in 1 Kings 19, (2) the fall of Jerusalem and collapse of the Temple in 587bce, (3) the conversion of Saul, and (4) Alison's own experience of disorientation and loss of self-confidence amidst a period of scrutiny. For Alison, all depict the fundamental dynamic of what in most places he calls a "subversion from within," but in this essay he describes more vividly as "a heart close to cracking." In his telling of each of these stories, Alison attends to the loss of confidence that accompanies the collapse of the interior structures that have maintained the subject's identity without the subject having been explicitly aware of them. Alison's personal experiences of interior collapse (understood through his appropriation of Girard's work) enable him to see the same dynamic in these biblical and historical narratives.

Describing the disillusionment of Elijah, Alison says, "Elijah sinks into a depression, and doubts the value of [the contest on Mount Carmel that he had just won]."[107] Speaking of the destruction of the Temple, he describes the collapse of external "sacred" structures, which led to the interior collapse of the identities tied to those structures:

> The process [following the destruction of the Temple] is likely to have been experienced as one of total annihilation. All the structures of group belonging, or personal, family, tribal belonging, in the dust. The whole imaginative world within which Yahweh was worshipped, torn to shreds.[108]

These brief descriptions provide a clearer picture of what the phrase "subversion from within" points toward. It describes the dismantling or implosion of a false self that

---

[106] Alison, *Faith beyond Resentment*, 27–41.
[107] Ibid., 29.
[108] Ibid., 31.

has been entangled and lost in a deceptive web of relationships, a web that includes institutional structures, religious and otherwise. This web deceives because it forms persons in the delusion of the three false premises described above. The subject experiences the delusion that maintains the subject's identification with the false self as a fear of losing his or her being, which in turn leads the subject to misremember his or her past as some combination of shameful failures and remarkable accomplishments. The dismantling of this false self, therefore, begins with a letting go of the fear of nonbeing. Hence, the first words of the risen Jesus to the disciples are repeatedly recorded as "Do not be afraid." With the letting go of this fear, it becomes possible to receive the forgiveness that dismantles the false self from within by exposing it to the view of the subject who had identified with it completely, thereby enabling the subject to remember himself or herself rightly.

Thus, we can take Alison's use of the phrase "subversion from within" as his phenomenological description of the process of "conversion" enabled by the reception of forgiveness. Conversion, then, in Alison's view, is the reception of the capacity for right remembering, clear perception, and vivacious imagination that dismantles "from within" the false self and the false remembering, perceiving, and imagining that have perpetuated it. Similarly, Alison describes prayer as a practice of opening oneself to the "indwelling of the Spirit," who is able to move persons from within, bringing the true self into being, without displacing or overriding the subjectivity or the agency of the person.[109] This description of the activity of the Spirit in prayer helps us to understand what Alison means by describing conversion as a "subversion from within." By using the directional qualification "from within," Alison is saying that the movement of conversion as a subversion dismantles the false self, not by some exterior power of annihilation but by the calling forth of the conditions necessary for adopting a truer self, which requires uncovering and empowering a deeper interior agency. Alison is not only telling us that the subversion is a kind of interior collapse or implosion, but is also indicating that this collapse or dismantling does not involve any displacement of the person's subjectivity. Instead, the collapse becomes possible precisely through the calling forth and the nurturing of that subjectivity.

Here it is important to recall from the last chapter Girard's implicit distinction between the "subject" and the "self" because this distinction supports and clarifies what I suggest is Alison's intended meaning of "subversion from within." For Girard, the "self" is not something solid and unchangeable, nor is it something solidly held by the subject. Rather, the "self" in Girard's schema is the "world of possibilities" for the subject that is generated by the subject's imitation of the desires of his or her models.[110] In other words, the "self" is the subject's horizon of becoming as it is received from his or her models, who shape the limit of the subject's imagination and, therefore, the limit of the subject's becoming. The subject, then, *is* the possibility for becoming, which is always already formed within the network of desire. The subject is an already desiring

---

[109] Alison, *Jesus the Forgiving Victim*, 218–219. Also see "Prayer: A Case Study in Mimetic Anthropology," which can be found on Alison's website at http://www.jamesalison.co.uk/texts/eng54.html (accessed March 30, 2019).

[110] See Chapter 2 Section 2.2.2 for my earlier treatment of this.

imitator who receives various "selves" by imitating, either knowingly or unknowingly, the particular patterns of desire of his or her models. Thus, the "false self" that has been dismantled represented the subject's previous reception of a world of *im*possibilities or false possibilities that he or she mistakenly believed to be realizable, specifically, the impossibility of being the source or generator of his or her own desire—the impossibility of not being what he or she is: a desiring imitator of desire.

This distinction between the subject, as a desiring imitator of desire, and the self, as the world of possibilities that the subject receives through imitating the desires of his or her models, allows us to understand conversion as an interior undoing of the false selves while also making room for, and even requiring, a correlative interior emergence of what I described in the last chapter as "authentic subjectivity," with its capacity to perceive rightly the subject's own constitution as an imitator of desire.[111] In Girard's mature perspective, we could see that the emergence of this subjectivity includes the freedom to choose one's models and, subsequently, to receive selves that represent worlds of attainable possibilities—in other words, true selves in that they represent actually realizable identities. Thus, Alison's description of conversion as a subversion from within suggests that the conversion effected by the presence of the crucified and risen Christ subverts the false selves—identities received in blindness and consisting of unattainable possibilities—and does so by calling forth an authentic subject capable of freely choosing to imitate Jesus' imitation of his Father. Conversion, then, is first a transformation that cultivates the subject's most defining capacity, the ability to perceive itself rightly, remember its past clearly, imagine God and the future vivaciously, and the subsequent freedom to choose its models accordingly. Conversion is simultaneously the subversion of the false selves that the subject had received unwittingly from poor models and the reception of truer selves and attainable possibilities from more authentic models.[112]

In experiencing the crucified and risen Jesus as a forgiving victim, the disciples receive the intelligence of the victim, a perspective that reveals to them the series of false selves that they had adopted throughout their lives and that they continued to adopt even throughout their growing friendships with Jesus. Their adoption of these false selves is revealed to them precisely as the disciples are forgiven of their various

---

[111] See Chapter 2 Section 2.4.3 for my earlier treatment of this.
[112] I should note here that there is a certain degree of tension and even ambiguity within Alison's own writing with regard to the nature of the relationship between authentic subjectivity (or freedom) and the transformation effected through the reception of forgiveness. In some places, Alison's writing suggests that forgiveness imparts subjectivity and freedom where previously, due to sin, there was none (see, for example, *The Joy of Being Wrong*, 42–5, 100–2). In other places, it seems that Alison is suggesting that the reception of forgiveness uncovers, calls forth, and nurtures a subjectivity and a freedom that had previously been hidden and latent (see, for example, *The Joy of Being Wrong*, 46–7). Here I am introducing an interpretation of Alison's view that holds the latter thread to be more representative of Alison's understanding. But a coherent case could be made in favor of the opposite inclination. Ultimately, and here I believe that Alison would agree, it is not so important which of these lines of interpretation is emphasized as long as the reader of Alison's work acknowledges that Alison's understanding of conversion sees the divine offer of forgiveness as initiating and making possible a human cooperation with the divine offer. For a more extensive treatment of this tension within Alison's *The Joy of Being Wrong*, see my "The Self Prior to Mimetic Desire," 7–31.

forms of complicity in the construction of these more or less violent identities. The discovery of these various false selves, which had led most of the disciples to abandon Jesus during his suffering and death, in turn enabled them to begin to see the fear of death that had perpetuated their blindness toward their own natures as desiring imitators of desire.[113]

Through the reception of forgiveness, the disciples discover the intelligence that is operative in the mind of Jesus. That is, they find themselves receiving not only forgiveness, but also the intelligence that enabled Jesus to desire to respond to violence with love rather than vengeance. They receive a perspective that is made known to them through their reception of a love that meets them as forgiveness. This intelligence of the victim, which operated within Jesus as a clear perception of human violence and divine love in the present moment, began to operate in the disciples as a new perspective opening up on the present, the past, and the future simultaneously. They were enabled to *remember* rightly the various false selves that they had used to protect themselves from death. They were enabled to *perceive* God's deathlessness, which raised Jesus and offered them freedom from death through the forgiving presence of the crucified and risen Christ. They were even enabled to begin to *imagine* participating in a life that did not fear death. As we saw at the beginning of the chapter, Alison succinctly describes the identity between the forgiveness of the disciples' sins and the recovery of their memories, saying, "It is the forgiving victim who enables our memories to be healed. That is, the forgiveness of sins and the healing of memories is the same thing: what unbinds our past is what opens up our future."[114]

3.3 From "Conversion" to Theological Reflection

In Alison's view, truly perceptive theological reflection is only ever possible as an inevitable outgrowth of the initial experience of conversion that begins in the presence of the risen Jesus, who approaches his victimizers as a forgiving victim. We have seen that conversion as a "subversion from within" involves the reception of an intelligence that takes the shape of forgiveness to uncover within persons a capacity for right remembering of the past and clear perception of the present. For the disciples, the uncovering of this capacity for right remembering and perception is accompanied by a new capacity for imagining the kind of God that Jesus calls "Father." In the presence of the forgiving victim, the disciples recognize that God was not against Jesus after all, and God did not participate in or condone his death; rather, Jesus is risen and has

---

[113] In Girard's view, it is an underlying fear of death as the complete loss of being that seduces persons to imitate those others who appear to be self-satisfying with regard to their own desire and, therefore, appear to be the source of their own "more substantial" being. This is what Girard refers to as the dynamic of "metaphysical desire" which we saw contextualized within Girard's larger project in the last chapter especially in Section 2.2.1. For a more extended treatment of the relationship between the fear of death and a denial of one's own nature as an imitator of desire, see my essay "Being Freed from the Illusion of the Enemy," 1–16.

[114] Alison, *Raising Abel*, 115.

been raised by his Father.¹¹⁵ Thus, the disciples are confronted with an experience that immediately challenges their perceptions of God. Speaking of Paul's encounter with the crucified and risen Jesus in the essay I referred to above, Alison asserts that the experience of the resurrection makes known "the novelty, vitality, and exuberance of God" in a way that was not simply an addition to a pre-existing perception, but that instead corresponded to the collapse of a belief in the existing social order with its standards for determining who belongs and who does not.¹¹⁶ The collapse of Paul's belief in the existing social order was a necessary and corresponding condition for the possibility of his experiential discovery of God's utter vitality and exuberance through his encounter with the risen Jesus on the road to Damascus. Like that of other disciples who experienced the crucified and risen Christ, Paul's encounter includes the reception of a twofold insight into his previous blindness to the working of God in his midst and, correspondingly, into the true "nature" of God embodied in Jesus. The reception of this insight represents the beginning of Paul's and the other disciples' participation in God's address to humanity. It is the opening through which the disciples are enabled to participate in humanity's appropriation of the intelligence of the victim through their own active and self-implicating reflection upon this initial insight. That is, the reception of this twofold insight that comes with the recovery of right remembering, perceiving, and imagining is the beginning of theological reflection as Alison understands it.

It is not coincidental that Alison's presentation of these four accounts of collapse—Elijah and the still, small voice, the fall of the Temple, Paul's conversion, and one moment in his own experience of conversion—constitutes the opening of one of Alison's most explicitly methodological reflections on the nature of theological discourse. For Alison, theological reflection becomes possible through the reception of a perspective that can come only with the forgiveness-enabled collapse of the self who is blind to its own participation in violence. Referring to his accounts of the conversions of Elijah and Paul, Alison describes the beginning of theological reflection as the reception of a new perspective that each one finds opening up in front of him in the midst of what has collapsed:

> [T]hey had nowhere to start except from where they found themselves to be. There was no universal principle, all-embracing idea, or pre-formed discourse which they could simply adopt.... The only perspective which was available to them, and starting from which they might make sense of the stones and the dust, was their own... [and] in each case, the perspective from which they had to begin was a perspective received by the process of finding themselves to have been involved in something which had been knocked to the ground.¹¹⁷

---

¹¹⁵ Alison succinctly describes what was likely the beginning of the shift in the disciples' understanding of God as they found themselves in the forgiving presence of the risen Jesus by saying: "If such a person [one who was said by his enemies to have died under the curse of God according to Deuteronomy 21:23] rises from the dead.... in the first place it means that Jesus had been right in the testimony which he had given about God: God is indeed the one who Jesus had described and that means that God is not like Jesus' adversaries had claimed him to be." *Raising Abel*, 26–7.

¹¹⁶ Alison, *Faith beyond Resentment*, 32.

¹¹⁷ Ibid., 35–6.

For Alison, these stories illustrate the direct connection between, on the one hand, the reception of forgiveness that enables insight into oneself as having been complicit in a violent system that has been "knocked to the ground" and, on the other hand, the reception of a perspective from and through which one gains access to "right remembering" of one's past, "right perception" of the present, and "life-giving imagination" of God and of the future. From within this humbled place, in which one has become aware, through the light of forgiveness, of one's involvement in a system of human violence, one receives a perspective from which more explicit, truthful reflection upon self, God, and others is both possible and expected to develop.[118]

Alison's own experiences of the recovery of right remembering provides him with the lens for reading the disciples' experience of meeting the risen Jesus as a "subversion from within" that enabled clearer, more truthful reflection upon who they had been, who God is, and who God desired them to become. As we saw in the biographical introduction, Alison recounts one particular instance of his experience of "recovering his memory" through an interior collapse. Prepared to teach a theology course in Chile in February 1994, Alison was informed by his supervisor that religious superiors around Latin America were calling for him to be removed as an instructor on the grounds that, while living in Bolivia from 1992 to 1993 and, previously, in Brazil, he had shown himself to be an "internationally known homosexual activist."[119] On a Jesuit retreat in Santiago, Chile, in April 1994, "still devastated by what had happened" two months earlier, Alison underwent a moment of collapse in which the charge levied against him, because it contained an element of truth, became for Alison an occasion of an encounter with Christ as a forgiving victim. As Alison says, "[T]he charge that I was an 'internationally known homosexual militant' did not fall like lightening from a clear sky."[120] Indeed, a deep resentment and fear that God would not acknowledge him as a gay man had been driving Alison to seek out and virtually demand such acknowledgment from any ecclesiastical authority that might give him a hearing. Alison says that his rejection by this group of religious superiors allowed him to see for the first time what his accusers had perceived clearly from the beginning: that he had been on "a sort of crusade."[121] He was trying to take by means of forced "dialogue" with religious leaders what he had despaired of receiving gratuitously from God—an invitation to flourish as he was. Thus, Alison underwent a collapse of an identity that he had kept hidden from himself and had prevented him from perceiving God and others clearly. With this collapse of a false self, Alison gained personal insight into who God is and realized that "God had nothing to do with what had happened [to him]." God was not involved with the human mechanism of violence in which Alison

---

[118] In *Raising Abel*, Alison similarly describes the relationship between forgiveness and collapse saying, "the time of Abel [is] the time in which the innocent victim is made present to us as forgiveness, and thus, little by little, allows us to let go of all the sacred mechanisms of which we lay hold to fortify ourselves against our own truth. Of course, this process of letting go is violent, because we don't let go easily, or at once." *Raising Abel*, 135. I provided a brief account of Alison's experience in Chile in early 1994 at the very beginning of this book.
[119] Alison, "Theology amidst the Stones and Dust," in *Faith beyond Resentment*, 36.
[120] Ibid., 38.
[121] Ibid., 39.

was entangled both as a victim and a perpetrator.[122] His reception of forgiveness during this time of retreat enabled a jarring of his memory; the collapse of a hidden, but operative, false self; and new insight into who God is.

This moment of collapse and the reception of the perspective that accompanied it depict the kind of recovery of right remembering and clear perceiving that lead to the possibility of authentic theological reflection.[123] Alison describes the space in which theological reflection becomes possible in this way:

> [It is a] space where we learn to forge a way of talking about God in the midst of the ruins of the forms of the sacred which are in full collapse. A space where we recognize our own complicity in the sacred forms of the past, with all their violence and their victims.... but also *a space where we learn*, precisely in the midst of the destruction of all that, *new ways of speaking words of God so as to participate in the new creation*. That is to say, it is the Eucharistic space par excellence, *where Christ is present as the crucified one, and we as penitents* learning to step out of solidarity with our multiple and varied modes of complicity in crucifixion; but *where Christ is present as the crucified and risen Lord, so not as accusation of our participation, but as a fount of, and power for, a new, unimagined, and unending reconstruction.*[124]

With this description, we begin to see the contours of his conception of theology and the activity of theological reflection. For Alison, theological reflection is the subject-approaching-authenticity's participation in the "subversion from within" of the "intelligence of the lie" by the "intelligence of the victim" through self-reflexive appropriation and articulation of the latter. Theological reflection, therefore, is a necessary part of the process of conversion; it is part of the bringing into being of the subject as his or her mind is slowly conformed to "the mind that was in Christ Jesus."[125]

Theology for Alison, then, is what I will describe as "inductive." It induces a new self into being. In the presence of the forgiving victim, the penitent semi-traitor seeks out ways to speak about God (and, subsequently, about oneself and the rest of creation) that participate in effecting the vision of the new Israel that he or she is receiving from the crucified and risen Lord. This search for new ways of speaking

---

[122] Ibid., 37.
[123] I would like to note that, although according to Alison theological reflection can only begin following the reception of a revealed perspective via the forgiveness-enabled collapse of the false self, this does not negate the fact that an at least partially deceptive theology correlative with the false self already existed prior to the reception of the revealed perspective operative in the mind of the forgiving victim. In other words, the "intelligence of the lie" that had been operative in the minds of the disciples prior to their experience of encounter hid itself under the cover of a particular theological understanding of self, God, and the created world. This theological understanding, however, is necessarily undergirded by a lie that attributed some degree of violence to God. The theological reflection that is made possible through the initial reception of the "intelligence of the victim" that was in Christ Jesus is distinct from the theology that was correlative with the false self to the extent that it possesses the power to bring a new self into being through the subject's gradual self-reflexive appropriation of it.
[124] Alison, *Faith beyond Resentment*, 35; emphasis added.
[125] Cf. Philippians 2:5.

about God facilitates the subject's transformation from a penitent semi-traitor into a subject increasingly capable of forgiving his or her persecutors.[126] In the introduction to a more recent collection of essays, Alison gives fragmentary descriptions of theology that illumine his view of its essentially inductive character. Theology is a participation in God's self-communication to humanity; God is not its object, but its protagonist. Instead, "we [penitent semi-traitors] are... the relatively inert, distant objects which are, as it happens, being invited into this form of knowing, thus becoming subjects."[127] Emphasizing theology as part of the ongoing process of conversion into a subject, Alison describes theology as "the long and slow... path by which we enter into our right minds."[128] Theological reflection is a participative activity through which God works to induce authentic subjects into being as forgiven forgivers.

Alison's understanding of theology represents a fundamental shift from the direction of intentionality that Christians commonly associate with the activity of theological reflection. Ordinarily, we tend to conceive of the theological task as an activity carried about by a thinking believer who reflects upon, and expresses his or her understanding of, the divine "object." This conception is often present even within understandings of theology that carefully explain that they are speaking of God as "object" only in an analogical sense. Alison, however, is proposing an understanding of theology in which the direction of intentionality is reversed. In his view, God is the true subject acting on, for, and toward us thinking believers, who are "relatively inert, distant objects" being invited to participate in God's desire to bring us into being as subjects. Because articulating, advocating for, and participating in this fundamental shift in the conception of theology has been at the heart of Alison's work throughout his theological career, his conception of theology is "inductive."

In the next chapter, I will develop the second movement within Alison's conception of the reciprocal relationship between conversion and theology—the movement in which the activity of theological reflection continues to deepen the subject's conversion to the crucified and risen Christ by freeing the subject to trust more fully in the God whom he or she is now perceiving more clearly. This increase of trust, in turn, increases the subject's receptivity to forgiveness and frees the subject to recognize and admit his or her lingering complicity in violence. To develop this second movement, I will consider the importance of Alison's identification of the believing subject as a witness to the crucified and risen Christ. By developing the category of witness, I can articulate more clearly how the activity of theological reflection functions as an act of witnessing and how this act deepens the conversion experienced by the subject, as well as his or her readers and hearers.

---

[126] Cf. Matthew 5:44 and Luke 6:27.
[127] Alison, *Broken Hearts and New Creations*, vii.
[128] Ibid., xi.

4

From Theological Reflection to (Ongoing) Conversion: Sharing a Received Perspective through an Act of Witnessing

> *While Peter was still speaking these words, the Holy Spirit came on all who heard the message. ... they heard [the Gentiles] speaking in tongues and praising God. Then Peter said, "Surely no one can stand in the way of their being baptized with water. They have received the Holy Spirit just as we have."*
>
> (Acts 10:44–47)

In the last chapter, we examined Alison's reading of the disciples' experience of being encountered by the crucified and risen Christ and we saw that, in his view, it was an experience of conversion that has become the paradigm for the dynamic of Christian conversion. The experience of conversion within a Christian framework involves the reception of forgiveness, which brings about a new and transforming insight into who the subject has been, who God is, and who God is inviting the subject to become. The insight is made available by the initial reception of Jesus' intelligence—the intelligence of the victim. The insight sparked by this intelligence leads to a gradual and ongoing self-reflexive appropriation and expression of that intelligence. Alison understands this process as theological reflection. It is an activity in which God is the primary protagonist, inviting those being converted to participate in God's re-creation of them.

In this chapter, before moving to elaborate the second movement in the reciprocal relationship between conversion and theology, namely, the movement from theological reflection to ongoing conversion, I will articulate some of the fundamental theological implications of Alison's view of theological reflection: namely the resulting theological conceptions of (1) the relationship between the "order of discovery" and the "order of logic," (2) doctrines and apologetics, and (3) theoretical understanding in general, and mimetic theory specifically. I will then develop what I call the movement from theological reflection to ongoing conversion in Alison's perspective by considering how theological reflection catalyzes the deepening of the subject's initial experience of conversion and the occasion for others to experience an encounter with the crucified and risen Christ. With the help of Paul Ricoeur's work on the relation between texts and action, I will argue that, for Alison, theological texts are acts of witnessing that hold the potential to become occasions of encounter between the readers of the text and the living presence of the crucified Christ.

By focusing on the notion of witness and the role of theological texts as one type of witness, we will come to a fuller understanding of Alison's theology as inductive, that is, as an occasion of encounter enabling ongoing conversion into witnesses of the crucified and risen Christ. I conclude the chapter by placing this understanding in an ecclesial and liturgical context. Then, by considering Alison's characterization of his own writings, I set the stage for the final chapter, in which I will examine diverse excerpts from Alison's writings to more fully describe the "inductive" theology that Alison advocates and practices.

4.1 Distinguishing between the Order of Discovery and the Order of Logic

Alison's most frequent description of the kind of theology that he advocates and in which he engages is his phrase "theology in the order of discovery." Alison is not the first theologian to make use of this phrase, nor is he the first to distinguish it from some other theological order. Thomas Aquinas's distinction between the order of discovery and the order of teaching is perhaps the most well known. Aquinas's usage of "the order of discovery" indicates the direction of theology that first moves from the "facts" of revelation to the gradual elaboration of the contents of faith implied within those facts.[1] Alison's usage is similar but distinct, since he is writing from within a historical consciousness that recognizes the fundamental role of human experience as the medium in and through which persons and communities come to understand themselves and the created world. As a result, Alison's usage of "theology in the order of discovery" indicates the direction of theology that moves from the subject's discovery of the God of the crucified and risen Jesus through the reception of forgiveness to an increasingly elaborated self-reflexive understanding of that God and the implications of this discovery for the subject's understanding of self, the whole of creation, and his or her relationship to it.

Here we should recall from the last chapter that the immediate experience of conversion is comprised of a deep insight that already involves a certain kind of self-reflexive awareness. Conversion consists of the subject's reception of forgiveness enabling a recognition and collapse of the false self and accompanied by an openness to the reception of a new intelligence. The light of loving forgiveness from the approaching victim enables the subject to see something about oneself, the one approaching, and God that was previously hidden. This insight into the falseness of one's previous understanding provides a recognition of that which was previously occluded.

---

[1] In his introduction to Lonergan's *Insight*, Terry Tekippe describes Thomas's understanding of these two orders in similar way. See Terry Tekippe, *Bernard Lonergan: An Introductory Guide to* Insight (Mahwah, NJ: Paulist Press, 2003), 20. I first made this comparison in my essay, "From a 'Revealed' Psychology to Theological Inquiry," 121–130; see endnote no. 13.

For Alison, the direction of discovery continues as the self-reflexive process becomes the ground for new experiences of conversion for oneself and others and for the reception of deeper insight. The reciprocal relationship between the subject's experience of conversion and the elaboration of fuller understanding continues indefinitely. Thus, Alison's use of the phrase theology in the order of discovery includes this entire, ongoing, reciprocal dynamic that moves back and forth between the experiential insight that comes with the reception of forgiveness and the elaboration of understanding that develops as the subject's intellect gradually appropriates the intelligence of the victim operative within and "behind" the insight.

This order of discovery opens up further as the reciprocal dynamic continues within persons and communities and begins to have a cumulative effect. The increase and deepening of theological understanding eventually make possible the articulation and development of doctrines (and eventually the development of those doctrines). The next section will examine the status of doctrines and apologetics in Alison's view at more length, but for now it is important to see that these doctrines are part of Alison's order of discovery since they are a fruit of the community of believers' deepening and expanding theological reflection.

In contrast with this order of discovery, Alison identifies the order of logic. The order of logic, as Alison describes it, is a product of the order of discovery, but it can be (and often has been) investigated and developed apart from the order that has preceded and given rise to it. It is a way of ordering the doctrines of Christian faith to tell the story of Christianity without any explicit reference to the experiential dimension of how those doctrines came to be discovered and articulated. Thus, it tells the story of salvation history through a "logical" ordering of the doctrines from a third-person perspective. Within this perspective, the Christian narrative is told as the story of creation-fall-redemption-heaven.[2] Alison calls this the order of logic (or we could even say the "order of theory") since it is presented in an order that anyone could grasp intellectually without any direct or explicit experience of the truth or meaning of the narrative.[3]

When the same narrative is viewed from a kind of first-person perspective, that is, when it is reattached to the order of discovery within which it originated, then the "logical" ordering of the doctrines for telling a coherent narrative changes. Within this order, the Christian story is told, Alison says, in a "slightly, but significantly" new way; here, "redemption reveals creation by opening up its fulfillment in heaven and reveals at the same time the fall as that which we are in the process of leaving behind."[4] Thus,

---

[2] Alison, *Raising Abel*, 55.

[3] For a brief articulation of how Alison contrasts these two orders and of their implications for theological method, see *The Joy of Being Wrong*, 100. Alison gives some further insight into the motivation behind his use of this phrase in several places scattered throughout his writings. See, for example, "Theology amidst the Stones and the Dust," 27–55; "On Learning to Say 'Jesus Is Lord': A 'Girardian' Confession," 156–64; "Unpicking Atonement's Knots," 20–2; "An Atonement Update," 52–5; "Doing Theology Is a Slow Business," vii–x; "Introduction. Oracles, Prophets, and Dwellers in Silence," in Martin Laird and Sheelah Treflé Hidden, eds. *The Practice of the Presence of God*, 1–7.

[4] Alison, *Raising Abel*, 55–6.

within this first-person perspective, the experience of individuals and communities in discovering and receiving the forgiveness offered and the intelligence revealed through the presence of the crucified and risen Christ shapes the ordering of the narrative. It is only a "slight" change in the sense that the components of the story are the same, but it is a "significant" change since the point of entry into the story becomes a place where persons can actually enter it, that is, experientially, rather than only notionally. And this point of entry is the experience of receiving forgiveness.[5]

In the next section, we will see that Alison's distinction between the order of discovery and the order of logic will help us to relate Alison's conception of theological reflection to doctrines and apologetics. In the subsequent section, this same distinction will help us to make sense of the relationship of Alison's work to theoretical understanding, or theory in general, and to "mimetic theory" specifically.

4.1.1 The Status of Doctrines and Apologetics in Alison's Conception of Theology

Similar to his view of theological reflection, Alison's understanding of Christian doctrines and apologetics represents a reversal of a more common understanding. One view of doctrines would hold that they are the central tenets of Christian faith that demand intellectual and moral assent from believers as the necessary condition for participating in the Christian assembly's sacramental life. Such a view gives doctrines a foundational role in the formation of Christian ecclesial communities and their members.

Alison's view of doctrines and apologetics, on the other hand, follows from his understanding of the close connection between conversion and faith, and his advocacy for a theology in the order of discovery. In summarizing his view of the relationship between conversion and faith, I refer to the common theological distinction between two traditionally recognized dimensions of faith: *fides qua*, the faith *by which* Christians believe what they believe, and *fides quae*, the beliefs or tenets *that* Christians hold to be true.[6] The activity of theological reflection as I began describing it in the last chapter forms a bridge between these two dimensions of faith.

It is difficult to make a conceptual distinction between conversion and faith because the spheres of meaning of each of these terms overlap significantly, or as Alison says, "[F]

---

[5] I should note that Alison's perspective in no way excludes the possibility that a "logical" presentation of the narrative (creation-fall-redemption-heaven) may become for some people an occasion of encounter with the risen Christ in which they find themselves receiving forgiveness. His point in advocating for a theology in the order of discovery is not, as we will see below, that theoretical understanding is in itself an obstacle to conversion, but rather that it is the experience of receiving forgiveness that makes true understanding possible. Therefore, we should be suspicious of theoretical understanding that has become detached from the order of discovery. A primary aim of this chapter will be to develop explicitly Alison's recognition of the value and necessity of theoretical (theological) understanding for the process of conversion.

[6] For a more extended treatment of the historical development of *fides qua* and *fides quae* and their relevance for the work of Girard and Alison, see my essay "From a 'Revealed' Psychology to Theological Inquiry," 121–31.

Alison briefly makes use of this distinction within his own treatment of "faith" at the beginning of *The Joy of Being Wrong*: "Both elements, traditionally called *fides qua* and *fides quae*, are simultaneously indispensable for the proper relaxation into the hypnosis of the other 'Other'" (p. 60).

aith, because it is what permits us to live on the interface between the old other which formed us and the new other which seeks to form us anew, is intrinsically related to conversion."[7] Yet, making a conceptual distinction between the two is necessary if both terms are to be seen as useful for describing the human reception of divine revelation. Drawing on Alison's understanding developed in the last chapter, I will refer to conversion as the gradual subversion from within of the subject's perception, memory, imagination, intelligence, and desire through his or her reception of divine revelation, which approaches in the form of a forgiving victim. I will refer to Christian "faith" in its primary usage as *fides qua* as the spiritual disposition of the subject—a disposition of receptivity to God in Christ—which is itself received as part of the conversion effected by forgiveness and which makes a deepening of conversion possible.[8]

The activity of theological reflection is the participation of the subject's intellect in response to the subject's reception of the forgiveness that effects faith. We have seen that theological reflection is the subject's attempt to attend to, appropriate, and express in language an unexpected encounter with God in Christ. This active reflection leads, in part, to increased theoretical understanding of the dynamics of the divine-human encounter, the kind of God that could have initiated it, and the kind of creatures that we human beings are, have been, and are called to become.[9] The engagement of the believer's intellect in theological reflection eventually makes possible propositional statements of what the community of believers holds to be true about God, Christ, the Spirit, humanity, etc. In other words, theological reflection allows for faith as *fides quae* (statements of belief) to be gradually distilled from faith as *fides qua* (faith as the receptive disposition of an individual and/or community).

This understanding of conversion, faith, and theological reflection requires a reversal in a common understanding of doctrines that I described above. Doctrines are officially accepted formulations of propositional statements of belief, and, as such, they are much more the result of the process of transformation than they are prerequisites for embarking on it. Doctrines, for Alison, act as a kind of "grammar" of faith in that they are tools that the Christian community employs to determine whether particular theological expressions are authentic expressions of Christian faith or not.[10] These "tools" are a fruit of ongoing theological reflection as it has been pursued by the community of Christian believers over the centuries. That is, in the order of discovery, the formulation of doctrines comes after, and as a result of, the experience of conversion

---

[7] Alison, *The Joy of Being Wrong*, 62.
[8] For Alison's detailed account of faith, see *The Joy of Being Wrong*, 55–62. The distinction between "conversion" and "faith" that I make here within Alison's perspective is consistent with the broader Christian tradition. See, for example, St. Thomas Aquinas's treatise on faith in the Summa Theologica II-II, 1–7; also Paul Tillich, *Dynamics of Faith* (New York: HarperOne, 2009); and Roger Haight, *The Dynamics of Theology* (New York: Orbis, 2001), especially chapter one.
[9] Thus, theological reflection moves deliberately into the territory that, as we saw at the end of Chapter 2, Girard largely chooses to avoid.
[10] This understanding of doctrines as a kind of grammar is developed much more fully by Robert Schreiter who draws upon Noam Chomsky's conception of language. See his *Constructing Local Theologies* (Maryknoll, NY: Orbis Books, 1985), 113–14.

and an ongoing engagement in theological reflection by individuals and communities. Doctrines are not the foundations of faith but are instead regulative boundary markers that test the capacity of theological expressions to remove obstacles to the faithful's reception of forgiveness. In other words, doctrines have a negative function in that they delimit the perimeter within which "authentic" theological reflection can develop and move. In Alison's view, the guiding principle around the development of such a perimeter is the understanding that theological reflection should facilitate the removal of obstacles to persons' reception of forgiveness from the forgiving victim—obstacles that almost always have an intellectual or theological component. For Alison, doctrines are needed to guard against the church's potential acceptance of theological formulations that obstruct, rather than facilitate, human receptivity to the forgiveness offered in and by the Spirit of the crucified and risen Christ.

The story in Luke's Gospel of the woman who washes and anoints Jesus' feet at the table of a Pharisee (Luke 7:36–8:3) illustrates the centrality of receptivity to forgiveness for conversion to Christ. Jesus says, "Therefore, I tell you, her sins, which were many, have been forgiven; hence she has shown great love. But the one to whom little is forgiven, loves little." In an Alisonian reading of this story, it is having been forgiven much, not having sinned much, that enables the woman to love much. The way that Jesus contrasts the woman with the Pharisees suggests that in his eyes the most significant difference between them is each one's receptivity to the forgiveness that God offers in Jesus, not a difference in the number or gravity of each one's sins. For Alison, it is human receptivity to forgiveness that is both the ground and the fruit of conversion. His understanding of theological formulations and doctrines follows from his effort to draw attention to this question of human receptivity. Theological formulations and doctrines are, therefore, aimed at fostering this receptivity.

Doctrines move beyond their regulative function when they are pressed to act as the source of theological reflection or as the foundation for faith in the resurrection. In such a view, doctrines demand assent as the necessary precondition for the reception of faith. This reversal in the order of discovery is dangerous, according to Alison's perspective, not because doctrines are essentially unhelpful or empty formulations, but because, as human expressions, doctrines are not *of themselves* capable of effecting conversion through an offer of forgiveness. This view fundamentally misunderstands

---

It is also quite consistent with George Lindbeck's understanding of doctrines as rules that function similarly to grammatical rules. Lindbeck's helpful demonstration of how doctrines are both propositional and regulative coheres with the Alisonian view of doctrines that I am developing here. See *The Nature of Doctrine*, especially pp. 84–7. Yet, Lindbeck's proposal of a cultural-linguistic theory of religion, upon which his regulative theory of doctrine is based, bears only a partial resemblance to Alison's understanding of induction through theological reflection. This resemblance can be seen in the centrality for each of the Christian narrative in shaping the identity of believers. However, Alison's theology places strong and unreserved emphasis on the reality of God and on the capacity of language to refer to that reality or to be disrupted by it. Thus, for Alison it is clear that language and culture are not generative of the reality to which they refer. And as a result there is no possibility of agnosticism in Alison's approach. While Lindbeck himself may very well affirm the reality of God and the capacity of language to point to God as its referent, his cultural-linguistic view of Christianity could be read and applied in such a way as to be compatible with an agnostic perspective.

the nature of doctrines and tries to substitute adherence to "truth" claims for the painful and uncharted process of personal and ecclesial conversion. Only an experience of meeting the living presence of the crucified Christ has the capacity to effect faith, which almost inevitably comes in the wake of a collapse of old structures of belief in the "sacred" and which then stimulates the intellects of believers to reflect upon their discovery of God through their reception of forgiveness.[11]

This view of doctrines as regulative boundary markers that test theological expressions also suggests an alternative to a common understanding of apologetics. One unhelpful but common approach of contemporary Christian apologists involves constructing some rational foundation, which will possess a degree of cultural influence, from which to persuade hearers to assent to a set of Christian theological and moral propositions. Such a view of apologetics attempts to make rational argumentation the foundation for faith and also to delimit apologetics as a distinctive and essential subdiscipline of theology. An opposing, but equally unhelpful, view of apologetics is one that is highly suspicious of any appeals to reason made in the public, and therefore "secular," sphere. In this view, any use of an intellectual system that does not come "directly" from the person of Jesus Christ or Scripture is unable to communicate the message of the Gospel. This second perspective considers reason and "culture" to be inherently inimical to faith.

Alison's understanding of doctrine, however, implies that apologetics can only ever be a confessional task and that, rather than designating a subdiscipline in theology, it is an inevitable characteristic of much, if not all, of authentic theological reflection. The apologetic character of theological reflection is expressed as believers strive to articulate the coherence of faith from within, and as an outgrowth of, their experience of receiving faith. In other words, the activity of theological reflection is inherently apologetic because it consists of the subjects' self-reflexive appropriation and expression of the intelligence being received in and through the faith that is transforming them. This appropriation and expression inevitably make use of culturally relevant language since subjects are formed in and by that language. By reflecting upon this received intelligence, which is acting as a light that reveals the subjects to themselves as it simultaneously reveals God, subjects use this intelligence to make sense of the culture in which they are immersed. By this very process and without explicitly attempting to do so, the subjects are participating in an attempt to communicate this same understanding of self, God, and the particularities of their culture to those others immersed in the same, or a similar, cultural milieu.

Believers necessarily make use of culturally laden and relevant language to come to understand and express the transformation they find themselves undergoing and the intelligence of forgiveness that drives it. This is so even as the culturally laden language

---

[11] I should reiterate here that this view of doctrines as "not of themselves capable of effecting conversion through an offer of forgiveness" does not deny that doctrines themselves, as well-formulated articulations of the truths of Christian faith, can act as occasions of encounter between a human subject and the crucified and risen Christ. Rather, a view of doctrines from Alison's perspective would firmly assert that it is precisely this encounter with the risen Christ (whatever its occasion happens to be), and not the doctrines themselves, that provides the necessary opening and transformation that becomes the foundation for authentic faith and theological reflection.

that they are making use of itself is being subverted, along with their own memories, identities, and desires. Speaking of this intelligence as appropriated by the church, Alison says,

> The ecclesial intelligence of the faith is, then, a divine impulse toward a constant purifying of language and practice so as to allow God an ever less obstacled possession of us, precisely because it is through human words and practices that God wishes to have access to us. The theologian seeks to [put into practice]...the vertiginous belief that words themselves need not be stumbling blocks, but can also be vessels of God.[12]

Thus, the revelation of the intelligence of the victim through the presence of the crucified and risen Christ becomes more immediately accessible to the contemporary culture precisely through the ecclesial process in which believers are made more fully human through their appropriation and expression of this intelligence. This process of theological reflection occurs whether or not the believers have been trained as theologians or not. Part of what is received through the experience of conversion is the belief that words need not act as obstacles to persons' receptivity to forgiveness. Instead, words themselves can be "subverted from within" and made into instruments of the presence of God through the participation of human subjects in the appropriation and expression of the intelligence operative in the mind of Christ.

It is true for Alison that, as a confessional undertaking, apologetics, like doctrines, is non-foundational. It cannot and, therefore, should not attempt to provide the ground that makes the reception of faith possible. At its best, theological reflection in its apologetic capacity offers an invitation to nonbelievers, first, to suspend disbelief in order to honestly consider the coherence and integrity of the meaning being communicated via the believer's appropriation and expression of a received perspective, and then to consider, not only with their intellects, but with their imaginations, what kind of experience might have been necessary for the believer to receive such a perspective. If accepted, such an invitation has the potential to create an opening for faith in those who operate unknowingly from a belief that God is untrustworthy and death is ultimate. In this view, any explicit attempt at apologetics for a particular audience must operate with an awareness that the presence of the crucified and risen Christ always provides its own ground. Thus, Alison's theology exhibits a fundamental trust in the presence of the crucified and risen One, who does and will continue to communicate himself to persons and communities.

4.1.2 The Status of Theoretical Understanding and "Mimetic Theory"

Alison's perspective on doctrines and apologetics and his development of a theology in the order of discovery provide the basis from which I can fill out his view of theoretical understanding in general and mimetic theory specifically in relationship to his conception of theological reflection and conversion. As we saw in the last chapter, for

---

[12] Alison, *The Joy of Being Wrong*, 61–2.

Alison, intellectual understanding always occurs in the context of an "intelligence" that includes spiritual sight or blindness, relational perceptiveness or lack thereof, and true or false remembering of one's past identities, and their constitution in and through more or less rivalrous relationships. Thus, Alison's work emphasizes that theoretical or intellectual understanding, theological or otherwise, is deprived of its integrity and usefulness if it is isolated from the relational context that shapes the horizon of knowing in which it has arisen.

Alison's sensitivity to the fact that theoretical understanding exists within and is made possible by a specific relational context—a sensitivity that has been inherited from, and cultivated by, his reading of Girard—fosters in him a heightened awareness of the negative effects of the abstraction of theory from the context that gave rise to it. He believes that, in modern Western culture, fixation on the value of theoretical understanding in itself—as an "objective" statement of something true—often leads to the illusion that understanding the "theory" constitutes knowledge. With regard to theological understandings more specifically, this same Western bias leads to the dangerous misperception that grasping the most widely accepted, or authoritatively endorsed, theory of salvation is equivalent to a real knowledge of the mysteries of faith. This grasping the theory becomes all that is necessary for undergoing "conversion," receiving "faith," and being "saved." Faith, in such a perspective, is reduced to *fides quae* and looks more like something one possesses or grasps rather than something one receives and into which one is inducted more and more fully. Speaking of his approach to an understanding of atonement in particular, Alison says,

> [T]he principle problem with [the] conventional account [of atonement] is that it is a *theory*, while atonement, in the first place, was a *liturgy*.... In fact treating atonement as a theory means that it is an idea that can be *grasped*—and once it is grasped, you have "got" it—whereas liturgy is something that *happens to and at you*.[13]

In an earlier essay, Alison implies that this "conventional" view of atonement often functions as an unrecognized attempt on the part of subjects and communities to protect themselves from the process of conversion and collapse that is necessary for actually receiving faith. In Alison's words, it often becomes an attempt to substitute "understanding" for "undergoing."[14]

This problematic Western view of theory and theoretical understanding undermines the reciprocal dynamic between the experience of conversion and theological reflection that Alison believes to be essential to the healthy formation of Christian persons and communities. His repeated call for theology to remain within the order of discovery is his primary language for urging theologians (himself included) and all Christians engaged in "faith seeking understanding" to remain aware of the link between their personal or communal experiences of receiving forgiveness and the theological understandings that they develop through their ongoing reflection upon those experiences. Maintaining an explicit awareness of the order of discovery means

---

[13] Alison, "An Atonement Update," 51–2; Alison's emphasis.
[14] Alison, "Unpicking Atonement's Knots," 28.

keeping alive the personally experienced awareness of the way in which theological understanding, Christian beliefs (*fides quae*), and doctrines have all arisen from a profound experience of conversion made possible by the forgiving presence of the crucified and risen Christ. As a result of this awareness, we are able to accept and recognize that the discovery first made possible by the initial encounter with Christ opens up into a process of ongoing and deepening discovery and invites believing subjects and communities to maintain their spirit of receptivity, that is, faith (*fides qua*).

Alison's use of Girard's mimetic theory provides us with an opportunity to elaborate upon his view of apologetics and theoretical understanding through an assessment of the relationship of mimetic theory to his own process of theological reflection. Alison describes "mimetic theory" both as an "insight" into, and an "understanding" of, "the workings of human relationships at both a cultural and a personal level."[15] First, we should note that he is telling us what this theory is about, namely, how human relationships operate at the interpersonal and cultural/societal level. Second, and more importantly for my purposes here, he is telling us that mimetic theory consists of *an insight and an understanding*. In his view, "mimetic theory" is a theory that, even as it articulates a theoretical understanding of human relationships, is presented from an awareness of its connection to an experienced insight or discovery. In other words, it is a theory that, at least in Girard's usage, explicitly maintains its connection to the experiential order of discovery that has enabled Girard to formulate it.[16] This description of Girard's work indicates that, in Alison's view, "mimetic theory" is a theory in that it is an elaborated understanding. Yet, it is not the kind of theoretical understanding about which Alison is cautious, since its genesis from an experienced insight is kept in view so as to enable the theory to act more effectively as a potential vehicle for the originating insight to be experienced by others. It is a theory, elaborated from an experienced insight, that builds upon and deepens the initial insight, while also acting as an occasion for others to discover it for themselves.[17] Alison says,

---

[15] Alison, *Raising Abel*, 18, 24.

[16] It is worth noting here that this description of Girard's "theory" as experienced insight combined with reflective understanding would be of considerable help in suggesting why it is that so many scholars have pointed to the difficulty of characterizing Girard's work on mimesis as a "theory." Alison's critique of our Western obsession with theoretical understanding asserts that the modern usage of "theory" indicates an understanding that has been separated from the experience(s) that led to it. Girard's "theory," on the other hand, is one that finds the experienced insight and the elaborated understanding to be inseparable from one another. It is perhaps, in part, this maintained connection to experiential insight that makes Girard's mimetic theory suspect to many Western theorists within many disciplines. For examples of scholars who have highlighted this difficulty with classifying Girard's work, see Kirwan, *Discovering Girard*, 113–25; Kirwan, *Girard and Theology*, 20–32; Paul Dumouchel, *Violence and Truth: On the Work of René Girard* (Stanford, CA: Stanford University Press, 1988); Chris Fleming, *René Girard: Violence and Mimesis* (Cambridge/Oxford: Polity, 2004), 152–64, James G. Williams, ed. *The Girard Reader*, and Alison, *The Joy of Being Wrong*, 20–1.

[17] We can recall from Chapter 2 that the experienced insight included two experiences for Girard. First, Girard experienced the initial insight vicariously through his perception of the deep structural similarities in his readings of his five modern novelists. Second, Girard experienced the same insight personally through what he describes as the religious conversion that occurred during Holy Week of 1959. Then, in the years following, a period of self-directed education occurred, which produced the "elaborated understanding" of mimetic theory articulated in many books and essays, but perhaps most notably in *Violence and the Sacred* and *Things Hidden*.

[M]imetic theory is first of all a very small understanding or insight, a little glimpse of a *sagesse* [wisdom] that is of almost infinite application; such is its flexibility. It is both a very simple idea and a very difficult idea, precisely because it is only insofar as one allows it to illuminate one's own relationships that it yields anything.[18]

Ultimately, Alison is able to make use of this theory because, when he encountered it himself, the insight behind it practically jumped off the page he was reading and shed new light on Alison's whole life. This theory told him who he was. Because it illuminated the truth of his own identity and his own relationships, it has subsequently been able to illuminate much of his understanding of theology, psychology, sociology, etc.

Yet, despite the fact that Girard's "theory" remains connected to his initial experiences of discovery, we saw at the end of Chapter 2 that Girard manages to articulate it in a primarily psychological and sociological perspective that brackets off virtually all reference to faith in the God whose self-revelation provides the ground for the possibility of that initial discovery. That is, Girard's articulation of the theory is able to maintain an explicit connection to the originating experience without reflecting upon the source or the conditions for the possibility of the experience. Even when Girard explicitly connects the ability to formulate mimetic theory with the New Testament and the historical experiences recorded therein, he places almost exclusive attention on the revealed psychological and sociological content of Scripture in an attempt to allow those who are not Christian believers and those who don't believe that faith claims should shape intellectual inquiry to engage with his understanding of mimetic theory.[19]

Alison's use of mimetic theory, however, attempts to put Girard's somewhat agnostic account of New Testament revelation (in the sense of bracketing off any consideration of the source of revelation to focus on the content of what is revealed) in creative collaboration with a more traditionally confessional account in order to elucidate the latter (although, as I will argue in Chapter 5, this collaboration also clarifies mimetic theory). Based on his own experience of first encountering mimetic theory, Alison seems to develop and pursue a twofold hunch: first, that Girard's theory will have the capacity to illuminate the disciples' experience of the resurrection and, second, that the reason why it has such a capacity is that the disciples' experience of the resurrection is precisely the event that made it possible for such a penetrating insight into, and understanding of, human relationships to be discovered and articulated at all. Speaking of mimetic theory as a necessary background story for his work on eschatology and the imagination in *Raising Abel*, Alison writes,

> We are going to put it [mimetic theory] to work to see what it helps us recover from the apostolic witness: that is to say, we're putting it to theological use. To do this we have to return to first principles and ask ourselves what it is which makes this story, this theory, possible in the first place.[20]

---

[18] Alison, *The Joy of Being Wrong*, 21.
[19] Again see my "From a 'Revealed' Psychology to Theological Inquiry," for an extended treatment of Girard's approach to Scripture and revelation.
[20] Alison, *Raising Abel*, 24–5.

This twofold hunch becomes the motivating insight that leads Alison into serious theological investigation and, as it is gradually confirmed through his theological pursuit, it becomes a foundational premise within his ongoing theological reflection. Thus, mimetic theory leads him to discover what he has come to believe to be the meaning of the love communicated by God to human persons in and through the crucified and risen Christ, which eventually leads to the development of his understanding of the reciprocal relationship between conversion and theology that guides his approach to both theological reflection and Christian formation.

I would like to draw out two implicit points from the above quotation to highlight Alison's understanding of his own theological method and of the relationship of mimetic theory to Christian revelation. First, Alison says that putting mimetic theory to theological use consists of "seeing what it helps us recover from the apostolic witness." Alison's description of the theological task in relation to mimetic theory confirms my suggestion that the task of theological reflection involves employing our newly received capacity for right remembering to recover a true remembering of our individual and collective histories. Mimetic theory has led Alison to recognize that the apostolic witness is, for Christians, the foundational component of our collective memories. Therefore, theologically investigating the apostolic witness is not primarily a matter of studying texts via any number of methods (although studying texts is a necessary component of the larger task); rather, it consists of engaging in a process of gaining access to and recovering our own foundational memories as Christian believers. We investigate the apostolic witness through a process of right remembering of ourselves. This view of theological reflection as both gaining access to and recovering our foundational memories suggests that, through our reception of forgiveness and the intelligence of the victim, *believers are actually inducted into a new set of memories*. By being inducted into the community of Christian believers through conversion, persons receive the collective memory of that community as part of their own memory and as constitutive of their own identities.[21]

Secondly, Alison's statement about his theological use of mimetic theory confirms my assessment of his view of theory and theoretical understanding while also illuminating the relationship between mimetic theory and Christian revelation. He says that to make use of mimetic theory to see what can be recovered from the apostolic witness we will need to "return to first principles" by "asking what makes this theory possible in the first place." For Alison, the first step for making use of any theory consists of inquiring into its origin or, as I was calling it above, the relational context that allowed it to be discovered in the first place. Thus, to do something theologically fruitful with mimetic theory, Alison believes that we first have to connect it more explicitly to the relational context that originally made its central insight fully discoverable. He has come to believe, through his own experiences of conversion and his intellectual engagement with those experiences, that this context was in fact the disciples' experiences of encountering the crucified and risen Jesus as a

---

[21] We will consider this view of memory more in the next section below when I give an account of the nature and purpose of witness consistent with Alison's view.

forgiving victim. Alison's use of mimetic theory is quite consistent with his concerns about what he sees as modern biases toward theoretical understanding. And his "first principles" for theological inquiry (and for intellectual inquiry more generally) include the following premise: making good use of a theory requires that one understand the relational context that made its discovery possible. We could add that failing to heed this principle often results in the use of theoretical knowledge as a substitute for, and even protection from, undergoing the kind of collapse and conversion that make true understanding possible.

We can now see that Alison believes Christian theology (which, in some sense, is always a theoretical understanding of redemption) and mimetic theory both became discoverable via the disciples' experience of the crucified and risen Christ. Because of this common origin, they are able to elucidate one another. However, elucidation of either is possible only if the relational dynamics surrounding their origin are seen as the context within which either theory has something meaningful to communicate. To gain real insight into these relational dynamics at the origin of mimetic theory and Christian theology, the person reflecting must become attentive to their own experiences of forgiveness leading to collapse and conversion. In the last chapter, we saw that Alison's attentiveness to his own experiences of receiving forgiveness clarifies his investigation into the relational dynamics surrounding the resurrection. Alison's insight into this shared origin of mimetic theory and Christian theology allows him to put mimetic theory "to theological use" first to understand what Christian conversion and Christian theology are (*fides qua*) and then to better understand much of the content of Christian faith (*fides quae*).

As I turn now to present my view of Alison's implicit understanding of the movement from theological reflection to ongoing conversion through witness, I will begin by offering an interpretation of how, in Alison's view, the disciples' experiences of meeting the crucified and risen Christ are related to the deepest experiences of conversion of all Christian (and non-Christian) persons since the resurrection. This account will offer an Alisonian way of describing what Christian theology has often referred to as "the communion of saints."

4.2 From Theological Reflection to Conversion through Witnessing

Now that we have further clarified Alison's conception of theological reflection by placing it in relation to the traditionally related categories of doctrines and apologetics, as well as in relation to theoretical understanding in general and mimetic theory in particular, we are better equipped to consider the end or goal of theological reflection as Alison might conceive of it. This will require a more extended treatment of what Alison might mean by terms like "witness" and "testimony," since theological reflection is directed toward and becomes fruitful through an act of witness or testimony.

Alison sees the New Testament texts as the fruit of a series of encounters made possible through the reception by others of the disciples' testimonies to their encounters with the crucified and risen Jesus. Becoming a witness of, and giving witness to, the resurrection is central to Alison's understanding of the relationship between conversion and theological reflection. Alison himself explains with exacting succinctness his reason for making the category of witness significant within his account of Christian faith: "We have a faith at all because we receive a witness,"[22] and "for that is how we know anything at all about Jesus: our access to him is the apostolic witness."[23] The disciples' acts of giving witness to their encounters with the risen Jesus are the historical origin of the entire chain of witnesses that together make up the communion of saints. In an account of Christian faith based on the assertion of a reciprocal relationship between conversion and theological reflection, the category of "witness" is the glue that holds the pieces together. Therefore, a substantive understanding of witness is essential to Alison's perspective on conversion, theological reflection, and their continuing reciprocity throughout the history of Christianity.

In Alison's statements quoted above, two components of his understanding of witness are evident. First, a witness is something that persons *receive*. This description is significant because it parallels Alison's understanding of the disciples' experience of meeting the crucified and risen Christ with the experience of any person undergoing a conversion through their reception of the "witness" of another who has encountered the Spirit of the crucified and risen Christ.[24] As we develop an Alisonian account of witness, we will see that the structure of every believer's reception of a preceding witness parallels the disciples' reception of forgiveness through their encounter with the risen Jesus.

Second, Alison's description implies that a witness is someone who the disciples, as well as believers after them, become, since this is what makes it possible for there to be a witness for others to receive. At the outset of the first chapter of *Knowing Jesus*, Alison begins to develop the understanding of witness as that which the disciples are transformed into through their encounters with the risen Jesus. He depicts the disciples' transformation as one of becoming "witnesses *to*" and "witnesses *from*" the resurrection:

> [T]hat [apostolic] witness is not merely a witness to the fact of the resurrection, though it certainly is that.... But even more than bearing witness to an event..., [the apostolic witnesses] are witnesses *from* the resurrection. That is to say, it was a happening that profoundly changed them...causing them to rethink the whole of their lives, their relationship with their homeland, their culture, its values, and radically altering their understanding of who God is.[25]

Alison's understanding of the disciples' transformation into witnesses is complex. First, becoming a "witness" refers to the disciples' experience of encountering the crucified Jesus, whom they had known during his life and who had died by crucifixion, but who was now returning to them alive. The apostles were witnesses *to* some encounter in which they were deeply involved and that enabled them to know that Jesus was

---

[22] Alison, *Knowing Jesus*, 5.
[23] Ibid., 4.
[24] Cf. Phillipians 2:5.
[25] Alison, *Knowing Jesus*, 7; Alison's emphasis.

no longer dead but had been raised.[26] That is, they became witnesses to the *existence* of what Alison calls the intelligence of the victim or, perhaps more descriptively, the intelligence of forgiveness incarnate.

Alison's use of this phrase "witnesses *to*" seems to indicate that the first part of becoming a witness of the resurrection consists of becoming a receiver of forgiveness and the intelligence of the victim that made such forgiveness possible, since the disciples became witnesses to this forgiveness and its corresponding intelligence as they became receivers of it. They became witnesses in the sense that they now had a profound experiential knowledge of both forgiveness and the intelligence operative in the mind of Christ, such that they could no longer deny the reality of either.

The disciples also became what Alison refers to as "witnesses *from* the resurrection." The disciples' experience of the resurrection was a paradigmatic and transforming experience; this encounter gradually transformed those who witnessed it to the point that the presence of the risen Jesus became the paradigm from which they would learn to understand anew every past, present, and future experience of Jesus and, eventually, of everything else. The presence of the risen Jesus would become their paradigm, their hermeneutical key, for interpreting all of reality, and their mode of relating to everything around them would gradually come to bear the imprint of this presence. Thus, the process of being fundamentally transformed made the disciples into witnesses *from* the resurrection in that their presence and actions in the world would become an ongoing testimony to, and proclamation of, the living presence of Jesus the Christ. Their thinking, doing, and being would be shaped *from* their encounter with the crucified and risen One. Thus, for Alison, becoming a witness of the resurrection also involves becoming a bearer, or a vehicle, of the intelligence of forgiveness incarnate. Being a witness from the resurrection means that the disciples moved from knowing the fact of this intelligence to be undeniable toward having their identities and modes of relating to others became vessels of that intelligence.

Thus, the disciples become witnesses of the crucified and risen Christ in two senses. First, they become profoundly, experientially aware of the existence of the intelligence of the victim, which has become incarnate in Jesus Christ and which has approached them personally and gratuitously in the presence of the crucified and risen Lord. They have become witnesses to this intelligence as they receive the forgiveness offered. As a result of this reception they are irreversibly changed. They cannot be "unforgiven" and, therefore, they cannot "unwitness" it. The resurrection has happened, and they have more than simply observed it. They have been personally involved in it. This happening cannot be undone.

Being a witness to the fact of this event and, therefore, to the existence in history of the intelligence of forgiveness incarnate deepens as the disciples are slowly "subverted from within" by the forgiveness and the intelligence that they have received. As they cooperate with the movement of this intelligence, their minds, patterns of desiring,

---

[26] We already saw in the last chapter, especially Section 3.2.4, that Alison describes in some detail the apostles' ability to witness the resurrection as fruit of their friendships with him; cf. *Knowing Jesus*, 8.

modes of relating to others, and identities are transformed, through the work of the Holy Spirit, into bearers, or sacraments, of the presence of the crucified and risen Christ.[27] As bearers of his presence, the disciples *witness to/from* it more and more. In other words, as the disciples increasingly become witnesses of the resurrection, they eventually develop intentional and active ways of giving witness or testimony to the presence of the risen Christ, which is continually transforming them. The form or medium that their acts of witness take is varied. Paul's attestation to the various gifts of the Spirit in his first letter to the Corinthians identifies many of these varied means of giving witness to the presence and intelligence of the crucified and risen Christ. He speaks of the gifts of wisdom, knowledge, healing, prophecy, miraculous powers, speaking in tongues, and interpretation as many gifts that manifest the one Spirit of Christ.[28]

Before I develop Alison's understanding of theological reflection and theological texts as one form of witness to the presence of the Spirit of the crucified and risen Christ, I would like to offer briefly an interpretation of Alison's view of the relationship within the chain of witnesses to the crucified and risen Christ through history, beginning with the experiences of the first witnesses and moving forward to all others who have come to faith in Christ through their reception of a witness. I will also say something about the variability of place within Alison's understanding of encounters between the Spirit of the crucified and risen Christ and those persons being transformed into witnesses of that Spirit.

4.2.1 The History of a Chain of Witnesses

The category of witness is also essential for addressing a more specific theological problem that arises if one enquires into the kind of relationship that exists between the conversion experiences of the disciples and the conversion experiences of all who have come to believe in the resurrection of the crucified One. My assertion in the last chapter—that Alison identifies the disciples' experience of being encountered by the crucified and risen Christ as an experience of conversion and sets it as the paradigm for the dynamic of Christian conversion as such—requires an account of how we might understand the conversion experiences of the disciples and the conversion experiences of believers after them as intrinsically and structurally linked. Alison's understanding of the Holy Spirit as the creator of witnesses and the divine protagonist of conversion and theological reflection provides the essential element of such an account. The activity of the Holy Spirit, in Alison's perspective, consists of continually making present the crucified and risen Christ so as to reproduce for others the possibility of encountering him. Commenting on Luke's account of Pentecost in Acts (Acts 2:1-31) and John's account of the risen Jesus breathing the Holy Spirit into the disciples (John 20:22), Alison writes,

---

[27] Alison, *Knowing Jesus*, 26–7.
[28] 1 Corinthians 12:4-11.

> [I]n both cases the Holy Spirit is the Spirit of the risen Lord, the Spirit that was in Christ. The Spirit constantly makes present the crucified and risen Lord, thus perpetually reproducing those changes of relationship which the risen Lord had started to produce as a result of his resurrection. What I'm trying to say is that outside the group of apostles who were physical witnesses to the resurrected Lord, no one gets to see the physically risen Lord. But instead, all the really important elements of the resurrection—the irruption into our lives of gratuity as forgiveness, permitting a recasting of relationships—all that, is made constantly available to us by the Holy Spirit, so that we are able to become witnesses to the resurrection in our own lives.[29]

Alison distinguishes between the first disciples' experiences of conversion in and by means of the physical presence of the crucified and risen Jesus, and the experiences of conversion for all persons and communities who come to receive faith in Christ outside of that initial group. He doesn't say much about the difference other than that the first set of encounters involves a presence of the risen Christ that is "physical" in a way that the experiences of encounter made possible through Jesus' sending of the Spirit are not.

More importantly, however, the similarity that holds the chain of witnesses together through history is both intrinsic and structural, despite this difference in the kind of presence that subjects (personal or communal) encounter. The "link" in the chain is intrinsic since the Holy Spirit *is* the Spirit of the crucified and risen Lord, and it is the presence of this same Lord that the Spirit makes present to others, albeit in a manner that lacks some form of physicality. The link is also structural since the Holy Spirit makes present all of the essential elements that enable the encounter to become the beginning of a process of conversion for persons, namely, the gratuitous offer of forgiveness and the possibility of reforming one's mode of relating in and to the rest of creation. By making this same forgiving presence of the crucified and risen Lord present, the Holy Spirit makes it possible for others to have an encounter that transforms them into subjects freed from enslavement to death precisely by making them into witnesses of the resurrection.

Alison goes even further in identifying the Holy Spirit as the Spirit of the crucified and risen Christ by describing Jesus' going to his death as simultaneously an act of giving the Spirit:

> The whole process by which Jesus went to his death as a real, historical, conscious act of subversion of violent human practice: that *was* the act of giving the Holy Spirit. All the Gospels without exception bear a subtle witness to this when they

---

[29] Alison, *Knowing Jesus*, 26-7. In *The Joy of Being Wrong*, Alison defines faith in terms that also describe how it is passed on through a chain of witnesses: "So supernatural faith, the suggestion into being of a new other, becomes possible precisely through a certain historical enactment, kept alive by certain historical persons, who maintained alive for others the possibility of encounter with this suggestion by the construction and transmission of certain repeatable, historical actions... and certain historically repeatable words and texts" (p. 58).

describe Jesus on the cross "giving up" his spirit, or "breathing out" his spirit, which is the same thing as his dying. That is, the Holy Spirit is given us as the possibility of re-creating the same witness to the Father.[30]

By linking the gift of the Holy Spirit with the historical and conscious act of Jesus in willingly going to his death, Alison highlights a historical and embodied expression of the intrinsic relationship between the crucified and risen Christ and Christ's Spirit. Even further, this link suggests that one way that the Spirit might make the crucified and risen Christ present throughout history is by making it possible for others to "re-create the same witness to the Father" that Jesus gave, that is, by sustaining and strengthening those who are persecuted and by inviting others to become capable of seeing and understanding the relative innocence of their unrecognized scapegoats.[31]

Alison elaborates upon his identification of Jesus' dying with the sending of the Holy Spirit by linking this dual movement with the opening of a new and creative human practice as a constructive response to the hidden human mechanism of violence.

> So Jesus is making possible as a normal human practice the infinitely creative dynamic of the continuous re-presentation of the passion. He is not doing this independently of other human people: his purpose is to make available the divine inner dynamic as a new human story in the midst of the usual human story of expulsion and death. One part of the sending of the Holy Spirit *is* the preparation of the witnesses and is the making possible texts which call to mind who Jesus was, and what he was doing.[32]

The work of the Holy Spirit, then, includes preparing witnesses who, through their acts of witness, make available to other persons the possibility of creating a new human story through their participation in the inner dynamic among Father, Son, and Spirit as made accessible to humanity through the life, death, and resurrection of Jesus. And even further, the work of the Spirit also includes the inspiration of texts that act as one form of witness. Although here Alison is referring specifically to the first witnesses of the resurrection and the writing of texts that came to be included in the New Testament canon, we can also understand that this work of the Spirit among the first witnesses continues through history, inspiring an abundance of theological texts that give witness to the crucified and risen Christ. This ongoing work of the Spirit of Christ, then, forms a chain of witnesses to the crucified and risen Christ. Through their reception of the testimony of a preceding witness, they undergo an encounter with Christ in which they

---

[30] Alison, *Raising Abel*, 66; Alison's emphasis.

[31] In a section below, I will consider more fully the fruits of encounter with the Spirit of Christ, which will include an elaboration of how such an encounter might strengthen those that are being persecuted and might invite others to see more clearly the nonnecessity of their participation in violence.
  Alison's description of the work of the Spirit as recreating the Son's witness to the Father also recalls Girard's description of the saints as links in the historical chain of imitators of Christ's imitation of the Father. See Section 2.4.2.

[32] Alison, *Raising Abel*, 66–7; Alison's emphasis.

become transformed into forgiven forgivers and self-aware imitators and are enabled to create occasions of encounter for others through new acts of testimony. The reception of faith in the risen Christ and the creation of communities of faith become possible through a series of encounters between persons and the Spirit of Christ through which that Spirit creates a chain of witnesses of the crucified and risen Christ. Catholics often call this chain "the communion of saints."[33]

4.2.2 The Variability of Place

Given this understanding of the Spirit's work in forming a chain of witnesses through history, it would make sense to ask about the historical conditions that make possible the encounters that form persons into witnesses. In other words, such an understanding naturally raises a question about the fixity or variability of the "place" in which an encounter with the Spirit of the crucified and risen Christ might occur.

Alison's attention to what he sees as "some lost understanding" in the theological significance of the doctrine of the ascension is a helpful starting point for our consideration of his view of the place of encounter between the Spirit of Christ and persons. For him, this doctrine preserves a basic principle of the dynamic of divine revelation and human discovery.[34] Drawing out an understanding of the importance of the doctrine of the ascension at the end of the first chapter of *Knowing Jesus* and setting it as the framing question for his entire inquiry in *Raising Abel*, Alison argues that what the disciples came to believe and understand through their experience of Jesus' ascension to the Father was that "[b]eing human was from then on permanently and indissolubly involved in the presence of God."[35] In Jesus' ascension, this particular human story of the risen Christ enters into the life of God. Because the life and death of Jesus have been subsumed into the identity of the risen Christ, Jesus' ascension means that God's life can never again be known apart from this human life. Thus, Alison concludes that, as a consequence of the ascension, all future manifestations of the divine to humanity in and through the Spirit of Christ must take place "on an entirely human level."[36]

---

[33] Elizabeth Johnson's historical and constructive study of the symbol of the communion of saints places repeated emphasis on the centrality of the working of the Spirit as "Sophia" in producing a wholly inclusive communion of witnesses to Christ. She begins her study by quoting Wisdom 7:27, which provides the "guiding intuition of [her] exploration": "Although she [Sophia] is but one, she can do all things, and while remaining in herself, she renews all things; in every generation she passes into holy souls and makes them friends of God, and prophets." See *Friends of God and Prophets: A Feminist Theological Reading of the Communion of Saints* (New York: Continuum, 1998), especially p. 2.
  Johnson even makes direct use of Girard's work in her description of the power of narrative to transform the one telling it and the power of a subversive remembering of the dead as testimony against persecutors. See pp. 173–4.

[34] Alison begins to develop a theology of the ascension in *Knowing Jesus*, 23–5. However, the bulk of his work in this area is found throughout the guiding argument of *Raising Abel* (see especially pp. 16–17 and 174–7). He tries to show how the disciples, after their experiences of encounter with the crucified and risen Lord, had to gradually recover or appropriate Jesus' eschatological imagination in their ongoing attempt to tell Jesus' story.

[35] Alison, *Knowing Jesus*, 24.

[36] Ibid., 24–5.

This is a significant statement for Alison. It does not mean, of course, that God's self-revelation will confine itself to the limits of human understanding. Instead, a human level indicates the interpersonal level of relational dynamics in which patterns of desire and belonging shape the identities of persons and communities. In the ascension, these human patterns have been taken up into God and, as a result, they are suffused with God's presence in a more immediate way and, according to Alison, they become the primary (perhaps even sole) domain of God's ongoing self-revelation to persons through the Spirit of Christ. Thus, we can say that, for Alison, the place of potentially effective encounters with the Spirit of Christ is the interpersonal patterns of desire and networks of belonging that constitute our identities as persons and communities. This is indeed a broad and variable "place" of encounter.

Alison gives further indication of such an understanding of the variability of place with his use of the phrase "the universal christoformity of grace" in *The Joy of Being Wrong*.[37] With this phrase, Alison is asserting that all grace and, therefore, the possibility of all conversion have the form of Christ, who for him is the forgiving victim or, as I might put it, the intelligence of forgiveness incarnate. As he says, "There is no grace available to human beings that does not involve a turning toward the victim, that is, a certain form of conversion."[38] Inversely, we could also say that a turning toward the victim enabled by a reception of forgiveness *is* grace. This is so whether or not any thematically Christian language, symbols, or persons are present within the encounter.

Considering Luke's parable of the Good Samaritan, Alison expands upon his description of the christoformity of grace. He says that, with this story, Jesus

> was identifying the concrete way in which divine grace is made humanly present: as a turning toward the victim.... We can say, then, that grace is always christoform: the gratuitous presence of the self-giving victim is simultaneously a critique of the way humans are and a constructive forgiveness of humans permitting the construction of a creative sign of a new human reconciliation.[39]

In using this parable, Alison refers to both the man on the side of road and the Samaritan as victims. The Samaritan turns "toward the victim" on the side of the road and in doing so he becomes "the gratuitous presence of the self-giving victim." This

---

[37] Alison, *The Joy of Being Wrong*, 91. Alison first develops this phrase as an alternative to what he views as a problematic within Rahner's term "the anonymous Christian." Alison's reading of the meaning of this term as well as Rahner's "supernatural existential" tends toward a misreading of Rahner. Alison believes that with these terms Rahner is proposing an anthropology in which all human beings are imbued with a universal saving grace and, therefore, the Church and the sacraments merely explicate and make visible what is an already present and salvific gift of grace. For a fuller treatment of this misreading, see my "The Self Prior to Mimetic Desire: Rahner and Alison on Original Sin and Conversion," 7–31.

Despite Alison's misunderstanding of Rahner on these points, however, his development of the phrase "the universal christoformity of grace" is very helpful for understanding Alison's perspective on what I am calling the "variability of place." Beyond this application, I believe that it could also become a real contribution to a Christian theology of religions and Christian dialogue with non-Christians, both religious and secular.

[38] Alison, *The Joy of Being Wrong*, 93.

[39] Ibid., 91–2.

subtle identification supports an understanding of the forgiving victim that is *not* simultaneously a demand that all victims forgive their victimizers, but which instead invites all of us caught up in the victimization of others to turn and see our victims. Alison is saying that, in the transformative exchanges in which persons turn toward victims in such a way as to enable sorrow and repentance for their own complicity in victimization, an encounter with the Spirit of Christ takes place, whether thematically so or not. The authenticity of the encounter can be known through two fruits: first, an identification of and a moving away from a way of being human that generates identity and belonging through exclusion and, second, "a constructive forgiveness of humans" that becomes "a creative sign" of the possibility of "a new human reconciliation." Alison then goes on to explain that

> the self-giving of the victim ... is constantly pushing wider the human limitations of the contingent historical sign [the crucified and risen Christ] and is perfectly capable of creating anonymous proto-signs of the reconciliation of humanity with God *wherever there are humans to be reconciled—the field of opportunity is universal.*[40]

Thus, the "place" of potential encounter with the Spirit of Christ cannot be made any narrower than "wherever there are humans to be reconciled." The human need for reconciliation, then, is the only necessary condition for the Spirit of Christ to effect an encounter with the crucified and risen One, which need not be experienced thematically as such as long as it takes the form of a "turning toward the victims" in Alison's sense. This is, in fact, what Alison meant when he asserted that, as a consequence of Jesus' ascension into heaven, all future workings of the Spirit of Christ would be on a "human level." The human level is the level of interpersonal, social, and cultural *relationships in need of reconciliation*.

4.2.3 Theological Reflection and Theological Texts as a Form of Witness and Place of Encounter[41]

Having provided a sketch of the larger context of Alison's understanding of witnesses to the crucified and risen Christ and the kind of encounter that transforms persons into such witnesses, I will now consider theological reflection and theological texts as particular forms of witness or particular places of potentially effective encounter with the Spirit of Christ. Alison gives these forms of witness a great deal of attention. This is due in part to his own experiences of encounter via theological reflection and via

---

[40] Ibid., 92; my emphasis. With his use of the phrase "anonymous proto-signs of the reconciliation of humanity with God," we can see that Alison is offering an alternative to Rahner's "anonymous Christians."

[41] An earlier version of this section was given as a conference paper at the Colloquium on Violence & Religion conference in July 2013 at the University of Northern Iowa in Cedar Falls, Iowa. It was part of panel with Grant Kaplan entitled "James Alison and Theological Reflections Influenced by Girard." Alison served as the respondent on the panel.

texts and in part to the influence of Girard's work, which focuses a great deal on texts as instruments of conversion for both their writers and their readers.[42]

Earlier I developed Alison's distinction between two ways in which the disciples and all Christian believers are witnesses of the resurrection: they are witnesses *to* an event of encounter in which they are deeply involved, and they are witnesses *from* this encounter that effected their reception and gradual appropriation of the intelligence of forgiveness incarnate. As witnesses in both of these senses, the disciples and Christians after them give testimony to the Spirit of the crucified and risen Christ through a variety of actions. Within contemporary Christian culture, some of these kinds of actions include various forms of social engagement, parenthood, personal and communal prayer, and the corporal and spiritual works of mercy. In reality, all aspects of a person's life become potential domains for witnessing to the Spirit of the crucified and risen Christ. This witnessing does not necessarily include explicit, confessional statements of one's faith. Rather, the believer's witness consists primarily of a mode of relating to others that is shaped by his or her ongoing reception of forgiveness and an appropriation of the intelligence that motivates an ongoing offer of forgiveness. In short, witnessing for Alison is an embodied and relational expression of the believer's spirit of receptivity to the ongoing offer of forgiveness incarnated most fully in the crucified and risen Christ.

Given this understanding of witnessing, theological reflection, which in Alison's view consists of the believer's ongoing self-reflexive appropriation and articulation of the intelligence operative in the mind of Christ, constitutes one form of such witness. Theological reflection is the witness given by the mind of the believer as it allows itself to become increasingly receptive to the mind that was in Christ Jesus.[43] In becoming receptive to the mind of Christ, the mind of the believer is gradually subverted from within. As this happens, the mind attempts to make sense of both the transformation of its own mode of perceiving and the intelligence effecting the transformation. This interaction between the mind of the believer and the intelligence operative in the mind of Christ is the generative source of theological reflection. As the mind of the believer is engaged in this process of reflection, the transformation that it is simultaneously undergoing and reflecting upon becomes an occasion of encounter between other persons and the Spirit of the crucified and risen Christ. Even without explicitly attempting to witness to others, the mind's effort to reflect upon the intelligence to which it finds itself exposed, as it is simultaneously exposed by it, does in fact become a witness to others.

Theological texts for Alison are a preservation and a communication through distance of the fruit of a believer's theological reflection that extend the believer's

---

[42] Alison helpfully describes the place of theological reflection in his own life as well as the influence of Girard upon him and his experiences of encounter via texts in one key essay as well as in a recent interview. The first we will look at in some detail below: "On Learning to Say 'Jesus Is Lord': A 'Girardian' Confession," 147–69. The second is an interview published by Commonweal magazine: "Theology as Survival: An Interview with James Alison," March 6, 2012, http://www.commonwealmagazine.org/alison (accessed April 6, 2019). The unabridged version of this interview can be found on Alison's own website at http://www.jamesalison.co.uk/texts/eng67.html (accessed April 6, 2019).

[43] Cf. Philippians 2:5 and 2 Corinthians 3:14.

witness to the Spirit of the crucified and risen Christ so that it can become a potential occasion of encounter for persons beyond the immediate context in which the reflection is taking place. Paul Ricoeur asserts that this communication of meaning in and through distance enables texts, theological, or otherwise, to become "much more than a particular case of intersubjective communication"; instead, they display "a fundamental characteristic of the very historicity of human experience."[44] Ricoeur's understanding of texts supports Alison's attentiveness to theological texts as a form of witness that extends and strengthens the chain of Christian witnesses through history.

To draw out Alison's view of texts as a particular form of witness, or a potentially effective occasion of encounter between the readers of the texts and the Spirit of Christ, I will first reconsider one of Alison's reflections on his own experience of encounter leading to conversion, which was precipitated by his discovery of Girard's text *Things Hidden*. This will set the stage for developing a fuller account of Alison's implicit understanding of texts as acts of witness that make possible occasions of encounter with the Spirit of Christ or occasions of turning toward victims. I will then make use of some insightful reflections from Paul Ricoeur on hermeneutics that depict vividly the potential dynamic of exchange between text and reader—an exchange that effects a transformation in the reader's self-understanding. I will then return to Alison and his view of the divine protagonist to consider how we might understand an encounter via a text (theological or otherwise) as an encounter with the Spirit of Christ. Finally, I conclude this exploration of Alison's understanding of texts with a consideration of the possible fruits of such an encounter, as well as the possibility of receiving a false witness.

4.2.3.1 Alison's Experience of Encounter via Girard's Text

In *Faith beyond Resentment*, Alison recalls his first encounter with Girard's work in 1985, when he stumbled upon a copy of Girard's *Things Hidden*. We considered some of Alison's reflection on this experience at the beginning of the first chapter.[45] In *Faith beyond Resentment*, Alison describes his time reading *Things Hidden* as an experience of being "ambushed" by the Spirit of Christ. His reflection on this experience vividly depicts how he imagines that texts can serve as potential occasions of encounter with the Spirit. Alison says,

> Instead of reading that book, I found myself being read by it. I came away certain that I had met someone who had told me everything that I had ever done—an experience of being exposed to a massive amount of truth about the world I live in and about myself in particular. Glimpses of course, no immediate capacity to give a coherent account of myself; but glimpses which pointed to a coherence in

---

[44] Ricoeur, *From Text to Action*, 76.
[45] My treatment of Alison's reflection on this experience at the beginning of the first chapter was based on his short 1996 article, "Girard's Breakthrough," 848–849. This article can also be found on Alison's website at http://www.jamesalison.co.uk/texts/eng05.html (link last tested on April 7, 2019).

the voice telling the truth. And, along with those glimpses and that coherence, the knowledge of being pulled out of myself to know more about a truth which might be very challenging, but would never frighten me or bind me up.[46]

He goes on to say that he was aware of how this experience closely paralleled that of the woman at the well of Samaria.[47] It seems fair, then, to designate Alison's first interaction with Girard's work as the moment of reception of profound insight into himself and his way of relating to others in the world. His reading of the text became the occasion of an encounter, not with Girard, but with the voice of one who was able to tell him the truth about himself and to whom Alison could eventually confess, "It is the Lord."[48]

Alison's description of this encounter with the Spirit of the crucified and risen Christ via his reading of *Things Hidden* suggests that the text acted for Alison as a witness to the intelligence operative in the mind of Christ, and this particular act of witnessing was effective in opening Alison's spirit to being spoken to by the Spirit of Christ. We can sense the depth and abruptness of his discovery with his description of the experience as one of being "ambushed." We can also see that the Spirit led him to more than insight into his own identity and the world around him; it also pulled him "out of himself" to know more about the truth that was being spoken to him and about the voice of the one speaking.

In Alison's description of this significant moment of discovery, we see one possible origin in his own experience of an understanding of texts as potentially effective instruments of encounter and communication between the Spirit of Christ and the readers or hearers of the texts. Toward the end of the same essay, Alison articulates that the intended objective of theological texts is to attempt to reproduce for others "the possibility of dwelling in a particular experience of being told the truth."[49] Again, he says that theological texts should be written in such a way as to offer the reader the potential of "being spoken into being with words of truth which [open] up new vistas" into whom he or she has been and is being invited to become.[50] Still again, theological texts should aim to be "conduits for the Spirit of God to speak words into [the hearts of others]." These descriptive phrases give us a glimpse of Alison's view of texts that are "theological" in their composition, which, through their authors' reflection upon and appropriation of the intelligence in the mind of Christ, provide an authentic witness to the crucified and risen Christ that invites others into an encounter with the Spirit of Christ. These descriptions, along with Alison's account of his experience of reading *Things Hidden*, provide enough context for me to use Paul Ricoeur's work to support and fill out Alison's view of texts as potential occasions of encounter.

---

[46] Alison, "On Learning to Say 'Jesus Is Lord': A 'Girardian' Confession," 149.
[47] Ibid., 150; cf. John 4:29. Alison's account of this experience in *The Tablet* also explicitly makes this connection as we have already seen in the first chapter.
[48] Ibid.
[49] Ibid., 150–1.
[50] Ibid.

4.2.3.2 Turning to Ricoeur—Texts as Occasions of Encounter

Ricoeur defines "text" rather straightforwardly as "any discourse fixed by writing."[51] If we understand that Ricoeur characterizes discourse "as an event," then his apparently simple definition of a text is useful in my attempt to draw out Alison's understanding of theological texts as potential acts of witness for their readers. According to Ricoeur, a text preserves an event of communication and makes it possible for that communication to take place "in and through distance" by means of an encounter between the reader and what Ricoeur calls "the world in front of the text."[52] Ricoeur's attentiveness to the process of appropriation and disappropriation that makes up this encounter can help us to see how we might view texts in general and theological texts specifically as mediums for receiving a witness that has the potential to transform the reader by effecting within her a new and more consciously held self-understanding.

To my mind, the power of Ricoeur's insight into the potential encounter between text and reader lies in his recognition of the capacity of a text to communicate meaning to the reader in a way that disorients her and exposes the limits of her horizon. This disorientation makes possible the receptivity needed for transformation and new self-understanding. In an essay entitled "Phenomenology and Hermeneutics," Ricoeur describes the exchange between reader and text as a process of appropriation and disappropriation that uncovers the vulnerability of the reader and engenders receptivity:

> [W]hat is appropriation from one point of view is disappropriation from another. To appropriate is to make what was alien become one's own. What is appropriated is indeed the matter of the text. But the matter of the text becomes my own only if I disappropriate myself, in order to let the matter of the text be. So I exchange the *me, master* of itself, for the *self, disciple* of the text.[53]

We see here that the text offers the reader an opportunity to make herself receptive to the possibility of "being spoken into being," to use Alison's phrase, precisely by letting go of her self-delimited identity and becoming open to the meaning communicated through the text. The text acts as an occasion of an event, an encounter, in which the reader learns to become disciple and recipient.

Ricoeur adopts and develops Gadamer's phrase "the matter of the text" to identify the content that the reader appropriates through the encounter. That content is a proposed world of discovery that opens up in front of the text. Ricoeur explains that this world is not determined solely by a recovery of the intention of the author but instead makes a space for something new to be revealed.

> [T]he [content] of appropriation is what Gadamer calls "the matter of the text" and what I call here "the world of the work." Ultimately what [the reader] appropriate[s]

---

[51] Ricoeur, *From Text to Action*, 106.
[52] Ibid., 76, 37.
[53] Ibid., 37; Ricoeur's emphasis.

is a proposed world. The latter is not *behind* the text, as a hidden intention would be, but *in front of* it, as that which the work unfolds, discovers, reveals. Henceforth, to understand is *to understand oneself in front of the text*. It is not a question of imposing upon the text our finite capacity for understanding, but of exposing ourselves to the text and receiving from it an enlarged self.[54]

It is rather bold to claim that the essence of understanding is understanding of oneself in front of the text. Yet, Ricoeur is arguing that the height of understanding is in fact the new and enlarged *self*-understanding that becomes possible for the reader when a world opens up between herself and the text. Ricoeur's description of the event of interpretation makes it clear that the reader learns to interpret herself through the text, rather than the reader interpreting the text. That is, the text "invites the reader into a process of self-interpretation."[55] Thus, Ricoeur helps us see that, in the act of interpreting a text, there is ambiguity about the source of the interpretation and the resulting new self-understanding of the reader. He deemphasizes the influence of any unstated intention of the author in favor of the world in front of the text, which is the place of exchange between the text and the reader. He suggests that, for this exchange to be fruitful, the reader must refrain from "imposing" upon the text her "finite *capacity* for understanding" and instead "expose" herself to the text. The reader's capacity for understanding is not the active agent, nor is it the author's intention. The text itself "unfolds, discovers, and reveals." This assertion suggests that the text has a spirit, subjectivity, or intentionality of its own. Yet, it seems to me that Ricoeur's analysis makes room for the possibility that the source of the new self-understanding is neither the text nor the reader. Instead, an unidentified source of interpretation enters the encounter through the receptivity of the reader toward the text. While Ricoeur does not strive to name or even point directly to this source, his description of the encounter opens a space for it to enter, which can be explored further. On this point I believe that a dialogue between Alison and Ricoeur would be most fruitful.

4.2.3.3 The Protagonist of the Encounter via the Text

Ricoeur's understanding of texts as events of discourse that make possible transformed and enlarged self-understanding through the readers' appropriation of the world of discovery in front of the text supports Alison's view of theological texts as potential occasions of encounter in which readers find themselves being spoken into being. Ricoeur can help readers of Alison's work to see how theological texts can be occasions of encounter through which real transformation can take place within the readers as a result of the text's capacity to disorient its readers and push them to recognize and relinquish their sense of being masters of themselves. In my view, Ricoeur's

---

[54] Ibid., 87–8; Ricoeur's emphasis.
[55] Referring specifically to the New Testament using the work of Girard and Alison, Brian Robinette describes the Gospel as a text that addresses its readers and "draws [them] into its narrative world in order to deconstruct the stories [they] frequently tell about [themselves]." See *Grammars of Resurrection*, 293.

highlighting of the ability of texts to uncover the vulnerability of their readers and engender receptivity in them increases the plausibility of Alison's assertion that texts have the potential to act as occasions of encounter with the Spirit of the crucified and risen Christ in a way that parallels the disciples' experiences of conversion through their encounter with Christ.

I suggest that Alison's explicitly theological approach to understanding the potential encounter between texts and readers allows him to develop further than Ricoeur an account of the source of the readers' transformed and enlarged self-understanding. Ricoeur's strictly hermeneutical approach leads him to identify and observe the space that opens up in front of the text and the exchange between the reader and the world of the text that takes place there. However, he remains rather agnostic (at least professionally) about the source of the text's capacity to engender receptivity in its readers, as well as the source of the discovery and revelation that become possible for readers as they appropriate the world of the work.

Alison's account of the discipline of theology, on the other hand, is explicit about the divine protagonism that effects the dynamic of conversion leading to theological reflection. Alison's reversal of the traditional understanding of theology as the work of human subjects coming to understand a divine object leads to an understanding of God and, more specifically, the Spirit as the protagonist and we humans as "the relatively inert distant objects which are, as it happens, being invited into this form of knowing, thus becoming subjects.... We are not so much searchers as ones who are being found."[56]

This view of theology and theological reflection naturally carries over to inform his understanding of the source of the receptivity, discovery, and revelation that become possible in an encounter elicited by a text. Alison, not unlike many of the Reformed Protestant theologians (Karl Barth for example), asserts that the Spirit as divine protagonist makes the witness communicated in and through theological texts *effective* as potential occasions of encounter between the Spirit of the crucified and risen Christ and the readers of the text. The Spirit as divine protagonist makes it possible for the readers to "exchange the me, master of itself" for an "enlarged self,"[57] as Ricoeur says, or, in Alison's words, to "[dwell] in a particular experience of being told the truth."[58]

This conception of the activity of theological reflection and of theological texts as acts of witnessing and, therefore, as occasions for others to encounter the Spirit of the crucified and risen Christ is fundamental to Alison's development of an understanding of theology as inductive. Persons being drawn to engage in theological reflection and to put that reflection into writing, as well as those persons who become readers of the theological reflections of others, are being led into a dynamic and ongoing encounter with the Spirit of the crucified and risen Christ. This encounter inducts them into being as authentic subjects as they receive the forgiveness offered by Christ and as they continually appropriate the intelligence in the mind of Christ that makes such forgiveness possible.

---

[56] Alison, *Broken Hearts and New Creations*, viii.
[57] Ricoeur, *From Text to Action*, 37, 88.
[58] Alison, *Faith beyond Resentment*, 150–1.

In Alison's perspective, both the writing and the reading of theological texts constitute potential acts of witness in which the Spirit of Christ can move to make the crucified and risen Christ present to the writers or readers. As acts of witness and occasions of encounter, theological texts forge the growing chain of witnesses that extends through history in that they are able to simultaneously heighten and soften the attentiveness of their readers to their need for reconciliation. That is, theological texts become effective as occasions of encounter through the movement of the Spirit insofar as they open their readers to a more vivid and explicit awareness of their need for reconciliation, while at the same time softening any inclination to become scandalized by such an awareness. In other words, texts are effective as occasions of encounter to the extent that they foster a greater receptivity to forgiveness in their writers and their readers.

4.2.3.4 Distinguishing Theological Texts—Composition vs. Effect

The view of texts that I have tried to draw out from the above interchange between Alison and Ricoeur also helps us to distinguish between texts that are theological in their composition and texts that may be theological in their effect. From Alison's perspective, texts that are theological in their composition would be texts in which the authors use thematically Christian language to reflect upon and articulate their own experience of conversion, their need for reconciliation, and their gradual appropriation of the intelligence that they find themselves in the process of receiving from one who has told them who they are. In other words, texts that are theological in their composition have some explicit quality of testifying to the author's experience of conversion and to the Spirit of the crucified and risen Christ who is transforming their imaginations to become capable of perceiving and appropriating the intelligence in the mind of Christ. These texts are written both for the sake of the one writing and for their various potential readers, since the process of articulation is part of the process of appropriation and ongoing conversion.

Building on the view of apologetics that I developed at the beginning of the chapter, we could say that texts that are theological in their composition, like the activity of theological reflection, have an intrinsically apologetic character. The writers of such texts express the coherence of Christian faith as they continually strive to appropriate and articulate it for themselves. That coherence is most effectively demonstrated to the extent that the intelligence of the crucified and risen Christ can be seen, over time, to bring greater understanding, truthfulness, and freedom into the lives of those whose minds have become increasingly receptive to it. As the Jesus of Mathew's Gospel says about false prophets, "By their fruits you will know them" (Mathew 7:20), so too the truth of the intelligence of the crucified and risen Christ will be known by the fruits of understanding, truthfulness, and freedom that it is able to bring about in persons.

Yet, in my use of Ricoeur's work and Alison's own experience of conversion via *Things Hidden*, we see that texts that are not theological in their composition, that is, texts that do not have an explicit quality of testimony, still have the potential to become occasions of encounter for their readers to the extent that they are fruits of an experience of conversion. Based on Alison's view of the reciprocal relationship between conversion and theological reflection, I would say that we can see such texts as potentially "theological" in their effect. In other words, they still might open up a space "in front of the text" in which the readers are enabled to "disappropriate" themselves and thereby become receptive to being spoken into being by someone who has a capacity to tell them "everything they have ever done" in such a way as to enable them to be who they are more freely—uncovered imitators and forgiven sinners.

The above exploration of Alison's view of the wide variability of the potential "place" of encounter that leads to the reception of forgiveness is relevant here because it aids in an articulation of how texts that are not explicitly theological in their composition might still serve as an occasion of encounter leading to conversion. As I concluded above, Alison's understanding of Jesus' ascension into heaven and his assertion of the universal christoformity of grace lead to an understanding of the place of encounter with the Spirit of Christ as wherever there are people in need of reconciliation. Thus, understanding texts that are not explicitly theological in their composition as potential places of encounter means that these texts become places of encounter if they are able to evoke in readers a deeper awareness of their need for reconciliation by enabling them to receive forgiveness or at least to imagine the possibility of forgiveness. This capacity is the criterion that would make any text a potential place of encounter in Alison's view.

4.2.3.5 *The Fruits of the Encounter via the Text and the Possibility of False Witness*

Ricoeur's description of the exchange between text and reader that leads to a new and enlarged self-understanding, along with Alison's description of the aim of theological texts to speak authentic subjects into being "with words of truth that open up new vistas" of self-understanding, points us toward the kind of fruits that we should look for when considering the capacity of a text to be an occasion of conversion. These fruits are twofold and interrelated: the opening up of a process of learning how to speak truthfully about oneself and the corresponding process of learning how to become "a living sign of the new unity of humanity."[59]

The process of learning how to speak truthfully about oneself is one of being led to see more and more deeply within oneself the various patterns of deception that have operated below the surface of one's attentive awareness. Alison describes this process as one of becoming increasingly dissatisfied with telling lies:

> We find ourselves ever less able to be happy telling lies about ourselves. Precisely because we can detect the deep structure of the sacrificial melody, we are less and less happy to reproduce that in our own little accounts of our marital difficulties, our dealings with our employers and so forth.[60]

Like the disciples' encounters with the crucified and risen Christ, which gradually revealed to them their own participation in violence, the experience of encounter

---

[59] Alison, *The Joy of Being Wrong*, 62.
[60] Alison, *Faith beyond Resentment*, 163.

with the Spirit of Christ via a text reveals to persons their own habituated tendencies to cover up their more or less violent identities formed through exclusions. Whether these exclusions are as obvious as murder, or as subtle as gossip or half-conscious biases, a person begins to see that the "sacrificial melody," as Alison calls it here, is exactly the same. This is true whether the stories persons tell about themselves sacrifice themselves or others. In either case, one has been engaged in the same practice of trying to preserve one's own identity as "good" (or perhaps as "bad") through the "necessary" degradation or dismissal of those (perhaps oneself) who are unworthy of being acknowledged as "good." Thus, one fruit of conversion is the exposure of this habituated lying, along with an ability to recognize its identity with all other forms of sacrificial exclusions, and a growing sense of dissatisfaction with participating in this practice any longer. Such persistent dissatisfaction, if it avoids the extremes of despair or disgust, is the beginning of the humility that enables one to speak more truthfully about oneself.

It is important to draw attention to (1) the strong resonance between the language of recovering a capacity for right remembering of the past and clear perception of the present in Chapter 3 and (2) the language here regarding the growing awareness of one's habituated patterns of lying, which fosters a greater capacity for speaking truthfully. The exposure of, and growing dissatisfaction with, one's pattern of "sacrificial" lying is simultaneous with the recovery of a capacity for remembering one's past rightly. Both make possible a humble receptivity to the intelligence of forgiveness that allows for an increasing capacity for speaking truthfully about God, oneself, and others in the present.

The process of recognizing one's patterns of lying as a form of scapegoating, accompanied by dissatisfaction and an increasing capacity to tell the truth, eventually transforms one's mode of relating to others. Gradually one's perception of one's neighbors changes such that one begins to see that, for the designation "neighbor" to be meaningful, it has to be applicable to all people indiscriminately. This change in perception leads to the development of a new human practice of enacting solidarity, especially toward those one has victimized. Alison writes,

> [It is not] difficult to show how this conversion is intrinsically ecclesial. The new heart is created in us by the old heart ... being broken. ... The conversion works as we recognize our complicity in creating victims, cease to regard ourselves as a victim, and begin to see ourselves as covictimizers. This is a first step toward ... learning how to create concrete acts of solidarity with our own and other's victims, even though, as we will discover, this increases the likelihood of ourselves being victimized. In the concrete circumstances of humanity, what the new unity looks like is the beginnings of the gathering of penitent persecutors around the body of the self-giving victim, whose forgiveness made their new perception possible, and the creating of acts of worship of the victim, both in celebration and in acts of fraternal service.[61]

---

[61] Alison, *The Joy of Being Wrong*, 62. Alison gives a similar description of the fruits of conversion in the last chapter of *Knowing Jesus*. See pp. 94–5.

Learning to see one's own habituated lying as a form of victimization is the beginning of discovering the relative innocence of one's own victims, which in turn makes it possible to seek out concrete ways of supporting and strengthening those who are being persecuted. By "relative innocence," I mean to indicate that for Alison, what persons discover about their victims through conversion is not that they are absolutely innocent of participating in any violence themselves, since participation in violence is part of the human condition as sinful. Instead, they discover that their victims are innocent of much or all of the particular guilt that they had imputed to them as the motivation for their violence against them. They discover that, in their actions toward the victim, they were guilty of violence at least as much, if not more than, their victim, and that a false belief in their own righteousness has led them to develop rather egregious misperceptions of the guilt of others.[62]

The resulting attempts to stand in solidarity with one's own victims and those of others place one at risk of being victimized alongside them, but herein lies the power of such actions. The desire to alleviate the isolation of victims and to make their relative innocence more visible through acts of standing with them becomes more compelling than one's own fear of being victimized. This is a fruit of the transformation of one's imagination through the gradual self-reflexive appropriation of the intelligence of the victim, that is, through theological reflection. The transformation of the subject's imagination brings about the deepening of desire into a compassion that prefers to stand with the victims rather than to protect oneself from potential violence. Such acts of solidarity, regardless of the magnitude of the sacrifice or the degree of risk involved, are fruits of an encounter with the Spirit of the crucified and risen Christ.

This identification of the basic fruits of an encounter with the Spirit of Christ raises the question of whether it is possible to receive a false witness and in what might such falsity consist. The possible sources of falsity within a particular act of witness are diverse and cannot all be enumerated here. I will limit myself to considering briefly two sources of falsity that parallel Alison's identification of two related aspects of becoming a witness of the crucified and risen Christ: witnessing *to* the fact of an encounter in which persons were approached and addressed and witnessing *from* this encounter, which called them into being authentic subjects and forgiven forgivers.

As witnesses *to* a personal or communal encounter with the living presence of the crucified Christ, persons never have unimpeded and pure access to the event of encounter, much less to the Spirit who makes the risen Christ present. This encounter, while taking place within history as a movement toward and for humanity and creation, is always also an encounter with an Other who is completely other than all of creation. This divine Other, who is the origin and end of history, can never be communicated fully within history. As we saw in the last chapter, Alison asserts that

---

[62] Brian Robinette's clarification of the meaning of "innocence" as applied to victims within a Girardian framework was helpful for me in coming to understand this distinction between relative and absolute innocence. Robinette writes, "By innocence I do not mean that such victims are without any moral culpability whatsoever. I mean that the guilt their accusers project upon them in order to justify violence is shown to be deceptive and unjust." *Grammars of Resurrection*, 258.

this utter otherness of the divine Other is what makes it possible for the crucified and risen Christ to return without any hint of violence toward those human beings who have enacted violence against him.[63] Thus, the gap between the One who approaches with complete and unhindered forgiveness and those who are being invited to become witnesses of this divine Other can never be bridged. Such a gap creates the possibility, and even likelihood, that those witnessing the encounter will have only limited perception and understanding of the forgiving victim and of the Father who raised him from death.

Due to the blindness created by the disciples' own formation in the cultural mechanism of violence that led to Jesus' death, limited perception and understanding, as well as an initial misperception and misunderstanding of the crucified and risen Christ and his Father, are possible. We see evidence of this in the Holy Spirit's correction of Peter via Cornelius on the scope of the gospel as good news for more than only the Jews (Acts 10). Peter had not fully perceived and perhaps even partially misunderstood the God revealed by the risen Christ. Yet, Cornelius and his household discover themselves to be witnesses of the crucified and risen Christ as well, and the Holy Spirit confirms their testimony. This circumstance highlights the way in which a community of witnesses to the resurrection is necessary to help overcome the limited perception or misunderstanding of any particular witness (even Peter himself) or group of witnesses. If a possibility of limited perception and misunderstanding existed for those first witnesses of the crucified and risen Christ, then it certainly also exists for all those since that time who have become witnesses through the working of the Spirit.

A second potential source of falsity corresponds to the witnesses' gradual and ongoing transformation into a witness *from* the crucified and risen Christ. The appropriation of the intelligence in the mind of Christ, the resulting transformation of the witnesses' modes of relating to others, and the authenticity of the acts of witness (whatever form those acts take) are all open to being skewed by human finitude and the blindness that results from sin—that is, formation and participation in violence. In other words, beyond the witnesses' initial perception and understanding of their encounter with the crucified and risen Christ, there is the possibility of skewed or inauthentic appropriation and expression of the revelation of God in and through the presence of the crucified and risen Christ. The "subversion from within" of the witness's intelligence, imagination, and modes of relating to others is an ongoing and gradual process; therefore, it is likely that one's acts of witness, theological or otherwise, contain significant vestiges of the "old self" or the old intelligence. Only through one's ongoing openness to encounters via the Spirit of Christ and in fellowship with a community of diverse witnesses can the lingering vestiges of a sacrificial imagination be more fully undone.

These possibilities for some degree of falsity, or "cover-up," in various acts of witness to the crucified and risen Christ can also find expression in texts that serve as potential occasions of encounter with their readers. Alison, as well as Jeremiah

---

[63] We saw this in relation to Alison's description of the presence of the crucified and risen Christ as both gratuitous and forgiving in Section 3.2.5.1.

Alberg, a fellow Girardian, makes explicit a strategy for reading texts that contain some element of falsity. First, Alison describes the task of many "Girardians" as one of enabling texts that express some degree of false witness to become agents of truthfulness through forgiveness. He writes:

> [W]hat Girard does is read texts. Most of those of us who attempt to learn from his thought do likewise. Again, it is not just that there is an idea, and that the idea needs texts in order to show itself. I think that there is a more profound point here about the nature of truth-seeking: the idea can only be made present as the undoing of the various forms of sacrificial cover-up to which our texts and stories are prone. The idea just *is* the gradual, and contingent undoing of lies. There is no 'idea' without the contemporary putting of it into practice as a detection of sacrificial structure and the learning to tell a different story.[64]

While Alison's descriptions of texts as being prone to sacrificial cover-up refer here to texts that are not the fruit of an experience of conversion, they also can be applied usefully to texts that are acts of witness to the resurrection but that still express vestiges of a lingering sacrificial imagination. Alison is telling us that texts that tend to be part of an act of violence by acting to cover up violence can become occasions of discovery and of learning to speak more truthfully. This is especially true of texts that explicitly strive to be witnesses to the risen Christ but still contain some elements of the intelligence of death. In these texts, the tension and the inconsistency between the unveiling and the veiling of violence are much closer to the surface and more easily detectable. These texts provide tangible expressions of a pivotal moment in the process of "the gradual and contingent undoing of lies."

In his book *Beneath the Veil of the Strange Verses: Reading Scandalous Texts*, Alberg pushes Alison's suggestion further by developing what he sees as the Gospels' approach to texts that could function as a source of scandal.[65] Engaging in a comparative reading of Nietzsche, Rousseau, Dante, the Gospels, and Flannery O'Connor, Alberg defines scandalous texts as texts that simultaneously allow and block access to meaning, insight, or true perception, sometimes as part of the author's intention (as is the case with Nietzsche), but most often despite the author's intention and effort to express meaning. This definition of scandal as applied to texts is a helpful way of understanding texts of Christian theological witness that contain and express some degree of falsity or the lingering effects of a sacrificial imagination. These texts attempt to give witness to the risen Christ through an articulation of the intelligence of the victim, but the perception and the imagination of the authors of the texts, while in the process of being subverted by the intelligence in the mind of Christ, are not fully freed from the influence of the lingering effects of a sacrificial intelligence.

---

[64] Alison, *Faith beyond Resentment*, 162; Alison's emphasis.
[65] Alberg, *Beneath the Veil of the Strange Verses*.

Alberg claims that the Gospels suggest a way of transforming potentially scandalous texts into bridges through forgiveness.[66] He concludes his book by summarizing what he sees as a Gospel hermeneutic of forgiveness that enables readers to engage scandalous texts or potentially false witnesses such that these too become occasions of conversion.

> We [readers] take up an attitude toward texts that is in some ways analogous to the attitude Christ claims is God's own: I desire mercy not sacrifice. We do not sacrifice the texts that scandalize. As always, this scandal is neither purely in the text nor purely in us but in the space between. We read such texts with a quality of mercy, with forgiveness. Furthermore, this forgiveness is also not unidirectional. It may well be us who need forgiveness but it can also be the text. We interpret these writings with an awareness of what they would have us reject or what we would reject [within] them. In this way they point us toward either what we would sacrifice from them or what they themselves have rejected. This reveals the dependence of our interpretation on some expulsion or it allows the texts to reveal its dependence on both the rejection and what was rejected. Restoring what was rejected will undo both ourselves and those writings at the same time that it brings them and us to our true completion.[67]

This summary parallels well the interchange that I drew out between Ricoeur and Alison. Alberg goes further, however, because he suggests that we need to approach potentially scandalous texts (which I have suggested is an accurate way of understanding theological texts that contain elements of false witness) with a particular posture or attitude. Readers who desire to be led more fully into true perception, insight, and deeper meaning, whether they are Christian or not, would be wise to see these scandalous texts as ripe occasions of discovery and conversion. Such a perception may lead readers to adopt attitudes of forgiveness, enabling them to approach the "strange verses," as Alberg calls them, in which the tension between expression of meaning and obfuscation of meaning points toward what the text wishes to sacrifice. This same attitude of forgiveness will also heighten the reader's attentiveness to his or her own inclination to be scandalized, thus pointing toward what the reader would like to reject. By focusing on scandal and advocating for a hermeneutic of forgiveness, Alberg shows how the "world" between the text and the reader (Ricoeur's "world in front of the text") can become an occasion of discovery and conversion. Alberg's definition of scandalous texts provides an accurate description of theological texts that attempt to give witness to the risen Christ but contain some degree of falsity or misunderstanding of the intelligence of the victim. Such texts exhibit a tension between their attempt to express meaning, on the one hand, and the lingering distortion of perception that continues to obscure that same meaning, on the other.

---

[66] He sees Flannery O'Connor as a kind of modern mystic that tries to lead her readers to discover the capacity of forgiveness to make even violence an occasion for returning "to reality, that is, to the non-violent truth of love." Ibid., 119.

[67] Alberg, *Beneath the Veil of the Strange Verses*, 120.

4.3 From Theological Reflection to Ongoing Conversion: An "Inductive" Theology

Our discussion of the possibility of false witness in theological texts that attempt to confess explicitly the risen Christ leads directly into the central aim of this chapter, which is to show how theological reflection, especially as expressed in texts, is an act of witnessing to the presence of the crucified and risen Christ that becomes a potential occasion of new or renewed encounter with Christ for the readers of the texts, as well as for the subject giving witness through his or her writing. While most of this chapter has focused on the reader's potential encounter with the risen Christ through the working of the Spirit in and through the texts, our discussion of the possibility, and even likelihood, of false witness points to the interplay among the various degrees and kinds of witnesses who find themselves participating in an act of communication from God to humanity. The intelligence of forgiveness incarnate made available by Christ operates in varying degrees and in distinct but inseparable ways upon the witnesses writing the texts, the potential witnesses reading the texts, and the acts of witness that are the texts themselves. The question of the possibility of false witness necessitates a discussion of the communion of witnesses as the *communal subject* most capable of perceiving, appropriating, reflecting upon, and expressing its reception of forgiveness and its discovery of the intelligence of forgiveness incarnate in the crucified and risen Christ.

In Alison's perspective, the writers, readers, and texts themselves can all be described fundamentally as witnesses, albeit in somewhat different ways. The writers of theological texts have become witnesses through the reception of forgiveness and are invited to become so more fully through the activity of their writing, which is part of their attempt to appropriate for themselves and to express for others the faith (*fides qua* and *fides quae*) that they have received. The readers of the texts may become witnesses to the presence of the crucified and living Christ through the working of the Spirit in making the words of the texts effective as an occasion of encounter with Christ. And the texts themselves are acts of witness that are fruits of the authors' reception of forgiveness and their gradual self-reflexive appropriation of the intelligence of the victim. Together these witnesses and the acts of witness that connect them exist within a history of witnesses that embody, enact, and express God's communication to humanity in and through the crucified and risen Christ. This communion of witnesses formed by the Spirit of Christ and their various acts of witness make up the church as the space in which authentic and false acts of witness to Christ are discerned.[68] This discernment can be carried out more or less well in particular contexts within this communion, but the need for discernment in the face of the possibility of false witness confirms the necessity of a communion of witnesses that acts as a communal subject

---

[68] Elizabeth Johnson's *Friends of God and Prophets* provides a superb historical and constructive study of the church as a communion of witnesses, or saints, or, in the language that she borrows from the Book of Wisdom, "friends of God, and prophets." In this respect, the third (constructive) part of her work, entitled "Theology of the Friends of God and Prophets," is particularly illuminating as she describes this communion as "companions" in memory, in facing death, and in hope.

or communal recipient of the intelligence of forgiveness incarnate. Thus, Alison's Eucharistic theology moves into an ecclesiology.

Alison describes the Eucharistic celebration as the gathering together of those who find themselves being offered and receiving forgiveness from the crucified and risen Christ, gathered around and gathered by this forgiving victim himself, who is in their midst as a gift, rather than as something that they conjure up for themselves.[69] Whether these witnesses first encountered the forgiving victim individually or communally, witnesses gathered in the celebration of the Eucharist find themselves being drawn out of a particular story of being victim and victimizer and led into the shared worship of One who became our victim to open us to receive the love of God as forgiveness.[70] In this common worship of the forgiving victim, the Father who sends him to us, and the Spirit who makes him present, the witnesses of the crucified and risen Christ become a communal subject empowered to receive, appropriate, and be subverted by the intelligence of the victim that is operating within and behind the forgiveness that each finds him- or herself receiving in particular ways. Thus, the induction of an ecclesial subject into being as a community of witnesses provides the necessary context for the continuation and culmination of each individual subject's induction into being as a witness.[71]

4.3.1 Alison's Own Theological Texts as "Inductive"

We have seen in this chapter Alison's view of the significant role that theological texts can play in the initial or deepening conversion of persons, for they can be occasions of encounter with the crucified and risen Christ. To conclude this chapter, I will consider a few of Alison's explicitly stated hopes regarding the role that his own theological writings might have for his readers.

In speaking about how Girard's writings affected him, Alison says that his own writings are attempts to participate in the Spirit's desire to communicate with persons.

> No one needed to tell me that it was not Girard who was speaking to me all that truth. Little in Girard's works points to René Girard. I sense it to be a sign of the presence of the Spirit when what is taught points the pupil outwards, beyond the teacher and towards a discipleship richer than any clinging imitation could begin to yield.... The truth was coming from the source to whom he points, the one he recognizes as having made possible what he has to say, the same source who had given the experience of truth to the woman at the well. Since I embarked upon the adventure of following that voice ... [t]he journey, one of uncertain faithfulness on my part, is one in which the one thing that matters is the merciful honesty of that

---

[69] Alison, "Worship in a Violent World," 40–3.
[70] For a more lengthy treatment of Alison's Eucharistic theology and its relationship to his understanding of prayer see my "Being Freed from the Illusion of the Enemy," 10–14. Also see John Baldovin's *Bread of Life, Cup of Salvation* (New York: Rowman and Littlefield, 2003), especially pp. 154–61.
[71] For a fuller development of an ecclesiology developed from Alison's work, see chapter 5 "Imagining a Mimetic Ecclesiology," in Kaplan's *René Girard, Unlikely Apologist*.

voice. If in the chapters preceding this one, you have had no inkling...of being told the truth by someone other than the author of those pages, then I have, quite simply, failed you as a theologian, failed to be a conduit of the Spirit of God to speak words into your heart. If, however, you have found that you are able in some measure to discover yourself within the stories I have told, if you found yourself being spoken into being with words of truth which opened up new vistas of the sort, "Oh, so that's what I've been doing all along", then this is not because James Alison is a natural storyteller. It is because James Alison would be being seriously unfaithful to what he has received if he were not at least to try to make available to you something of the "well of Samaria" experience, which he takes to be "what it's all about."[72]

Much can be unpacked in this conversational description of Alison's understanding of his own vocation as a theologian. First, it becomes evident how central the story of Jesus speaking to the woman at the well of Samaria is for Alison's perception of the dynamic of encounter leading to conversion. The subject is spoken into being through an encounter with someone who tells the subject everything he has ever done while simultaneously offering the forgiveness that can free him from the violent forms of identity that have defined his past.

Alison sees this type of encounter with the Spirit of the risen Christ as gradually transforming him into a participant in God's act of communication to humanity. His own theological reflections and writings are attempts to allow the Spirit, which has spoken him into being, to speak to his readers as well. They are efforts to point others toward the source of forgiveness, the One who makes a new kind of imitation possible by simultaneously revealing one's past and freeing one from enslavement to the violent identities that made it up. By becoming an instrument of this "mercifully honest" voice, Alison hopes his own writings might become occasions of encounter between his readers and the Spirit of Christ, thereby participating in his readers' being "spoken into being" as witnesses of the resurrection, imitators of the risen Christ, and forgiven sinners becoming conduits of forgiveness for others.

Alison's stated hopes for his own theological writings align well with his understanding of the primary role of theological texts in general. The theologian, as a witness of the resurrection, attempts to articulate coherently for herself and for others (believers and unbelievers) the intelligence of forgiveness that is transforming her. In doing so, the theologian and her writings increasingly become conduits of the Spirit of Christ for others.

In the next and concluding chapter, I will first present a sampling of Alison's writings to various audiences (academic and ecclesial) and written in varying styles (historical, apologetic, systematic, constructive, and pastoral) to point toward what is distinctive about each and, more importantly, to draw out and reflect upon the common underlying character of each of these writings despite their differences in style and audience. This common character, the guiding tone and intention of Alison's writings, is best described as "inductive."

---

[72] Alison, *Faith beyond Resentment*, 150–1.

5

Theology "in the Order of Discovery" or an Inductive Theology

My investigation over the last two chapters into the understanding of the relationship between the experience of conversion and the activity of theological reflection that is foundational for Alison's theological work has contributed to a more developed articulation of the meaning of Alison's call for a "theology in the order of discovery." It has led me to suggest that, for Alison, theological reflection is the participation of the subject undergoing conversion in God's ongoing action of creation, which is working to induct the subject more fully into being as a forgiven forgiver and a witness to the crucified and risen Christ.

In Chapter 3, we saw that Alison's imaginative reading of the disciples' experience of conversion (via their encounters with the crucified and risen Jesus) enabled him to develop a psychologically descriptive understanding of conversion as a subversion from within—a constructive (rather than annihilating) collapse leading to the reception of a new intelligence and the possibility of new life—made possible by the divine offer of forgiveness in and through God's raising Jesus from the dead. The subject's engagement in theological reflection begins to happen almost inevitably as he tries to make sense of the collapse and the operation of forgiveness that has brought the collapse about. As a result of this collapse, the subject can engage in theological reflection authentically and creatively because he has begun to recover his capacity for right remembering, perception, and imagination of God, self, and humanity. Therefore, he can begin to see clearly each one's relationship to violence, victimization, and death. We also saw that Alison's view of theology as inductive leads to a reversal of a common understanding of theological reflection. God, rather than the theologian, is the primary protagonist, enabling us to continue to appropriate and give expression to the intelligence of forgiveness.

In Chapter 4, we saw that the movement from conversion to theological reflection develops into the reciprocal movement from the activity of theological reflection, seen as an act of witness, to ongoing conversion for the one engaging in that reflection and for others. Alison's understanding of theologians (as witnesses to the crucified and risen Christ whose thinking and writing enact their witness) and of readers and hearers of theological works (as potentially newly converted or more fully inducted witnesses) leads him to advance further his ecclesial and liturgical vision of the communal subject in and through which individuals come to know themselves ever more completely as witnesses of the crucified and risen Christ.

In this concluding chapter, I will first consider several substantive excerpts from Alison's writings to show, and then articulate more clearly, the underlying aim of what I have been calling an "inductive" theology. By reflecting on these excerpts, I will clarify some of the essential characteristics of Alison's inductive theology. In particular, we will see that his inductive theology actively seeks to elucidate and preserve the nature of human knowing as a process of discovery. It does so by keeping open the possibility of an encounter for the reader that produces a certain kind of collapse and by depicting how true understanding necessarily involves a process of transformation. Alison's inductive theology operates out of a deeply experienced trust that the Spirit of the crucified and risen Christ will and does come. As a result of this trust and his underlying intention to invite his readers into an encounter, Alison maintains a tone of speaking directly to his readers, regardless of the theological question he is pursuing, from a place that always remains close to his own experiences of collapse and transformation. In drawing out these characteristics of Alison's inductive approach, I will show how his understanding of the reciprocal relationship between conversion and theological reflection operates in his own theological writings so as to become an occasion for the Spirit of the crucified and risen Christ to induct his readers into a way of being more fully alive.

After illustrating Alison's inductive theology, I will conclude this study by developing what I see as two of the most significant Girardian and theological fruits of Alison's theological approach. First, I will argue that the fundamentally inductive aim of Alison's theology reinforces my assertion that Alison's primary objective in engaging theologically with mimetic theory is to articulate more clearly an understanding of the nature of Christian conversion and theology. Only as a result of his use of mimetic theory to develop a theological method is he secondarily able to apply mimetic theory to other theological questions. I will show how Alison's much more explicitly theological and methodological employment of mimetic theory brings into relief some of the unclarities produced by the historical development in Girard's usage of some of his own terms and by his partial entrance into the discipline of theology. To do this, I will return to my conclusions in Chapter 2 and then show how Alison's theological method includes a theological anthropology that intentionally brings Girard's mimetic theory into a fully theological perspective.

Second, in conversation with the work of other Girardian theologians, I will employ Alison's Girardian epistemology to articulate more fully a theology of Christian doctrines and a theology of revelation from within Alison's inductive perspective.

5.1 Depicting the Inductive Aim of Theology

Having developed the two reciprocal movements that together constitute Alison's conception of theology, I will now consider short excerpts from his various theological writings that embody a variety of theological styles, including apologetic, historical, systematic, constructive, and pastoral, and that are directed toward various audiences from academic to "lay" and from practicing Christians to LGBTQ persons questioning or rejecting any relationship to the Christian churches. I will attend to and draw out from each of them the fundamentally inductive aim operative in each example of Alison's theological reflections. We will see the reciprocal movements in these excerpts, despite the differences in each one's more immediate objectives and intended audiences. This will allow me to articulate more fully the identifying characteristics of an inductive approach to theology.

Alison's description of the work of the theologian identifies the fundamental aim of theology as allowing God an "ever less obstacled possession" of persons:

> This consideration [of the ecclesial nature of faith] also suggests the function of the theologian in the Church, which is to help in ... the detachment of human thought processes from their bases in the rivalristic understanding proper to the old other.[1]

By serving this function, the theologian participates in "a divine impulse toward a constant purifying of language and practice so as to allow God an ever less obstacled possession of us, precisely because it is through human words and practices that God wishes to have access to us."[2] My consideration of the following excepts will depict what this fundamentally inductive aim of theology looks like within Alison's treatments of specific theological questions.

5.1.1 "A Beneficent Understanding of Natural Law"—An Apologetic Excerpt

One of the theological fruits of an understanding of conversion that consists of a fundamental transformation of human subjects is a certain understanding of creation. The experience of conversion in the presence of the risen Christ transforms the doctrine of creation from a narrative about how the world and the human race came to be into an articulation of the (always) contemporary experience of wonder at (1) the fact that there is something rather than nothing and (2) the discovery of the gratuity of the ongoing act that holds all things in existence.[3] This discovery of the gratuity of creation results from the subject's reception of forgiveness, which first enables the prior discovery of God's complete non-involvement in death and violence.[4] Gradually, reflection on this experience of God's non-violence and utter vivaciousness leads to the realization that God's act of creation is always a gratuitous act of giving in the present

---

[1] Alison, *The Joy of Being Wrong*, 61.
[2] Ibid., 61.
[3] Alison, *On Being Liked*, 49–50. For a much fuller development of a theology of creation informed by mimetic theory, see Brian Robinette, "The Difference Nothing Makes: *Creatio Ex Nihilo*, Resurrection, and Divine Gratuity," *Theological Studies* 72 (2011): 525–57.
[4] It is important to keep in mind here my earlier clarifications regarding Alison's frequent descriptions of God as completely uninvolved in death. See the end of my treatment of the spiritual valence of the disciples' experience of Jesus' resurrection in Section 3.2.5.2 of Chapter 3. This language is not a denial of the natural place that death holds in the biological cycle of living creatures, nor of the essential role that death plays in the Paschal Mystery. Instead, it is an assertion that death is not a sign or enactment of divine judgment against persons, nor it is an obstacle to God's loving self-giving toward persons.

that is fundamentally distinct from, and subversive of, forms of creation that involve at least some degree of exclusion, expulsion, or condemnation.[5]

Within this context of Alison's elaboration of a Christian understanding of creation and its relationship to salvation, Alison develops a view of natural law as a constructively creative principle that arises from the intrinsic relationship between creation and salvation. I consider this text as an example of a more explicitly apologetic style of theology because in it Alison strives to recover a creative principle of Christian faith that has often been misused as a basis for accusations against various "modern" and "secular" beliefs perceived by some Christian authorities to be a threat to Christian faith. That is, this passage is apologetic in that it argues for the contemporary validity of the Christian principle of natural law by arguing against certain misuses of it. This passage is also inductive in that it articulates the rational grounds for the removal of a common obstacle to persons' discovery of the gratuitous self-giving of God in the present who is always enabling persons to be and to flourish.

The following excerpt on "a beneficent understanding of natural law" is taken from the end of an essay entitled "Creation in Christ," which Alison originally wrote as a lecture given at the Universidad Iberoamericana in Mexico City in April 2002. This essay was later published as the fourth chapter of the collection of essays entitled *On Being Liked*.

> [N]atural law is in the first place an indispensable element of the Christian doctrine of creation precisely because it is the indispensable link between creation and salvation. *That is to say, it is our way of insisting that there is not an absolute rupture between that which we see here and now and that which is the divine plan for the fullness of creation. What is now, and what will be, have an organic relationship between themselves, and in principle we can learn from what is now something about its definitive plenitude.* In other words, there is a trustable continuity between that which is in need of salvation and that which will appear once saved.
>
> [O]ne of the firmest consequences of the insistence on natural law is the denial of the arbitrary or capricious nature of divine commandments. This is evident traditionally in the rejection of the voluntarist and nominalist positions with respect to morals. If God forbids us something it is because doing it does us no good. Which is to say, the holiness of the commandment is in fact that it is for our good... *To put it another way: natural law would thus be a very powerful bulwark against the group tendency to constitute itself into the ghetto of the saved, making of its beliefs something independent of a process of discovery.*
>
> [W]e can see that natural law is, in the first place, and before any of its possibly polemical use in the world of non-believers, *a very powerful instrument of self-criticism with respect to our own moral teaching.* If it is used correctly, the first consequence of the use of this instrument would be having confidence that we can change our own understanding of morality in the light of our growing appreciation of what is.

---

[5] Alison, *On Being Liked*, 51–7.

> Now please notice that this is a two-edged sword. *On the one hand it [natural law] can serve as a critical instrument with relation to practices which are socially and economically 'convenient' with respect to the weak and vulnerable, in the case of abortion, euthanasia, the rights of immigrants, of racial minorities and so on.* That is to say, it allows the discovery of values which will in fact change the composition of the [socio-cultural] group which has a tendency to reject the possibility that such vulnerable people should be an intrinsic and constitutive part of it. *On the other hand it serves as an internal critique of ecclesiastical doctrines which start from aprioristic principles and which do not correspond to the discovery of what is, but rather refuse to participate in that discovery,* like for instance the critique, made by the sixteenth-century Spaniards who defended the Indians, of the intellectual structure which allowed the inhabitants of the New World to be treated as slaves; or closer to home, of the current teaching of the Vatican congregations with relation to gay people.
>
> In any case, I am seeking to demonstrate that within the relationship between salvation and creation which I have been sketching out, there lies the possibility of an understanding of natural law which is much less open to the real criticism which is made of it. *The criticism is that it is a subtle a priori defence of doctrinal positions which are never submitted to the possibility that in the light of what is discovered as the world is progressively demystified, these same doctrinal positions might be revealed to be the enemies of the very natural law which they espouse, by being sacred bulwarks erected against enemies, which are necessary to a certain group self-understanding.*[6]

This elaboration of an understanding of natural law exhibits an apologetic style by addressing a persistent and relatively widespread misunderstanding of natural law to recover a meaning of the principle that has frequently been pushed aside because particular groups within and outside of the church tend to generate a "certain group self-understanding" that is dependent upon the existence of "outsiders," "intruders," "perpetrators," "heretics," or "schismatics." This diagnosis of a particular form of group bias does not negate all theological or ecclesial validity of the terms heresy, heretic, schism, or schismatic. However, the meaning of natural law that Alison attempts to recover here seeks to cultivate a healthy suspicion about the extent to which these terms are used to perpetuate the sacrificial "sacred" that Girard's work has helped to expose. To that same extent, they demonstrate a fundamental lack of trust in the God who makes Godself knowable to persons via the process of human discovery of what is.

While I asserted at the beginning of the last chapter that, within Alison's conception of theology, apologetics should not be seen as a distinct subdiscipline of theology but rather as an intrinsic characteristic of all theological reflection, it is still also true that this apologetic character can be more pronounced in some theological reflections and writings than in others. The above passage advocating a view of natural law not commonly held in contemporary Western culture is more explicitly apologetic than many other of Alison's writings in that it responds to what Alison sees as legitimate

---

[6] Ibid., 61–3; my emphasis.

cultural criticisms of a common (mis)understanding of natural law. These criticisms point out the way that "natural law" is often used as an a priori weapon of defense for specific doctrinal formulations and cultural values. This approach serves to protect these doctrines and values from having to engage with the always contemporary process of human discovery, which is simultaneously personal and sociocultural and, therefore, furthered by every discipline of the physical and social sciences. Such a (mis)use of natural law has led to significant opposition to it as a principle of Christian reflection and argumentation.

Alison's style above becomes apologetic because it is guided by a fundamental trust in God's desire to make Godself known through the human discovery of what is. This trust allows him to hear the criticisms leveled against the church's use of natural law arguments with the belief that doing so in a spirit of openness will lead to a fuller discovery of truth. Alison then offers an understanding of natural law that cannot be used to dismiss or protect against authentic human discovery concerning the created world. Nor can it be used to formulate a priori accusations of "unnaturality" that are largely based on long-held social, cultural, and religious perceptions. Instead, natural law is a "two-edged sword" intended to expose both ecclesial and sociocultural tendencies to interrupt the process of human discovery in order to protect a group self-understanding that requires a certain view of "nature" to legitimize some form of group identity arising from exclusion. That is, natural law insists that we investigate the created world guided by the assumption that this investigation is capable of disclosing something of the God whose fullest self-revelation occurs in and through the crucified and risen Christ.

Alison employs this more explicitly apologetic style in the service of his fundamentally inductive approach to theological reflection and writing. He describes his understanding of natural law as "beneficent," which I take to mean that it is an understanding that aims to produce good; that is, it will, he hopes, have a constructive impact on persons. Within the context of this essay, which offers a reimagining of the doctrine of creation in light of the resurrection, Alison's retrieval of a beneficent understanding of natural law can be seen as a response to the legitimate criticisms of a common (mis)use of natural law that dismisses the fruits of ongoing human discovery rather than remaining open to them. Alison's response invites persons who have been formed according to such a misuse of natural law to become open to a new understanding of creation and creation's intrinsic relationship to redemption, which Alison believes to be revealed in the crucified and risen Christ. This understanding, which views the doctrine of creation as an affirmation of God's ongoing and always present relationship to all that is, seeks to invite persons to become open to and to participate in the process of human discovery in and through which God makes Godself knowable to us.

Thus, Alison articulates an understanding of natural law that takes seriously contemporary criticisms and simultaneously invites people to engage in honest curiosity and inquiry about the created world. By encouraging such curiosity and inquiry, Alison exhibits his fundamental confidence in God's unchanging desire to make Godself known to God's people. By engaging with contemporary criticisms, Alison expresses his conviction that authentic Catholic/Christian doctrines have the capacity to speak to the experiences of both Catholics and non-Catholics who are willing to think critically while also remaining open to the newness of God that is made available in and through their ongoing experiences of discovery. By articulating both sides of this "two-edged sword," Alison hopes to gently expose some of the blind spots that ecclesial and societal communities maintain with regard to their respective exclusions. In each of these ways, we can see that Alison's treatment of natural law is not only apologetic but also simultaneously inductive. He invites critics "on both sides" (secular and ecclesial) to challenge certain prejudices and to cultivate an openness toward the possibility of experiencing genuinely transformative encounters within the whole of the created world. More specifically, this excerpt expresses his effort to invite Catholics, non-Catholics, and even non-Christians to overcome a misunderstanding of natural law in order that each of them might be enabled to see *both* Christian doctrines and the created world as potential places of discovery of what actually *is*. Here Alison shows us that an inductive theology employs natural law as an instrument for striving to open persons, whether Christian or not, to opportunities for discovering what "is"—biologically, socially, psychologically, spiritually, etc.—by helping to identify and remove some of the entrenched intellectual obstacles or misunderstandings. Such a theology helps to facilitate potential new or renewed encounters with the crucified and risen Christ, which transform persons' modes of remembering, perceiving, imagining, and relating in the world.

5.1.2 "An Atonement Update"—A Historical Excerpt

Much of the theological work that makes use of Girard's thought is aimed at offering an understanding of Jesus' "atoning" death that is not beholden to a view of sacrifice in which an angry god needs to be appeased for some offense and, therefore, requires some form of human sacrifice as the necessary means of that appeasement.[7] To the extent that Alison's own work is motivated by his soteriological concern to invite persons into new or renewed encounters with the crucified and risen Christ who meets us as a forgiving victim, he, too, is engaged in this endeavor of rethinking atonement theology.[8] Offering an understanding of Jesus' death and resurrection as an atonement for our sins is essential for Alison's project of demonstrating that all authentic theological reflection should be an occasion for persons to find themselves encountered by the crucified and risen Christ.

In one of Alison's sustained attempts to articulate such an understanding, he takes up an explicitly historical approach to contribute to an authentic Christian understanding of atonement. In the following excerpt, Alison relies on the work of Margaret Barker,

---

[7] See, for example, Raymund Schwager, *Jesus in the Drama Salvation* (New York: Herder & Herder, 1999); Raymund Schwager, *Banished from Eden: Original Sin and Evolutionary Theory in the Drama of Salvation* (Leominster: Gracewing Publishing, 2006); Robert Daly, *Sacrifice Unveiled: The True Meaning of Christian Sacrifice* (London: Continuum, 2009); S. Mark Heim, *Saved from Sacrifice: A Theology of the Cross* (Grand Rapids, MI: Eerdmans, 2006); Simon Taylor, "Save Us from Being Saved: Girard's Critical Soteriology," *Contagion* 12-13 (2006): 21-30.

[8] See especially "Unpicking Atonements' Knots" in *On Being Liked* (2003), and "An Atonement Update," in *Undergoing God*.

a historical theologian, to consider the ancient Jewish understanding of the atonement rite as the context within which a properly Christian understanding of Jesus' death and resurrection, as well as the Christian celebration of the Eucharist, would have initially developed. The following excerpt on the ancient Jewish understanding of the atonement rite and its relationship to a Christian understanding is taken from an essay entitled "An Atonement Update," originally given as a lecture at Australian Catholic University in Brisbane, Australia, in 2004, and later published in the collection of essays entitled *Undergoing God* (2006). I insert it here as an example of Alison's historical style of theological reflection, which also exhibits his consistently inductive aim.

> I want to go back and recover a little bit of what the liturgy of atonement was about; because when we understand that we begin to get a sense of what this language of 'atonement' and 'salvation' is about.
>
> Let's remember that we are talking about a very ancient Jewish liturgy about which we only know from fragmentary reconstructions of what might have gone on in the First Temple. For this liturgy ... [b]efore the high priest went into the Holy of Holies he would sacrifice a bull or a calf in expiation for his own sins. He would then go into the Holy of Holies, having chosen by lot one of two lambs or goats – a goat which was the Lord, the other goat was to be Azazel (the 'devil'). He would take the first with him into the Holy of Holies and sacrifice it; and with its blood he would sprinkle the Mercy Seat ... , the Ark and so on.
>
> The priest emerged from that and came through the Temple Veil. This was made of very rich material, representing the material world, that which was created. At this point the high priest would don a robe made of the same material as the Veil, to demonstrate that what he was acting out was God coming forth and entering into the world of creation so as to make atonement, to undo the way humans had snarled up creation. And at that point, having emerged, he would then sprinkle the rest of the temple with the blood that was the Lord's blood.
>
> Now here is the interesting point: for the Temple understanding the high priest at this stage *was* acting 'in the person of Yahweh', and it was *the Lord's* blood that was being sprinkled. This was a divine movement to set people free. It was not – as we often imagine – a priest satisfying a divinity. The reason why the priest had to engage in a prior expiation was because he was about to become a sign of something quite else: acting outwards. The movement is not inwards towards the Holy of Holies; the movement is outwards from the Holy of Holies.
>
> So the priest would then come through the Veil – meaning the Lord entering into the world, the created world – and sprinkle all the rest of the Temple, hence setting it free. After which, as the person who was bearing the sins that had been accumulated, he would place them on the head of what we call 'the scapegoat', Azazel, which would then be driven outside the town, to the edge of a cliff and cast down, where it would be killed, so that the people's sins would be taken away.
>
> That was, from what we can gather, the atonement rite. But here is the fascinating thing: the Jewish understanding was way ahead of the 'Aztec' version

we attribute to it. Even at that time it was understood that it was not about humans trying desperately to satisfy God, but God taking the initiative of breaking through towards us. In other words, atonement was something of which we were *beneficiaries*. This is the first point I want to make when emphasizing that we are talking about a liturgy rather than a theory. We are talking about something that we undergo over time as part of a benign initiative toward us.[9]

This short excerpt from a lengthier retrieval of the historical practice and understanding of the ancient Jewish liturgy of atonement provides insight into Alison's view of the particularities of the history of God's self-revelation and its cumulative and unfolding impact on the formation of persons and communities. Relying on Barker's work, Alison gives a succinct description of the rite, which shaped their experience of atonement as an action of God's self-giving continually undertaken on behalf of God's people and all of creation. Alison uses historical theology and his engagement in this more explicitly historical mode of theological reflection to uncover and articulate as faithfully as possible persons' experience of the God of their forefathers. In this instance, his consideration of the atonement rite serves as a lens into a particular aspect of the ancient Jews' experience of God.

By highlighting the Jews' experience of God as expressed through their understanding of the rite of atonement, Alison implicitly argues in favor of his understanding of theological reflection as a fruit of the ongoing process of conversion. The Jewish understanding and practice of liturgy as a re-presentation of God's movement of self-giving toward God's people are the fruit of, and an occasion for, a personal and communal experience of God as one who acts in this way. Alison's historical description of this rite depicts the liturgical practices and the understandings that accompany them as having a reciprocal and mutually conditioning relationship with the people's experiences of, and faith in, God. This emphasis on reciprocal and mutually conditioning relationships is Alison's implicit and assumed perspective as he presents the Jews' experience, understanding, and liturgical practice as cohering with their fundamental belief that they are recipients and beneficiaries of God's self-giving and atoning action toward them and all of creation.

Although we don't see it developed explicitly in the excerpt above, Alison uses historical insights like this one to hypothesize about the overall shape and trajectory of the history of God's ongoing self-revelation, which culminates in the living presence of the crucified Christ. His forays into historical theology serve, in part, to fill out his Girardian sketch of the arc of God's self-revelation in history. The accumulating impact of God's revelation in history gradually re-forms the imaginations of God's people to be less under the sway of death such that they become capable of seeing more and more fully the aliveness of God made most accessible in the living presence of the crucified Christ. We get a sense of Alison's tendency to point to the arc of this growing impact through history at the end of this essay on atonement:

---

[9] Alison, *Undergoing God*, 52–5; Alison's emphasis. Alison's retrieval of the ancient Jewish atonement liturgy in its practice and meaning is dependent on the work of historical and biblical theologian Margaret Barker, *The Great High Priest: The Temple Roots of Christian Liturgy* (London: Continuum, 2004).

> Do you see that there is a huge movement in the atonement? This movement is from creation to us becoming participants in creation by our being enabled to live as if death were not. This is the *priestly* pattern of atonement; and it is the priestly pattern that Jesus had the genius to combine with the ethical, bringing together the ancient liturgical formula, the prophecies, the hopes of fulfillment of the anointed one, the true high priest, the true shepherd of the sheep who would come to create a new temple, ... and revealing what it meant in anthropological and ethical terms: the overcoming of our tendency to sacrifice each other so as to survive.[10]

The process of the human discovery of the self-revelation of God is long and slow, and, therefore, the corresponding reshaping of the human imagination is also slow. Only through the whole history of God's self-revelation to the Hebrews, culminating in the crucified and risen Christ, and continuing to the present day, are Christian communities (and, hopefully, through them, others) continuously invited and enabled to imagine the complete and utter vivaciousness of God, whose love is unhindered by death.[11]

This instance of Alison's more explicitly historical theological reflection exhibits his fundamentally inductive approach. At the end of the excerpt above, Alison tells us that his primary motive in describing the practice and understanding of the ancient Hebrew atonement rite was to demonstrate the significance of seeing that atonement is a liturgy before it is ever a theory. Therefore, when we talk about atonement, "[w]e are talking about something that we undergo over time as part of a benign initiative toward us." In other words, Alison recalls and examines this piece of our Judeo-Christian history to help Christians today see that atonement is God's always contemporary "benign," or, better, redemptive, action toward and for humanity and all of creation. This action, which God is always desiring and undertaking on our behalf, aims to free persons in the present who are unknowingly caught in an unnecessary pattern of violence through which they try to protect themselves from death by exposing others to it. Alison's retrieval of the ancient Jewish practice and understanding of the rite of atonement is his consciously chosen attempt to participate in this divine action, and to do so on behalf of those who are often caught in this pattern of violence in a particular way—those who, like himself, tend to perceive atonement and redemption as primarily designating an understanding of God's action (a theory), rather than as first pointing to the action itself, which is always unfolding in the present.

Alison is intuitively aware of how theologians and other intellectually adept Christians can be inclined to use their understanding of a theory of atonement as a substitute for, and even a subtle protection against, an encounter with the crucified and risen Christ. He is well-attuned to the ambiguity, instability, and fear that are part of the experience of anticipating such an encounter. As he says,

---

[10] Alison, *Undergoing God*, 66.
[11] Again, see the end of Section 3.2.5.2 in Chapter 3 for an explanation of Alison's description of God's utter vivaciousness and what it is intending to express about God's relationship to death.

> If you are *undergoing* atonement it means that you are constantly in the process of being approached by someone who is forgiving you.... The difficult thing for us is to sit in the process of being approached by someone.... [I]f the real centre of our universe is an 'I AM' coming towards us as our victim who is forgiving us then we are *not* in a stable place.[12]

Alison's retrieval of the ancient rite of atonement is an attempt to invite those of us who are comfortable understanding and discussing theories of atonement to learn from the ancient Jews a deeper trust in the God who approaches us. His hope is that we recognize and relinquish any illusions of control over our own salvation that we foster through the belief that our understanding of, and advocating for, the "right" theory of atonement is necessary for salvation. It is easy to believe that, by getting the theory right and understanding its nuances, we distinguish ourselves from those who have a much less sophisticated understanding or are perhaps unable to articulate much of an understanding at all. Holding this belief is just another form of the violent prejudice in which one tends to perceive oneself as much nearer than many others to being righteous. In drawing out the primary mode of atonement as a liturgy, rather than a theory, Alison hopes to create an opening for those of us afraid to place ourselves at the mercy of the crucified and risen Christ who is approaching—an opening for the beginning of trust that dispels fear and generates a receptivity for the faith that comes through forgiveness.

Like the passage concerning natural law, this treatment of the ancient rite of atonement exemplifies Alison's inductive approach. Both are interested in identifying and removing potential intellectual obstacles, misunderstandings, or deceptions that tend to insulate certain groups of people from opportunities for new or renewed encounter with God. His historical presentation of the rite of atonement strives to invite those who have been seduced by the apparent security of understanding the "right" theories to become open to the possibility of new and renewed (destabilizing) encounters with Christ as a forgiving victim. That is, Alison employs greater historical understanding itself as a means for creating an opening through which persons may be further inducted into an ongoing encounter with the risen Christ by acknowledging the fear produced by our anticipation of the destabilization and collapse of identity that such an encounter likely entails.

5.1.3 The Structure of Jesus' Creative Imagination and the Trinity—A Systematic Excerpt

We saw in our consideration of Alison's reading of the disciples' experiences of meeting the risen Jesus how central imagination is to the process of conversion, which Alison describes as a subversion from within. The disciples' imaginations are inescapably conditioned by an unthematized belief in the ultimacy of death, despite their years living with, and learning from, Jesus. Jesus' imagination, on the other hand, is "fixed on the things that are above," namely, the utter vivaciousness of God.[13] In the passage

---

[12] Alison, *Undergoing God*, 64; Alison's emphasis.
[13] Alison, *Raising Abel*, 15–17; cf. Colossians 3:2.

excerpted below, Alison uses the language of Jesus' imagination being untouched by death to unpack the Johannine belief that Jesus, the Son of God, lived as a human being among human beings with "all the creative power and freedom of God." What Alison finds most significant about John's testimony is the way in which he attempts to lay bare the interior dynamic and structure of Jesus' imagination. In doing so, John depicts that Jesus' imagination includes the ability to see how the reality of God's vivaciousness, which grounds Jesus' own identity, may, through him, come to subvert and re-form the imaginations of others.

This excerpt is taken from chapter 7 of *The Joy of Being Wrong*, which is entitled, "The Trinity, Creation, and Original Sin." This chapter and the excerpt below in particular have an explicitly systematic quality to them in that Alison uses his biblically grounded understanding of the disciples' experience of meeting the risen Jesus to illuminate the Johannine portrayal of Jesus' imagination and what that portrayal might help us to imagine about both the interrelation among Father, Son, and Holy Spirit, and the Trinitarian movement toward the reconciliation of the world in and through the crucified and risen Christ.

As can be seen in this series of excerpts from *The Joy of Being Wrong*, Alison links Jesus' creative imagination to the "creative power and freedom of God," who desires to bring life to those whose imaginations are bound in by death.

> At this stage of our analysis there seems to be no way of getting around a particular feature of the Johannine witness. This is John's sense of marvel at the extraordinary nature of Jesus' creative imagination.... John paints out the humanly unimaginable: the creative content of an imagination that is in no way touched by death, *how it is possible for a human imagination that is in no way marked by death to bring into being what amounts to the most prodigious human invention ever, the human structure by which what had appeared to be human nature is revealed, changed, and empowered to become something different.*
>
> John was convinced of nothing less than that the Son of God walked this earth with all the creative power and freedom of God as human creative power and freedom and made this creative power and freedom available through the human imagining into being of a way out of the systematic dead-end into which humans had locked the creative power and freedom which should have been ours.
>
> The original man [Jesus], then, with creative imagination intact because [it was] in no way shaded into futility by any sort of involvement with death, came among us and *imagined into being* the unleashing of the extraordinary possibility of our being allowed actively to share in that creative imagination and practice, bringing about our free creative movement into what we were originally to be.... John gives a clear picture of the structure of the identity of that original man in his positive depiction of the workings of the trinitarian image. This depiction is the exact inverse of the understanding of rivalistic mimetic desire that we have seen Girard set out[.]
>
> Thus we have, in John 5:17[-19], the content of Jesus' equality with God. Jesus' identity is entirely dependent on that of the Father and is brought into being as a human in a quite specific way: the perfect imitation by the Son of the Father. In

the original man, because there is no rivalry between Father and Son, the love between Father and Son is not worked out in blindness and shadow, but the Father is able to show clearly to the Son what the Father is doing. *That is to say, the Father's creative expansion is able to flow directly into the Son's creative imagination such that the Son can bring that expansion into being in the midst of humanity.* Thus Jesus is able to understand how the completely deathless nature of the Father, who raises the dead and gives them life, will enable himself to make available life to whom he will through his creative going to death to bring into being the visible living out of human life-beyond-death.

Jesus is perfectly clear that he is in absolute dependence on the Father: there could be no clearer indication of an interdividual psychology than this. The Other, the Father, is absolutely constitutive of who he is. Yet, because there is no appropriation of identity over against the Other who forms him, the complete dependence on the Other rather than being a limitation or a source of diminishment is exactly what enables the creative flow of life bringing about life to be made manifest and, being made manifest, to be made actual.[14]

Jesus' creative imagination, being unshaded by death, had as the constant background to his action and project the real creative sense of God's creative reality. It was this which lay behind the project he inaugurated to enable humans to become active participants in this creative reality, a project which depended on his being able to treat death as if it were not.... I am going to refer to this creative imagination which rests on and derives energy from the creative alterity of God as the "eschaotological imagination."[15]

In these passages and in the chapter from which they are taken, Alison draws out the coherence among a Christian understanding of the person and work of Jesus, original sin, and the Trinity. In the highlighting of the creative power of Jesus' imagination, its source, its aim, and the obstacles of human history that it must confront, we begin to sense the intrinsic interdependence of these central mysteries of Christian faith. Only the utter vivaciousness of God made ever present to the mind of Jesus could make possible the creative power in and through which he lived, died, and was raised. It is only through Jesus' "eschatological imagination" that both the reality and the non-necessity of the human system of violence, which has locked away the creative power and freedom for which we were created, are fully revealed. And only the content and power of Jesus' imagination, which shaped his living, dying, and rising, were and are capable of effecting "the most prodigious human invention ever, the human structure by which" humanity can be freed from living under the power of death to participate in the raising of others bound by this same power.

We see in these passages, then, Alison's systematic skill in elucidating the essential coherence of these central mysteries of Christian faith—the person and work of Jesus, the

---

[14] Alison, *The Joy of Being Wrong*, 197–8; my emphasis.
[15] Ibid., 212.

relation of Jesus to the Father, and the historical dynamics of the Incarnation that make visible the effects of original sin. Alison's sense of the internal coherence of Christian faith, grounded ultimately in the coherence of God, is expressed in such a way that it continues to make apparent his underlying inductive aim, which has two parts. First, theological reflection is intended to be inductive both for the writer and speaker and for the readers and hearers. The experiences of receiving forgiveness from the crucified and risen Christ—that is, the experiences of the disciples as Alison has unpacked them and Alison's own experiences in the context of the faith communities that have contributed to his formation—begin a process of induction into penitent semi-traitors on the way to becoming forgiven forgivers. This process is partially facilitated by the encountered subject's reflection upon his or her experience of receiving forgiveness, its source, and his or her own previous blindness. Such a perspective informs Alison's approach in the passage above. He treats John's Gospel as the testimony of someone who has a strong conviction about Jesus' relationship to God based on the writer's own experiences of encounter with the crucified and risen Christ. John's reflections on the nature of that relationship are an outgrowth of his own experiences of encounter. In turn, Alison's elaboration upon John's articulation of the shared identity of the Son and the Father is part of the process of Alison's own induction into becoming more fully human through further reflection on Jesus' creative imagination made possible by his perfect imitation of the Father, which Alison recognizes as the source of Alison's own experiences of transformation through forgiveness.

Alison's depiction of Jesus' creative imagination lends itself to his "inductive" approach in a second way. He notes repeatedly that through the human (i.e., the relationally constituted and structured) imagination of Jesus, the creative power of God's vivaciousness becomes accessible and transformative for persons whose imaginations are formed according to rivalry and death. The process by which human persons come to encounter, appropriate, and live according to Jesus' eschatological imagination is a process of human discovery that unfolds within the context of their rather ordinary relationships. Alison's depiction of this human process of discovery repeatedly invites persons into such a process. It strives to open persons' actual imaginations to the possibility of an encounter with someone whose imagination is completely free from slavery to death. Alison remains close to "the order of discovery" that he advocates by offering a coherent account of the source of the forgiveness that he and others have received and desire to receive more fully. By doing so, Alison attempts to prepare the soil for new and renewed encounters with the crucified and risen Christ among his readers.

5.1.4 Original Sin in a Framework of Forgiveness—A Constructive Excerpt

Theologians familiar with Alison's work might suggest that he has made his most significant theological contribution with regard to the question of original sin.[16]

---

[16] For example in the "Foreword" to *The Joy of Being Wrong*, Sebastian Moore comments about the book's treatment of original sin by saying, "One should, one can, never say of a theological work that it is the definitive statement on its subject. But very occasionally one is tempted to do so, and this book represents that temptation in an acute form... I do not see how this book will not become a standard work on the subject" (vii–xi).

Although my argument throughout this project has worked to suggest that Alison's most significant theological contribution lies in his drawing out of a particular theological method that he believes to arise spontaneously from the experience of conversion in the presence of the crucified and risen Christ, his constructive treatment of the question of original sin is worthy of further theological investigation and is an area of his work in which the inductive aim of his theological reflection becomes quite evident.

In the following excerpt from the end of Part 2 of *The Joy of Being Wrong*,[17] Alison summarizes and makes explicit how he has attempted to return the doctrine of original sin to a framework of forgiveness in which it first became discoverable. He also contrasts this framework with a framework of accusation in which it is frequently presented but which distorts the doctrine and its fundamental value in communicating the salvific revelation made encounterable for all people in the crucified and risen Christ. In this passage, Alison articulates his understanding of the salvific and ecclesial function of the doctrine of original sin. This articulation both demonstrates and describes the inductive aim of theological reflection that he advocates.

> The function of the Church's doctrine of original sin ... is to keep alive the beam in my eye ... God keeps alive the beam in my eye by making that beam a living Cross, a beam on which there hangs a murdered victim.
>
> Does this keeping alive the murderous beam mean that God is involved in a noncomplicit accusation against us ...? Rather the reverse: it means that God was fully prepared to become similar to us, but in order to construct a forgiving sociality with us. *The doctrine of original sin is not an accusation against humanity, and by keeping it alive the Church is not engaged in an accusation against humanity. What the Church is keeping alive is the possibility that even those who bear the tremendous burden of being "right" may recognize their complicity with those who are not, and so construct a sociality that is not cruciform.*[18]
>
> My starting point has been rather limited. It is that in the Catholic faith we have no available explanation for evil or sin as such, not because we may not have many insights into such things, but because we don't have an explanation of anything at all. *We have a salvific revelation: what is revealed as something now operative is the mystery of God's plan of salvation for us.* This plan of salvation enables us to know the Father and share in his life by sharing in the life and death of his Son.[19]
>
> We have a contingent human transmission of a form, a shape, of salvation. This I have shown to mean that our only approach to the question of evil or sin ... is when we look at "that which we are on our way out of." This is a particularly difficult epistemological starting point, and we might do well to remember what happened to Lot's wife when she turned around to see that which she was on her way out of.

---

[17] Part 2 forms the body of this work and it is devoted to Alison's constructive reframing of the doctrine of original sin.
[18] Alison, *The Joy of Being Wrong*, 261.
[19] Ibid., 262.

> Much treatment of sin, and original sin, is the theological equivalent of a pillar of salt: something that is no longer on its way out of anything.... *My attempt has been rigorously to maintain the dynamic of salvation throughout, from which alone a certain limited insight can be gained into sin and original sin.*
>
> My plea therefore is in favor of respecting what I have called the *mysterium caecitatis*. We have only one way into an understanding of what sin, including original sin, might be, and that is starting from the resurrection. That is to say, there is a certain radical blindness as to both good and evil that began to be unveiled only as a result of the resurrection. *The forgiveness of sins, which became part of both the preaching and the power that flowed from the resurrection and is its central meaning, is what enables us to approach the question of sin.*[20]

> There is an important point that is worth making here lest it be thought that I am simply insisting that there is no way of knowing that something is evil outside of Christian faith.... My point is this: any understanding of good and evil that exists is not merely a piece of information about an act, but a part of a human social order, as part of the maintenance of that social order. There is no knowledge of good and evil that is not also part of a socially constructed relationality which is either inclusive or exclusive, but never neutral. So the question legitimately arises whether knowing that something is good or evil is known within the framework of accusation ... ,or within the framework of forgiveness.... *It is, as the Lucan text suggests, part of the particularly Christian understanding of sin that any accusatory knowledge of sin has a particular propensity to blindness about complicity and that only forgiveness enables us to see.*
>
> [I]t may not be an entirely unfortunate metaphor to see God himself as the ultimate master of suspicion. His suspicion is not, however, a reductive accusation, but is itself the beginnings of a creative forgiveness, letting us off the hook of our pretensions by suggesting to us that we are all actively involved in blindly creating victims, and need not be. *The ecclesial function of the doctrine of original sin is to participate in the Holy Spirit's keeping alive among us ... the creative suspicion of God. This essay has no other ambition (but no less ambition) than to be a contribution to that function.*[21]

This passage from the conclusion of Alison's reimagining of the symbol of original sin is an exemplary instance of Alison's inductive approach in that it makes explicit the aim of a theology that is attempting to participate in God's activity of reconciling the world to himself in Christ Jesus.[22] Alison has made the argument that the Christian doctrine of sin, which includes an understanding of original sin, is intended as the formal expression of the church's ongoing witness to the human necessity of undergoing a merciful discovery of one's (unknowing) complicity in the construction of "cruciform" societies. All understandings of good and evil, that is, all theologies and all human

---

[20] Ibid., 262–3.
[21] Ibid., 265.
[22] Cf. 2 Cor. 5:19.

knowing more generally, fluctuate between one of two possible forms. They either operate within a framework of accusation in which they participate in the creation of victims, or they operate within a framework of forgiveness in which they participate in fostering the humility capable of seeking repentance for oneself and others. Here Alison expresses with clarity the essential dynamic of what I have been calling an "inductive" theology, namely, it arises from the subject's interior knowledge of having received forgiveness. The subject's effort to better understand the power, source, and effect of that forgiveness (i.e., an effort to engage in theological reflection) is motivated by a desire to participate in making that forgiveness available to others, rather than by a misguided intention to secure his or her own life by withholding forgiveness from others. An inductive theology participates in the ongoing induction of the subject into a framework of knowing that makes forgiveness imaginable as the most fully human act in that it frees persons to construct families, communities, congregations, and societies that are not cruciform, that is, that do not depend on various forms of exclusion to maintain their identity and cohesion.

This language of being inducted into a framework of forgiveness is another and perhaps more illuminating way of describing the transformation that follows from conversion. The subject's appropriation of the intelligence of the victim involves, in part, the work of the subject's intellect in striving to come to an initial understanding of what is being made known to him about social reality and his participation in it. This intellectual participation gradually inducts him further into the framework of forgiveness that made the subject's initial and ongoing discoveries possible. As Alison indicated in the passage above, participating in one's own induction into this framework of forgiveness and seeking to make it available for others have the necessary function of keeping alive the possibility of discovering one's complicity in violence in such a way as to enable one to participate in the divine project of reconciling the world to God by reconciling persons to one another.

This is the essential content of the salvific revelation embodied most fully in the life, death, and resurrection of Jesus and into which we are inducted through the reception of forgiveness: accusation perpetuates blindness; receiving and offering forgiveness enable sight (which includes right remembering, clear perception, and a creative, or eschatological, imagination). An inductive theology is made possible by the human discovery of this revelation and seeks to make it both intellectually and personally discoverable for others. In other words, an inductive theology is grounded in and guided by a fundamental epistemological insight that was (according to Girard and Alison) made fully humanly discoverable for the first time through the historical and bodily presence of the crucified and risen Jesus to his closest friends and disciples. This insight is essentially that, historically speaking, no act of human knowing is neutral or purely "objective." Instead, human knowing always occurs, to varying degrees, either in a framework of self-justification and accusation, or in a framework of self-giving in free imitation of a forgiving model. According to Alison, "the ecclesial function of the doctrine of original sin is to participate in the Holy Spirit's keeping alive among us...the creative suspicion of God[,]" which gently exposes persons' blindness to creating victims and forgives us in order to set us free. Thus, in Alison's view, the doctrine of original sin, appropriated, articulated, and enacted in a framework of forgiveness, provides the impetus for what Alison calls a theology in the order of discovery, and for what I have been calling an inductive theology, which makes a framework of self-giving and forgiveness the means for seeing oneself, others, and God with any clarity.

5.1.5 A Gay Catholic Heart—A Pastoral Excerpt

Before introducing this next excerpt, I believe that a brief comment on the term "pastoral" is necessary. In one way the term "pastoral" as a descriptor of a theological approach should be considered synonymous with "inductive," since both words can be seen to indicate the intention of theology to make the essential revelation communicated in the life, death, and resurrection of Jesus Christ more immediately discoverable for persons. My use of the word "pastoral" here, however, is not primarily in this sense, since by it I am not suggesting that the "apologetic," "historical," "systematic," and "constructive" excerpts above are something other than "pastoral" and "inductive." I use the term "pastoral" here to indicate that this excerpt is directed toward a particular group of persons who have often felt misunderstood and excluded by Christian moral teaching and by Catholic and other Christian churches. It is pastoral in that it seeks to address persons who have been pushed to the margins of any group and to show compassion toward their particular experiences of exclusion.[23] This context of reaching out to persons who have traditionally been marginalized makes Alison's inductive approach more explicitly present. It also demonstrates that the reception of forgiveness that enables conversion can and does occur outside of official church structures and actions, and that members of the church hierarchy are also among those in need of new or renewed encounters with the crucified and risen Christ, who chooses to become incarnate among those who have been marginalized.

The following excerpt is the conclusion of a talk given as part of a panel discussion for LGBTQ persons held at Most Holy Redeemer Parish in San Francisco, CA, in September 2006. The title of the panel provided by the hosts was "Is it ethical to be Catholic? Queer perspectives," which became the title of the later published version of Alison's essay as the first chapter of *Broken Hearts and New Creations*. Alison's role on the panel was to offer a positive response to this question. He began his response by arguing that being or becoming Catholic is not a question of ethics, but rather a question of grace that begins a process of discovery in which one finds oneself being invited and inducted into a divine project of reconciliation. After explaining his confusion about the question presented and speaking about the working of grace to reveal to us who we are, he points out ways that research in the social sciences and even some of Pope Benedict XVI's writings have helped to create an opening for the possibility of gay and lesbian persons to occupy "an honest and straightforward" presence within the church. In the excerpt below, Alison begins to describe this

---

[23] This usage would cohere quite well with Friedrich Schleiermacher's description of "pastoral care" or "care of souls," in his "encyclopedia" of theology. Pastoral care is directed toward "those members of the congregation who, from internal or external causes, have lost their identification with the rest" (*Brief Outline of Theology*, 1830, translated 1966, §299).

shift in climate, and he invites LGBTQ Catholics to acknowledge themselves to be recipients of grace and to hold a more dignified posture both for their own good and for the good of the church.

> Something like this is going on at the moment for us gay and lesbian people in the Church. A certain sense of truth about who we are is beginning to become available to us in the midst of frightening and violent struggles, shouting and name-calling. It has begun to become available precisely in the degree in which we learn to stop defining a particular group of people as evil so as to hold on to what turns out to be a spuriously narrow sense of what is good.... It is only as we learn to see and love our neighbors as ourselves that we find out who *we* are, and find that we are much more than we thought we were.
>
> What is beginning to become apparent is that there is a more or less regular minority of people of both sexes who, entirely independently of circumstance, war, long journeys, imprisonments, cults and so on, simply are principally attracted to people of their own sex at an emotional and erotic level.... And it is even beginning to become clear that such people are able to develop and receive that full-heartedness of love for each other, that delicate birth of being taken out of themselves for the other which is not just lust, nor a defect of some other sort of love which they really ought to have, but don't seem to be able to, but is quite simply the real thing, which, when present, is recognized as a gift from, and an access to, God.[24]
>
> And one of the things which, as the Pope [Benedict] rightly insists [in *Deus Caritas Est*], we might find ourselves learning, is how the development of our love should feed into, and be fed by, our development of charitable practices, of practical Catholic outreach to the poor, the sick, the imprisoned and the marginalized.... Catholic faith without love of the poor is not the real thing, and the Catholicity of gay love will be seen by the way in which it is part of our empowerment to love the dispossessed. And this is something no one will be able to take away from us.
>
> My concern with the matter of ethics at the moment is this: let us be magnanimous victors. There are some people in our Church who have been seriously upset by the way that ordinary Catholicism in all its disputatiousness and diversity is breaking out again under Pope Benedict. They are going to be terribly sore as it becomes clear that the Church, in its stumbling, bumbling, chaotic way, is just learning how to deal with the reality of honest, straightforward lesbian and gay people, learning how to treat differences of opinion in this sphere as discussions concerning third-order truths which do not exclude from the life of the Church.
>
> There are also a good number ... of priests and bishops who genuinely do not know what to do, who are themselves to some degree implicated in all this and who have never been able to face for themselves the issues of conscience which go

---

[24] James Alison, "Is It Ethical to Be Catholic? Queer Perspectives," in *Broken Hearts and New Creations* (New York: Continuum, 2010), 11–12.

with the deep fear about just being gay; people who have been hoping against hope that Church structure would somehow save them from having to face the issue of their own truth squarely, and who are now genuinely at sea [in] coping with all of this. ... So, let us be gentle! Ethics is very much to do with how we extend mercy to the fearful, just as we have found ourselves the recipients of mercy at a time when we have been frightened, tortured, annihilated by voices telling us how evil we were.

For me, the real ethical challenge as a Catholic now is: I don't have any excuse any more. It is no good pretending that the Pope or the Church is really against me for the long haul, so that I have to fight him or them. Instead, I will have to grow up and learn to love starting where I am, and being aware that the gift of a gay Catholic heart is a heavy responsibility, pregnant with love and opportunity.[25]

In light of Pope Francis's papacy, this passage sounds profoundly prophetic in its description of shifts in the ecclesial climate toward gay people and even more so in its highlighting of Pope Benedict's assertion in *Deus Caritas Est* that the authenticity of Catholic faith requires an enacted love of the poor and the dispossessed.[26]

This particular address to gay Catholics (which is one of many written by Alison) acknowledges the ways that they have been fearfully and forcefully misclassified, marginalized, and degraded in both the universal church and the local churches. However, it does so with a view toward inviting the whole church to become more fully human by recognizing together the spuriousness and narrowness of a "good" that has required the identification and exclusion of a group of "evil" persons.

In this passage, first we see Alison inviting gay Catholics questioning their place in the church to become open to the love which is both "gift from, and access to, God" so that they might claim their place among the witnesses of the crucified and risen Christ who together reach out to the poor, the sick, the imprisoned, and the dispossessed. He is inviting them to become open to new and renewed encounters with the crucified and risen Christ by adopting a certain indifference and even playfulness toward the attempts at exclusion happening around them, because these encounters will lead them into becoming vessels of the love of God for one another, for the poor, and even for those who for a time have acted in some ways as their persecutors.

Then Alison goes further by challenging gay Catholics to become witnesses of mercy to those who now may find themselves undergoing the painful collapse of identities that were tied to structures mistaken for sacred pillars. Alison invites gay persons who have come to receive mercy, likely from somewhere or someone outside of the church, to identify with those who are frightened by various forms of collapse taking place within the church and, in identifying with them, to show them mercy. In so doing, those who have been marginalized can become occasions of encounter with Christ for those inside the church who are fearful and who may feel inclined to lock themselves in a kind of "upper room."

---

[25] Ibid., 15–16.
[26] Cf. Pope Benedict XVI, *Deus Caritas Est*, 15, 20, 23, 26, 30, 40.

Here we see that Alison's outreach to this group of dispossessed Catholics is both empathetic and challenging. He first offers theological reflections that arose from his own experience of conversion via a reception of forgiveness when he suggests that becoming Catholic is not about an ethical choice on our part, but instead about an interior response to a movement of grace toward us. In offering theological thinking from within his own experience, he attempts to invite his audience out of a framework of accusation and into one of forgiveness. Here he lays some ground for them to become open to an encounter not with the Catholic Church, but with the crucified and risen Christ who will transform the ground of their reasoning and of their relationality. Through his personal and theological reflections, Alison is trying to help open their imaginations to become "fixed on the things that are above" so as to transform their presence as they inhabit the spaces in which they find themselves below.

This is, I believe, an inductive, pastoral theology. It uses all of the tools at its disposal—personal experience, theological insight and knowledge, empathy toward those being addressed, knowledge of the ecclesial and social context—to point a marginalized group of readers and hearers toward the possibility of a new or renewed encounter with the forgiving victim in whatever place and by whatever means Christ chooses. An inductive theology operates out of a deep trust that the Spirit of the crucified and risen Christ will and does come because the subject doing the reflecting has been transformed by an encounter with that Spirit. The implicit communication of this trust, through whatever mode of theological reflection is undertaken—apologetic, historical, systematic, constructive, pastoral, etc.—is an essential component of a theological method that has as its primary objective inviting persons to a new openness to the possibility of such an encounter.

We saw at the beginning of this chapter that, without explicitly identifying his own understanding of his theological method as "inductive," Alison does describe the task of the theologian as keeping the possibility of discovery alive through a purification of language that strives to interrupt the attachment of human thought patterns to rivalrous understandings, or to a framework of accusation, so that we can participate in opening ourselves and others to the reality of the advent of God among and within us. I will quote here in full the paragraph that I quoted in part at the beginning of the chapter because now I will be able to break it down and show more fully how this description of the task of the theologian coheres well with, and develops, what I have been calling an "inductive" theology. Alison writes,

> This consideration [of the ecclesial nature of faith] also suggests the function of the theologian in the Church, which is to help [keep] the discovery alive by helping in the detachment of human thought processes from their bases in the rivalristic understanding proper to the old other. The ecclesial intelligence of the faith is, then, a divine impulse toward a constant purifying of language and practice so as to allow God an ever less obstacled possession of us, precisely because it is through human words and practices that God wishes to have access to us. The theologian seeks to make words formed in and through the old other become capable of transmitting, or at least not betraying too grotesquely, the new "Other"—the

vertiginous belief that words themselves need not be stumbling blocks, but can also be vessels of God.[27]

First, it is worth noting that this description of the task of the theologian assumes an ecclesial context. The identification of this context here does not imply that Alison fails to imagine a task for the theologian in the public sphere or the academy. It does, however, indicate that he sees the task of the theologian as first being an ecclesial one. In the New Israel, the continued presence of the Spirit of the crucified and risen Christ gathers persons, each undergoing a subversion from within of their own rivalrous identities, into a community of those being brought to life peacefully through a common reception of forgiveness and a common practice of repentance from which arises true and shared worship of the living God. Alison writes, "True Worship leads to a slow, patient, discovery of being able to like [one another] in their bizarre particularities, and see the beauty in those things."[28] Here theological reflection upon the forgiveness being received and the transformation it effects within oneself and the community facilitates the individual's and the community's gradual appropriation of the intelligence and the imagination that was in Christ Jesus, which is continuously being made available through his Spirit.

In this ecclesial context, the theologian is to help in the detachment of human thought processes from their bases in rivalrous understandings, or "intelligence," as we called it earlier. He or she is to help illuminate the ways that a framework of accusation has given persons a false understanding of self and others by generating rivalries that appear to be substantive or as arising from the "essence" of persons' identities, but which are actually generated by persons' basic misunderstanding of their own identities as something discrete, self-contained, and self-chosen. The theologian affirms and further develops the insight received through the reception of forgiveness—an insight that reveals to persons that their most basic and stable identity is and always has been something given freely by God through others. If such an insight is received freely, then persons are able to see the non-necessity of the rivalries that previously appeared to be the result of something substantive within themselves.

As Alison describes the task, the theologian is engaged in "purifying language" so that words that previously have been understood within a framework of accusation might be re-formed within the framework of forgiveness into which persons are being inducted. Words like "sin," "sinner," "intrinsic evil," "grace," "repentance," "life," "death," "self," "other," "creation," and many others both "religious" and "secular" are all reworked by the theologian into sacraments of, or pointers toward, the utter vivaciousness of the living God, who pours out life upon all persons and the whole of creation simply because it is of the very nature of God to do so. Re-forming the meanings of these words to become useful in this framework of forgiveness is an arduous and ongoing task, since persons' identities and their use of these and many other words have been so thoroughly formed according to the framework of accusation that they have learned to believe them to be fundamental and reflective of reality itself. The task of the theologian,

---

[27] Alison, *The Joy of Being Wrong*, 61–2.
[28] Alison, "Worship in a Violent World," 46.

then, is to participate in the induction of persons more and more fully into the ecclesial framework of forgiveness by working to make words into signs of the reign of the living God. Thus, this inductive task of the theologian is first an ecclesial one.

Second, it extends from its ecclesial context to become a task of striving to speak to all persons (or all nations) in such a way so as to (1) attempt to remove some of the obstacles that prevent persons from imagining the possibility of an encounter with the living God and (2) to identify shared ways of talking about how persons of other traditions (or no tradition) also find themselves in the presence of a force of forgiveness that has begun to transform them.

5.2 A Theological Anthropology Informed by Mimetic Theory

Alison's understanding of the inductive aim of theological reflection can be summarized as transforming human belonging and language from a framework of accusation in which rivalry and fear of death are the primary forces shaping persons' patterns of remembering, perceiving, and imagining, to a framework of forgiveness in which the vivaciousness of God, peacefully imitated by the forgiving victim, frees human beings to move through the world as forgiven forgivers. Alison believes that theological reflection arises from experiences of conversion and is oriented toward creating the possibility of further experiences of conversion for both the person doing the reflecting and those who receive that reflection. In other words, theological reflection (whether done by "trained" theologians or not, and whether written, recorded, published or not) is part of the process through which people are inducted into a new pattern of belonging, which involves new ways of remembering, perceiving, and imagining, and so it must also involve a new pattern of using language, whether specifically theological or not. Alison believes that theological reflection participates in this process if and when it serves as an occasion for the Spirit of the crucified and risen Christ to induct someone into being by making tangible for him or her the possibility of forgiveness within the particularity of his or her life.

We have seen that Alison views theology in its truest form and the activity of theological reflection to be a participation in God's communication of salvific and reconciling love for all of humankind. This divine communication of love ultimately inducts people into a new pattern of being human, which is characterized by forgiveness rather than accusation. By depicting how this inductive aim of theology is operative in the five excerpts above, I have argued that Alison's understanding of theology as inductive is not only theoretical but also consistently practiced in his own theological reflection. In other words, there is a congruence between his theory and his practice of theology. His experientially informed view of the impact of Jesus' resurrection appearances on Jesus' disciples grounds both Alison's understanding of theology and his understanding of mimetic theory, as well as Alison's own ongoing engagement in the practice of theological reflection.

This congruence and its source in Alison's understanding of the disciples' experiences of Jesus' resurrection appearances, in turn, make evident again that Alison's primary objective in using Girard's mimetic theory to clarify a Christian theological perspective is to develop a theological method; that is, it is a task in fundamental theology. More specifically, Alison's underlying aim is to use mimetic theory to clarify his theological understanding of the nature of Christian conversion and of Christian knowing. His inductive theology, which seeks to become an occasion for ongoing experiences of encounter with the Spirit of the crucified and risen Christ, is a fruit of his application of mimetic theory to an understanding of the disciples' experiences of Jesus' resurrection. His understanding of Christian conversion and of theological reflection (or Christian knowing) as reciprocal moments in an ongoing and deepening act of communication between God and humanity is the theological fruit of his application of mimetic theory to his reading of the disciples' experiences of Jesus' resurrection, and it forms the substance of his inductive theological method. Thus, Girardians interested in Christian theology and theologians interested in mimetic theory should understand Alison's entire theological project and his appropriation and application of Girard as essentially a work of fundamental theology. Only as a result of Alison's development of this inductive theological method is he then able to employ mimetic theory to better articulate an understanding of more particular theological and ethical questions, such as how we might understand original sin in our much more culturally and socially minded context, or how we might contextualize a Christian view of atonement within its Jewish roots, or whether and how LGBTQ persons might authentically participate within the Catholic church in the twenty-first century. Alison's reflection on these questions and on every other theological or ethical question that he considers is undergirded by his work in fundamental theology, which applies mimetic theory to articulate an understanding of the disciples' experience of the resurrection, Christian conversion, and theological reflection. In other words, any contributions that Alison might make to trinitarian theology, soteriology, ecclesiology, sacramental theology, apologetics, theological ethics, or theological anthropology are always a fruit of (and in that sense secondary to) his primary contribution to fundamental theology in his development and practice of an inductive theological method that is substantially shaped by his appropriation of mimetic theory.

Perhaps one of the most widely recognized fruits of Alison's work in fundamental theology is his articulation of a theology of original sin "through Easter Eyes", an excerpt of which we considered above. Alison argues that a clear perception of sin, and of original sin in particular, only ever comes through the rearview mirror, so to speak, as that which we are in the process of leaving behind. Sin can only be perceived clearly in the light of the resurrection (i.e., "through Easter eyes") as a set of relational dynamics from which we are being freed. Thus, one of the most significant fruits of Alison's fundamental theology is a theology of sin and grace, or a theological anthropology articulated as an interplay between the dynamics of accusation and those of forgiveness.

Through his patient attentiveness to his own experiences of receiving forgiveness unexpectedly and being freed from entanglements of which he had been unaware, as well as through his careful attention to the New Testament narratives of Jesus' resurrection appearances, Alison offers a view of being human—that is, of remembering, perceiving, imagining, and desiring (or belonging)—that can be formed according to one of two poles, a framework of accusation or a framework of forgiveness. And the character of a human being's or a human community's formation at any given time is determined by the patterns of desiring of the many models according to which the person or community is being formed.

The degree of persons' awareness of their formation according to the desire of their models also varies between the poles of accusation and forgiveness. Human beings are desiring imitators of those others whom we have subconsciously or consciously adopted as worthy of emulating. The degree to which we are aware of the kind of beings we are, namely, desiring imitators (or imitative desirers), correlates directly with the degree to which we have developed the capacity to receive forgiveness from those whom we have excluded, at least partially unknowingly. In other words, experiences of receiving forgiveness simultaneously reveal to us something of the kind of beings that we are (desiring imitators) and also provide us with new models whose patterns of desire are at least partially formed according to a framework of forgiveness rather than accusation. Alison's application of mimetic theory to his own experiences of being forgiven and to the New Testament accounts of the disciples' experiences of being forgiven by the crucified and risen Christ leads him to recognize the freeing influence that the reception of forgiveness has on a person or community such that they become more able to remember rightly and humbly their own participation in acts of exclusion toward others and to perceive themselves clearly as desiring imitators in need of models. Patterns of desiring that participated in the exclusion and marginalization of particular others become visible for the first time as they begin to be left behind and become undone by a gratuitous offer of forgiveness.

An illuminated reimagining of God's relationship to us and to death accompanies this right remembering of one's collapsing patterns of accusation, exclusion, and marginalization and the clear perceiving of one's identity as a desiring imitator. Through experiences of receiving forgiveness we see that our fear of death, which we had experienced as a fear of having no lasting value, led us into denial about who we were and enticed us into a pervasive rivalry with others. In fact, we believed that death was the ultimate and definitive reality. In receiving forgiveness, we begin to reimagine God as abundant and not limited by our experiences of life or death.[29] We glimpse God's "utter vivaciousness," which freely holds us in being before and after death. We see for the first time that our imagination of God as placing us in rivalry with one another to become worthy of love had been false, generated by our imitations of rivalrous earthy models. Instead, our imaginations, "fixed on the things that are above," can now begin to see God as completely uninvolved in our many experiences of violence, accusation,

---

[29] For a lengthier treatment of Alison's understanding of our fear of death and the gradual discovery of God's abundance through forgiveness, see my essay, "Being Freed from the Illusion of the Enemy," 1–16.

persecution, and marginalization, both as a persecutor and as the persecuted. God has always held us in being and desired our peaceful coexistence with one another.

Through our experiences of receiving forgiveness, we also begin to see that our previous patterns of mis-remembering, mis-perceiving, false imagining, and rivalrous belonging worked together to maintain their occlusion from our direct view and experience. The interpersonal and social dynamics that trapped us in a mechanism of accusation and rivalry and in which we were participating (albeit unknowingly) clouded our memory, perception, and imagination, and our clouded faculties, in turn, prevented us from seeing the arbitrariness of the mechanism of rivalry in which we were existing. This mechanism and our relationship to it come into view only as we find ourselves beginning to be freed from it through our reception of forgiveness, which allows us to see how unnecessary all of it had been as it offers us an alternative. These interpersonal and social dynamics of rivalry and accusation in which we unknowingly participate constitute Alison's understanding of the dynamics of sin on all of its traditionally recognized levels—original, social, and personal. They are perceivable only through the light of the resurrection, which simultaneously reveals the utter abundance and aliveness of God who has never desired any of these entanglements for us and who has been working to communicate to us an alternative pattern of remembering, perceiving, imagining, and belonging formed according to the peaceful imitation of self-giving love.

Alison's theological anthropology of desiring imitators formed according to a framework of accusation or a framework of forgiveness, depending on the patterns of desire of their models, arises from his ongoing inquiry into the nature of conversion and of theological reflection using the lens of mimetic theory. By drawing out an understanding of conversion and theological reflection from his Girardian reading of the disciples' experiences of Jesus' resurrection, Alison also brings the Girardian view of being human into a fully explicit theological perspective that sees the divine intention expressed in Judeo-Christian revelation as part of what is made knowable to human beings and as the light in which the dynamics of sin (experienced as a system of rivalry and accusation that involves its own occlusion) become directly perceivable. In other words, this Alisonian theological anthropology is a kind of a natural by-product of Alison's application of Girard's "revealed" mimetic anthropology to an understanding of the disciples' encounter with the crucified and risen Christ and to the development of an inductive theology of conversion and theological reflection.

5.2.1 Clarifying Girard

The resulting contributions of Alison's use of Girard's "revealed" or "Gospel" anthropology to shed greater light on the disciples' experiences of encountering the crucified and risen Jesus are not limited to an Alisonian inductive theology and theological anthropology, however. They are not even limited to the theological side of this relationship. Instead, they are reciprocal. Mimetic theory as Girard develops it over the course of his entire career is also clarified by Alison's theological application of it. I will argue here that the clarification of mimetic theory that results from Alison's development of his inductive theology arises most immediately from Alison's explicitly theological (and teleological) inquiry into what their encounters with the crucified and risen Jesus make knowable to the disciples—and the rest of humanity—about who God is and what God desires for them.

Before I make this argument, however, let us recall Alison's understanding of the primary source of the mutually clarifying effect that mimetic theory and Christian theology have upon one another, namely, their shared origin.[30] By "origin," Alison means the relational context that originally made both mimetic theory and Christian revelation fully discoverable, which was the disciples' experiences of encountering the crucified and risen Jesus as a forgiving victim. Near the beginning of Chapter 4, I quoted a key passage alluding to Alison's view of this shared origin:

> We are going to put it [mimetic theory] to work to see what it helps us recover from the apostolic witness: that is to say, we're putting it to theological use. To do this we have to return to first principles and ask ourselves what it is which makes this story, this theory, possible in the first place.[31]

For Alison what "makes this story, this [mimetic] theory, possible in the first place," or the relational context that allowed mimetic theory as Girard has articulated it to come into view, is the Judeo-Christian Scriptures and their culmination in the New Testament accounts of the disciples' encounters with the crucified and risen Jesus. This is the same relational context that gave rise to Christian theology, since, as Alison makes clear at the beginning of *Knowing Jesus*, we have Christianity at all only because of the witnessing to the crucified and risen Christ of his disciples.[32] Putting mimetic theory to "theological use" means seeing what it can help us recover from these first witnesses. Alison has devoted his primary theological focus to this task, and he has done so to great effect.

Because of this shared originating relational context, the clarifying effect of applying mimetic theory to an understanding of the crucified and risen Christ and Judeo-Christian revelation is reciprocal. Alison's application of mimetic theory to his theological inquiry into what is unveiled or made knowable to the disciples through their experiences of encounter with the crucified and risen Christ creates, in turn, a clarifying lens for mimetic theory as Girard has developed it. At the end of Chapter 3, I delineated Alison's understanding of the content of what is unveiled by examining what Alison means by two of his key phrases, "the intelligence [of the victim] operative in the mind of Christ" and "subversion from within."[33] Alison draws on the Pauline references to the mind of Christ and to minds fixed on the things that are above to argue that the intelligence operative in the mind of Christ is primarily a clear perception of God, namely, that God is totally, fully, and utterly alive.

---

[30] See Chapter 4, Section 4.1.3.
[31] Alison, *Raising Abel*, 24–5.
[32] Alison, *Knowing Jesus*, 5. I cited this passage early in Chapter 4 as well; see Section 4.2.
[33] See Sections 3.2.5.4–3.2.5.6.

This is precisely what the disciples discovered when they encountered the crucified and risen Jesus—"He is alive!" They discovered not only that Jesus who died is now no longer dead, but also that God, as the one who raised Jesus from the dead, has absolutely nothing to do with death and is not limited by death. God is alive in such a way that death (neither as a biological occurrence nor as the result of social exclusion and violence) has absolutely no bearing on God's ability to be in relationship to us human beings, that is, to love us. The intelligence operative in the mind of Christ perceives that death is not a limit for God; death is simply not definitive or ultimate. Alison thus chooses to describe God as totally and utterly vivacious because he sees it as essential to the intelligence operative in the mind of Christ that God is alive in a way that is not at all opposed to or threatened by death. For Alison, then, the disciples' experiences of the crucified and risen Jesus are most essentially an experience of who God is and of what God desires and has always desired for them and for the rest of humanity.

It is because the disciples had a life-shattering experience of God when they encountered the crucified and risen Christ that anything about themselves, their relationships, and the workings of desire and scapegoating also became revealed to them. The crucified and risen Christ, approaching the disciples as a forgiving victim who says, "Peace!", revealed to them fully for the first time that (1) their imaginations of God had been bound by an unseen but pervasive belief that death was the ultimate reality and that (2) a persistent fear of death had been shaping all of their remembering, perceiving, imagining, and belonging.[34] In being offered forgiveness by the crucified and risen Christ, they saw for the first time that death is not and never has been ultimate. God is ultimate, and God is completely and utterly alive. The relational context that made this discovery possible for the disciples was their relationships with Jesus leading up to and including his death, which, like the relationships of all other human beings, had been both rivalrous and loving to varying degrees. They believed that Jesus was the anointed one and they were his friends, but when he was crucified, they despaired and believed that the human judgment of Jesus as a blasphemer must have been true. Their own fear of death had led them to abandon Jesus rather than stand by his testimony.[35] But when the crucified and risen Jesus, whom they loved but whom they had also abandoned, approached them offering nothing but peace, they finally saw that throughout Jesus' whole life (and indeed throughout the whole of the Hebrew Scriptures), God had been actively trying to show them that death is not ultimate, and that God is wholly and utterly alive and desires that they too might have life.

This revelation of God's utter vivaciousness was the light through which the disciples could first see how their belief in the definitiveness of death had shaped everything that they had previously said and done to some degree or another. This belief had led them to misperceive themselves and their neighbors; it had generated

---

[34] I treated this initial recognition of and transformation of the disciples' false belief in the definitiveness of death in Section 3.2.5.2.

[35] See Section 3.2.3 which describes Alison's "Imaginative reconstruction of the Disciples' post-Crucifixion experience."

their rivalrous desires and relationships; and it had blinded them to the mechanism of rivalry and scapegoating in which they were participating unknowingly. Only the forgiveness offered by the crucified and risen Christ through its revelation of the utter vivaciousness of God to them and for them made this belief fully visible as it was demonstrated to be completely untrue.

Alison's putting mimetic theory to "theological use" in this way goes beyond what Girard was interested in or willing to pursue in his own articulation of mimetic theory, as Girard himself explicitly affirmed.[36] As a result of Girard's study of literature and cultural anthropology, when he discovered the unveiling power of the texts of Judeo-Christian Scriptures, he recognized that such a power could only be the fruit of an intelligence that could not be generated within the social framework of human relationships. Instead, it must have broken into human relationships and human understanding from outside of them. While he did, of course, personally identify this power with his own belief in God, in his writings Girard explicitly chose not to inquire into the nature of this power and intelligence because, for him, this appeared to be engaging in a kind of speculation that was beyond what could be found in the text themselves. To engage in this speculation would be to engage in theology. Although he believed that such speculation was in fact good and necessary, he did not believe that this was his task or his skill. He also feared that engaging in this speculation might distract from learning what could be learned from the texts of the Judeo-Christian Scriptures about the operation of human desire, relationships, conflict, and scapegoats.

To use a visual-spatial metaphor (which is, of course, limited), we can say that Girard saw clearly that the texts of the Judeo-Christian Scripture were like a crater that could only have been created by the tremendous impact from something completely outside of human societies. But Girard chose to focus his attention on what could be learned from the direct observation of the crater itself and to avoid using those observations to hypothesize about what kind of "object" might have made such an impact. Alison, on the other hand, begins with the premise that the crater itself bears within it the imprint of the "object" making the impact and so it is most effectively studied with an imagination of that object (along with its speed, trajectory, and source) in mind. Recall that when Alison talks about "imagination" with regard to the disciples' encounters with the crucified and risen Christ, he is specifically not talking about something "imaginary," but instead he is extrapolating from the texts what would have been the ordinary human responses to Jesus' life, death, and resurrection for his disciples who had given up everything to follow him.[37]

As a Catholic theologian and priest, Alison naturally brings a different set of premises and intentions to his reading of Scriptural texts than did Girard. Foremost among these premises is a fundamental belief that these texts have something to teach us about who God is.[38] Although Girard also held this belief personally, he chose not

---

[36] See especially Section 2.4.4.
[37] See especially Sections 3.2.2 and 3.2.3.
[38] See Section 3.2.1.

to take it as a premise for his own scholarly work, even when that work involved reading the texts of Scripture. I do not contend that Girard should have read the texts of Scripture differently or that he has not contributed greatly to our understanding of the anthropological and sociological content of what is made known to us in and through the texts of Scripture. My view of Girard's contributions is quite the opposite. Instead, what I am arguing is that Alison's explicitly theological premise—namely, that the Scriptural texts are evidence of a revelation to the disciples that was first and foremost a revelation about who God is and that resulted in an ongoing revelation about who they were, had been, and were being invited to become—clarifies an articulation of mimetic theory that Girard approached only toward the end of his career. Alison's explicitly theological inquiry is able to do this because the essential content of what became known to the disciples through the life, death, and resurrection of Jesus was a new and experienced understanding of who God is, and that understanding made possible and permeates all the texts of Christian Scripture.[39] By attending to what the texts of Scripture make accessible to us about what the crucified and risen Jesus revealed to the disciples regarding God, Alison places his engagement with mimetic theory fully within the light of the resurrection.

One of the most significant ways that Alison clarifies mimetic theory is by placing at the center of our attention the loving imitation of Jesus' imitation of his Father, as seen "through Easter Eyes." When Alison makes the disciples' experiences of the risen Jesus foundational for his entire theological project, the result is that the "first" or primary human interaction from which everything else is understood is Jesus' word "Peace." In response to the disciples' abandonment of Jesus to death and their expectations of disappointment, hurt, anger, resentment, and possibly vengeance from Jesus, the crucified and risen Christ who is fully assured of his being loved and held in being by the Father still has only one desire for his friends: to offer them peace. The centering of our attention on this human interaction makes it completely clear from the start to the disciples and to those of us attending to their witness that mimetic desire is not inherently rivalrous. If this encounter with the crucified and risen Christ is indeed where what we now refer to as mimetic theory first became fully unveiled (as both Girard and Alison attest), then at the point of its fullest unveiling it would have become evident to the disciples (though not yet discursively articulatable) that peaceful or loving imitation of Jesus' peaceful imitation of the Father not only was possible but was what God had desired for them and for all of humanity from the beginning.

Jesus' offer of peace and forgiveness as the crucified and risen One in response to abandonment and expectations of vengeance makes known to the disciples in an immediate, but still inchoate, way that God is fully and utterly alive, and offers to them the possibility of choosing to imitate the Son of the Living God. The "density" of this experience for the disciples, as Alison describes it and as I laid out in detail in Chapter 3,[40] leads to their gradual ability to remember their past rightly, perceive their present clearly, and imagine God and their future vivaciously and peacefully for

---

[39] See Section 3.2.4.
[40] See Section 3.2.5.

the first time. This unveiling of God as Jesus' Father and model who is fully alive and unhindered by death provides the disciples with an initial insight into their rivalrous past selves, the possibility of choosing peaceful imitation of Jesus, which could free them from their fear of death, and an undeniable experience of God and God's love as beyond death and as holding them in being in their past, present, and future.

Alison's ongoing reliance on the disciples' experience of the resurrection in his development of an understanding of the nature of conversion and of theological reflection provides other Girardians with the beginnings of what I suggested is needed to have greater consistency and clarity in the use of some key Girardian terms, including mimetic desire, mimetic rivalry, and conversion—namely, an understanding of being human in terms of the theological planes of sin and grace that is able to conceptually differentiate and relate mimetic desire from its two particular "modes" of mimetic rivalry and peaceful imitation. Because Alison focuses on the new revelation of God to the disciples through the resurrection appearances, his application of mimetic theory to his theological inquiry consistently refers to mimetic desire in relation to its modes of operation as either rivalrous or peaceful, and it treats the Christian Scriptures as revelatory of God's desire for human beings to imitate Jesus' loving imitation of the Father, even to the point of being unafraid of death. Alison's exploration of the process of religious conversion as first depicted in the accounts of Jesus' resurrection appearances makes clearer than Girard did both the transformation and the continuity in the disciples' self-understanding and subjectivity throughout their responses to the life, death, and resurrection of Jesus. Because Alison sees God's loving desire for human beings as foundational to what is being witnessed to throughout the texts of Scripture and as the light through which the Scriptures became possible at all, Alison's reading of the resurrection narratives provides us with a perspective from which to articulate Girard's mimetic anthropology that Girard himself does not. As a result of Alison's theological inquiry, he and other Girardians can articulate a theological anthropology informed by mimetic theory in which we perceive human subjectivity and relationality as grounded in God's regard for human beings, which is constant regardless of our human awareness of it. From this vantage point, it becomes clear that persons' and communities' patterns of belonging can vary between being formed according to the desires of more or less rivalrous models and being formed according to the desires of more or less peaceful models. The degree of a person's or community's perception or misperception of self, God, and others expresses the formation of their pattern of belonging. Human patterns of belonging that are characterized more by a framework of accusation and a misperception of God and others as rivals constitute human sinfulness from Alison's theological perspective. And human patterns of belonging that are formed by the reception of forgiveness and that relate to God as a loving father and others as neighbors constitute Alison's understanding of grace, which frees and enlivens human beings to live in peace with one another. Although mimetic desire in Alison's view never operates outside of one of these two modes, it is clear that, for Alison, mimetic desire in itself is neither inherently rivalrous nor inherently loving. Instead, it is simply the way human beings exist in the world as creatures always and everywhere formed according to various others who serve as their models. "Desiring imitators" or "imitating desirers" is the best way of describing the kind of creatures that human beings are. And mimetic desire is the network of connectivity in and through which human beings are formed.

In Chapter 2, I showed how Girard's own articulation of mimetic theory over the course of his career was moving in this direction in his effort to develop a "gospel anthropology." Alison's explicitly theological inquiry into the Scriptural texts allows him to bring Girard's shift from a literary-cultural anthropology toward a Gospel anthropology to greater clarity and consistency within a theological anthropology that views the crucified and risen Christ's revelation of God as the source and primary content of the New Testament texts, and that views the loving regard of God as the grounding of human subjectivity and relationality.

5.3 Contributions to Contemporary Christian Theological Questions

While it is beyond the scope of this study to consider the possible theological import of Alison's inductive theological method for any number of theological questions in fundamental, systematic, historical, moral, or practical theology, I will conclude by briefly considering how Alison's work of applying mimetic theory to the fundamental theological questions of Christian conversion and theological reflection bears significant fruit for developing a contemporary Christian understanding of the nature of doctrines and, specifically, the doctrine of revelation. With each of these fundamental theological questions, Alison's Girardian epistemology creates the capacity for deepening our understanding.

First, I will develop more fully my consideration in Chapter 4 of the status of doctrines within an inductive theology. My intent there was to help readers of Alison's work to conceptualize the difference that an inductive theology might make for how one approaches several basic theological questions. Here, I would like to extend my exploration to consider more specifically the nature and value of doctrines in light of Alison's conception of the ongoing ecclesial experience of conversion.

Second, I will consider the doctrine of revelation in particular as it might be expressed from a perspective shaped by an inductive theology. Drawing on Alison's treatments of both natural law and original sin presented earlier in this chapter, I will show how the doctrine of revelation might best be understood as both an attestation to God's ongoing self-communication, which culminated in the life, death, and resurrection of Jesus, and also a support for and a safeguard of the process of human knowing as one of ongoing discovery of self, God, and others.

5.3.1 An Inductive Theology of Doctrines?

At the beginning of the last chapter, I briefly considered the likely status of doctrines within a theological perspective informed by Alison's emphasis on the order of discovery.[41] There I asserted that the function of doctrines in relation to theological

---

[41] See Chapter 4 Section 4.1.2.

reflection is to delimit the perimeter within which "authentic" theological reflection can develop. And then I argued that, for Alison, the determining factor that makes theological reflection authentic is its capacity for either facilitating the removal of intellectual obstacles to persons' reception of forgiveness or appropriating and articulating in a new context the intelligence of the victim that is subverting the subject from within. This standard for discerning the authenticity of theological reflection within Alison's perspective is the result of his epistemology.[42] "Knowledge of salvation" (to use the Lucan phrase) or a deepening understanding of who God is and of God's desire for humanity can only ever be made possible through an ongoing reception of forgiveness that gradually exposes and removes the subject's blindness—a blindness that results from operating according to an intelligence of death.

From the perspective of Alison's inductive theology, we could understand doctrines as formalizing an aspect of faith that the collective experience of the community of witnesses to the risen Christ has consistently come to perceive and confirm as an essential component of the intelligence operative in the mind of Christ. These aspects of faith are "essential" in the sense that the community's reflection on their ongoing experience of conversion has led the community to conclude that without this particular understanding being operative in the mind of Christ, the offer of forgiveness received by the community of Christian witnesses would not have been, nor would it continue to be, possible. In *Why Doctrines?*, Charles Hefling explains that there is a reciprocal relationship between a community and its doctrines and that this is particularly true of the Christian community. Prior to the reciprocal relationship between the Christian community and its doctrines, there is a more foundational reciprocity between the community and their shared experience of conversion to the crucified and risen Christ.[43] Christian doctrines articulate what the Christian community comes to know in faith about God and humanity through the community's ongoing transformation into witnesses of the crucified and risen Christ.

By formalizing this knowledge known through faith, doctrines preserve and announce it, thereby delimiting a perimeter for theological reflection. Such a boundary is meant to keep reflection upon each mystery of faith attuned to the fullness of the life of God in Christ, which brings people to "the knowledge of salvation by the forgiveness of their sins."[44] Because they maintain an explicit acknowledgment of the essential components of Christian faith as it has been received, doctrines guide theological reflection toward elucidating the intelligence of forgiveness operative in the mind of Christ through an ongoing and deepening articulation of the coherence of that which persons have come to know through their induction into faith. Doctrines attest to the fullness of the intelligence of forgiveness, and they call those engaged in theological reflection to take account of that fullness in their effort to understand specific aspects of the intelligence of forgiveness for themselves and others.

---

[42] See Chapter 3 Section 3.1.1.
[43] Charles Hefling, *Why Doctrines?* (Cambridge: Cowley Publications, 1984), 65–70.
[44] Luke 1:77.

As formal statements of the intelligence of forgiveness, doctrines are the fruit of shared theological reflection through history and, therefore, the fruit of conversion. They represent, in acute form, the basic belief that language can become signs of who God is, who we have been, and who we are being invited to become in Christ Jesus. They are formal statements of belief that have been arrived at over time and as a result of a slow process of human discovery and appropriation of the intelligence of forgiveness. They are not ahistorical statements crafted by God and inserted into human minds. Rather, they are the fruit of the process of human transformation and reconciliation to God that God is effecting through Christ. As such, doctrines themselves are signs of redemption to the extent that they are signs of the possibility that human language, which from the beginning of human history has been formed in rivalry generated by the fear of death, can become an instrument for expressing the human proclamation of God's vivaciousness and triumph over death.

As historical proclamations of the vivaciousness of God, doctrines call for ongoing theological reflection to develop the meaning of Christian faith and its central mysteries within the specific historical and relational contexts of particular individuals and communities. They call for theological reflection that addresses persons in the midst of the circumstances of their lives so as to (1) foster authentic curiosity within them concerning the living God and (2) speak to the intellectual components of their honest objections to, and misunderstandings of, particular aspects of faith. This attentive and responsive address aims to invite persons to an interior awareness of how a still unthematized desire for and/or resistance to forgiveness might undergird their curiosity, objections, and misunderstandings. That is, theological reflection of this kind should invite persons into a curiosity about, and an awareness of, the intrinsic relationship between the mode of their relationality and their capacity for theological understanding.

With the help of theological reflection that addresses persons in the midst of their life circumstances, doctrines can facilitate new and renewed occasions of encounter by drawing out persons' ambivalent and hidden responses to their need for forgiveness. If an understanding of particular doctrines is articulated in such a way so as to foster an awareness of this need, they can prepare the way for an encounter with the crucified and risen Christ that offers forgiveness, not as a form of humiliation, but as an invitation into becoming fully human.

Thus, an inductive approach to doctrines is exceedingly pastoral in its aim and orientation. Charles Hefling affirms this pastoral aim of doctrines as he describes them as fruits of the experience of Christian conversion. He develops the thesis that

> [Doctrines] articulate Christianity's announcement, draw out its implications, state what it does and does not mean. Like the message itself, doctrines belong to the outer aspect of Christianity, and hence they are important in so far as the Christian story is intrinsically bound up with Christian conversion and the new life it generates.[45]

---

[45] Hefling, *Why Doctrines?*, 9.

Describing the relationship between doctrines and faith, Hefling writes, "For it is the unmerited and unconditional love which generates the convictions of faith, and it is in light of faith that one can discern the evidence, the warrants, the reasons that count decisively in choosing to believe the particular teachings of a particular religion."[46] Like Alison's inductive approach, Hefling's explanation of the value of doctrines strives to make explicit the intrinsic relationship between the "inner" and "outer" aspects of Christianity. Although doctrines may be part of the "outer" aspect in that they are external articulations, they are not "extrinsic to the church but intrinsic to its ongoing life."[47] Their meanings are not communicable if they are severed from the ongoing life and discernment of the community of witnesses of the risen Christ out of which they have arisen.

Yet Hefling also identifies the propositional nature of doctrines as performing a regulative function that coheres with the Alisonian perspective I have been developing here. He says, "Conciliar doctrines regulate what the Christian community *says* about the source of its salvation by means of propositions *about* what it says."[48] In other words, if theological reflection is part of the Christian community's act of "saying" what it says about its salvation, then doctrines constitute the boundaries, identified by the Christian community itself, that determine what counts as authentic reflection on the Christian story. Yet part of that reflection should also include a healthy and faithful questioning of the internal validity of specific boundaries. Thus, as we said above, the Christian community and doctrines reciprocally form one another.

This Alisonian view of doctrines, supported and developed by Hefling's thorough consideration of why doctrines are essential to the Christian community, can also be helpfully contrasted with George Lindbeck's classic classification of various approaches to understanding doctrines.[49] Lindbeck labels his identification of three basic approaches to religion, theology, and religious doctrines as (1) cognitive-propositional, (2) experiential-expressive, and (3) a Roman Catholic attempt to integrate them both. Lindbeck draws out the contrast between the first two approaches and describes what he sees as the inadequacy of each of them, as well as the third, before proposing his own model, which he calls a cultural-linguistic approach.

There is some significant commonality between the understanding of doctrines that I have been developing here and Lindbeck's cultural-linguistic model, which advocates a "regulative" or "rule" theory of doctrines.[50] In this view, doctrines are to theology and the Christian narrative as grammatical rules are to a particular language. Both doctrines and grammatical rules are articulated only as a language has developed to a point that its users are able to reflect upon it and come to a consensus about what constitutes proficient usage (of English, Chinese, or Christian narrative and symbols, Islamic ones, etc.). These rules articulate the present boundaries of meaningful and coherent speech.

---

[46] Ibid., 32.
[47] Ibid., 134.
[48] Ibid., 170; Hefling's emphasis.
[49] George Lindbeck, *The Nature of Doctrine* (Philadelphia, PA: Westminster Press, 1984).
[50] Such a view of doctrines is also consistent with Robert Schreiter's approach to the question of the Gospel and inculturation. See especially his *Constructing Local Theologies* (New York: Orbis, 1985).

We have already seen that Alison's inductive approach advocates a similar view of doctrines. Indeed, the very notion of "induction" as I have been using it to describe Alison's theological method resonates well with a view of religions that treats religion as a kind of culture with a corresponding language. Cultures, through the medium of language, induct subjects into being. That is, cultures give persons the words, symbols, behaviors, and, ultimately, the meanings of each, through which persons come to know, understand, and relate to themselves and others. "Induction" into the community of Christian witnesses, as I have used it to describe Alison's theological method, involves the gradual reception and appropriation of an intelligence (i.e., a set of meanings) that reveals the limitations and falsity of previously held understandings and enables persons to become themselves more fully and more authentically, and then to relate to others accordingly.

Yet, there is also a fundamental difference between Lindbeck's classification of these approaches to doctrine, including his own proposal of a cultural-linguistic approach, and the "inductive theology of doctrines" that I have begun to develop here. This difference can be seen most clearly by considering Lindbeck's treatment of the cognitive-propositional and the experiential-expressive approaches. His cultural and nontheological assessment of these two approaches continues and deepens a falsely dichotomous view of doctrines, to which Alison's inductive approach is an explicit response. Historically speaking, the development of an extreme "cognitive-propositional" view of doctrines, such as in segments of the Catholic Church around the time of the Reformation and to some extent codified by the Council of Trent, demonstrates the operation of a nontheological view of doctrines within the Catholic Church itself. A view of doctrines as cognitive propositions with little or no articulation of their intrinsic relationship to the experience of receiving the faith that makes such propositions understandable and potentially believable has already abandoned a truly theological perspective in which such an articulation would be foundational for any account of the nature and status of doctrines.

The development of what Lindbeck calls an experiential-expressive view of doctrines (such as that which might be associated with the school of Protestant Liberalism beginning in the 1800s) as a reaction against the previous nontheological, cognitive-propositional view only fostered an antagonistic and rivalrous relationship between what we could consider to be two equally nontheological approaches to doctrine. The fostering of such a rivalry leads to a strong climate of opposition between these two perspectives—the first of which could be labeled "objective" and the second "subjective"—which then leads to the entrenchment of this basic misperception of doctrines; namely, that they are not dependent upon an intrinsic relationship between interior experience and statements of belief.

Lindbeck's characterization of these two approaches maintains the common understanding that they are mutually exclusive positions with little or no room for mutual clarification or interdependence. And his dismissal of the more recent Roman Catholic attempt at integration could be seen as a confirmation of his underlying assumption of an intrinsic incompatibility between the previous two approaches. Alison's theological perspective, on the other hand, attempts to make clear the inadequacy of any understanding of Christianity or Christian doctrines that does not perceive the intrinsic relationship between the "objective" and "subjective," or "outer" and "inner," dimensions of faith. With his emphasis on the order of discovery, he deliberately intends to show the interdependency of these dimensions.

Lindbeck's equally nontheological presentation of his own cultural-linguistic approach can be seen as at least having the potential to continue the oppositional and dichotomous view of doctrines previously maintained by a rivalrous relationship between the "propositionalists" and the "expressivists." In Alison's perspective, only the intelligence of forgiveness, incarnate most fully in the crucified and risen Christ—that is, only a properly theological account of doctrines—is capable of showing doctrines' function as regulative propositions and their intrinsic relationship to the experience of receiving faith (*fides qua*). Only a theological perspective that arises from the transformation effected by forgiveness is also free of the blindness that results from an underlying fear of death and that generates the misperception of an irreconcilable dichotomy between the objective and subjective dimensions of faith specifically, and of being human more generally.

Lindbeck's cultural-linguistic approach to doctrines attempts to overcome the dichotomy created by the two previous approaches by comparing religion to a culture with a unique language and narrative. Here doctrines are the grammar that regulates how the story is told and sets the boundaries of competent or "orthodox" usage of a particular religious language. Such a cultural model allows room for both the propositional and the experiential elements of doctrines.

However, a Girardian theological perspective like Alison's would reply that, while Lindbeck's cultural-linguistic approach includes both the experiential and propositional elements of Christianity, it does not provide any means for discerning the truthfulness of its propositions or the goodness of its core experiences outside of its own system. From a thoroughly theological perspective, Alison asserts that a person or community's ability to perceive both the intrinsic relationship between the basic religious experience of conversion in the presence of Christ and the propositional statements of belief, as well as the connection of those experiences and propositions to something that is objectively true even "prior to" the subjects' experience and knowledge of them, requires the kind of conversion that gradually transforms persons' perception, memory, imagination, and mode of belonging. This conversion, via the reception of forgiveness, enables persons to see the world anew through a framework of forgiveness, which reveals the vivaciousness of God to be the deepest reality undergirding the whole of the created world. Alison describes reality or truth quite poetically in an essay on prayer, where he says, "rather it is [the] hugely leisured, creative abundance [of God] that is the underlying reality."[51]

Thus, Lindbeck's approach uses a model that allows for a truer understanding of the nature and function of doctrines to be possible, but his hesitancy to speak about an ultimate referent outside of the cultural and linguistic system of meaning that he delineates does not allow him to describe how someone might come to hold such a view

---

[51] Alison, "Prayer: A Case Study in Mimetic Anthropology," 15. This essay can be found online at http://www.jamesalison.co.uk/texts/eng54.html (accessed July 25, 2014) as well as in his recently published introduction to Christian faith, *Jesus the Forgiving Victim: Listening for the Unheard Voice* (Glenview, IL: DOERS Publishing, LLC, 2013).

of doctrines authentically or to offer any criteria on the basis of which someone might judge whether this particular system of doctrines and practices is capable of forming persons and communities in a way that approaches what is actually true and good.

Alison's Girardian perspective, on the other hand, could be used to develop precisely such criteria because it argues that the intelligence of the victim reveals what is true, while the intelligence of death continually conceals it. In a disagreement with the postmodern deconstructionists Jacques Derrida and Gianni Vattimo, Girard identifies the genuine concern for victims as the basic criterion for discriminating between a system that derives its meaning from that which is true and one that does not.[52] Along a similar trajectory, an Alisonian view of doctrines would assert that a doctrine that in fact points toward truth can be shown as supporting a genuine concern for victims and as facilitating the reception of forgiveness that is capable of healing the relationships between victims and perpetrators, outsiders and insiders.

5.3.2 The Doctrine of Revelation as a Safeguard of Human Knowing

Throughout the five excerpts above we have been able to see that Alison's inductive approach is formed by, and brings attention to, an epistemology that views the activity of knowing as a movement from blindness—false remembering, distorted perception, and death-bound imagination—to increasing sight that occurs through a process of discovery initiated and maintained by encounters in which the subject learns to receive forgiveness. Alison's treatment of the doctrine of original sin and his resulting theological anthropology suggest that this process of discovery is essential to the transformation and redemption of persons in that it is through the discoveries made possible by the reception of forgiveness that persons come to perceive the blindness that they are now beginning to leave behind, and to appropriate and articulate a new understanding of self, God, and others that gradually reforms their manner of relating. Alison also views the doctrine of original sin as keeping alive the possibility of an ever-deepening discovery of personal and communal blindnesses generated by a still unexposed fear of death. As a formal and visible expression of this possibility for discovering "the beam in my eye," the doctrine of original sin implies the central importance of this process of discovery in God's activity of reconciliation and redemption.

In my treatment of the excerpt on natural law above, we saw that Alison views the Catholic principle of natural law as an explicit affirmation in faith of the positive relationship between creation, that is, the whole of the created world as it exists here and now, and redemption, namely, the divine plan for bringing about the fullness of creation. This principle of affirmation provides the rationale for believers to attend to the human process of discovery with regard to the natural and social world and to employ those discoveries in light of their ongoing reception of forgiveness to develop, clarify, and correct their deepening understandings of self, God, and others. Thus, in

---

[52] See Girard's *I See Satan Fall Like Lightning*, 177 & 214. Cf. Wolfgang Palaver, *René Girard's Mimetic Theory*, 262–73.

affirming the existence of some positive relationship between what is now and what will be, the principle of natural law also implicitly affirms the inherent value of the process of ongoing discovery through which persons come to know.

Alison's inductive theological method, namely, theology in the order of discovery, affirms the centrality of the historical process of discovery as the means through which persons come to know themselves and the created world, and also as the means through which God chooses to reveal Godself to us. Alison views the doctrine of revelation as the Christian community's explicit pronouncement of this foundational affirmation—a pronouncement that acts as a human participation in the divine safeguard of the way that we come to know. The doctrine of revelation safeguards this aspect of humanity by affirming that God has chosen (and continues to choose) to make Godself known to us by becoming like us[53] and, therefore, becoming discoverable by us in the midst of our own historicity and under the conditions of our own process of discovery, distorted as it is by our formation in mimetic rivalry.[54]

According to Alison, one advantage of a theological anthropology informed by mimetic theory is its ability to offer a constructive view of the positive relationship between divine revelation and human history:

> [By] insisting on human alterity...as constitutive of what it is to be human, [this anthropology] permits us to consider divine revelation as a process of human discovery. That is to say, [revelation] is not frightened of the utterly contingent, human, historical process by which cultures arose and declined, events occurred, peoples were formed, events were reenacted, texts were brought in existence, [etc.]...It is not as though divine revelation needs somehow to be protected from all such happenings, in order to really be divine revelation. Rather it is precisely in the midst of such manifestly human happenings that divine revelation has occurred as a process of the self-manifestation of God that is simultaneously the coming into being of a certain intelligence regarding who human beings are.[55]

If human beings operate according to the dynamics of mimetic desire that Girard and Alison have elaborated, and if, therefore, we learn and develop through our fundamental orientation toward an "other," then we can understand the working of revelation throughout salvation history, and particularly in the person of Jesus Christ, as becoming accessible to persons precisely through our formation by the dynamics of mimetic desire within history. This means that God's self-manifestation to persons happens within the "normal" process of human discovery. This process occurs as

---

[53] Cf. Philippians 2:6-8; Romans 8:3.
[54] Grant Kaplan's chapter, "Mimetic Theory and Theology of Revelation," supports the theology of revelation as occurring within a process of human discovery that I am developing from Alison's perspective here. Kaplan's chapter also does the work of placing this understanding within the hermeneutical tradition of Hans-Georg Gadamer and Walter Ong which itself enabled a correction to the subject-object dualism that persisted in the Catholic theologies of revelation from the post-Vatican II era, particularly as articulated by Avery Dulles and René Latourelle. See *René Girard, Unlikely Apologist*, 69–101.
[55] Alison, *The Joy of Being Wrong*, 65.

persons find themselves undergoing an encounter with a new "other" who operates according to a truer understanding of who human beings are and who God is. This understanding or "intelligence" is not purely intellectual insight, since within this anthropology there is no such thing. Intelligence includes memory, perception, and imagination, and it both informs and is formed by the subject's relationships with particular others.[56]

Thus, Alison is describing an understanding of divine revelation that encounters human beings in our particular historicity and in our conscious or unconscious openness to such an encounter. This encounter makes both God and humanity discoverable for us. In Alison's words, "Revelation is the process of the discovery of who God is that is subversive of the culturally developed understanding of who humans are, and in turn is constitutive of a new identity of what humans are on the way to becoming."[57] He goes on to explain his assertion of an intrinsic and inseverable link between human knowing and the reception of forgiveness:

> I do not think that anything human could have revealed the constitution of the human consciousness in human victimization, because I do not think that we can accede to that sort of awareness of who we are without simultaneously being absolved of our complicity in violence.... I think all that because I believe in the forgiveness of sin. I would then refine my understanding of divine revelation to say that the discovery of who God really is has happened through the human process of discovery that human beings can forgive sin: that a divine prerogative has become human without ceasing to be divine.[58]

In other words, only the reception of forgiveness is capable of revealing to human beings who we are and who God is, and this revelation, as it is discovered by particular persons, is the necessary foundation for clear perception, remembering, and imagination of the whole of creation and of God.[59] If revelation is available and discoverable by humans through an encounter with an "other" who offers forgiveness, then within Alison's inductive theology, the doctrine of revelation should be understood in part as the church's official affirmation in faith of the validity and necessity of the process of human discovery within history as a means of access to knowing reality as it actually is.

Alison's view of the doctrine of revelation can be seen as consistent with other modern Catholic theological perspectives, while it also offers a valuable corollary

---

[56] Kaplan captures this distinction between the "purely" intellectual and the relational when he describes the truth being revealed through Jesus' message as "more closely resembling an interpersonal truth requiring conversion than an objective piece of information whose acceptance requires no particular effort." (Kaplan, *René Girard, Unlikely Apologist*, 93).

[57] Alison, *The Joy of Being Wrong*, 69.

[58] Ibid., 69–70.

[59] Drawing on both Girard and Alison, Kaplan beautifully describes revelation as a gradual reception of forgiveness: "Revelation occurs not so much in the suddenness of an event, but in the slow and painful coming-to-understand that unifies being forgiven with becoming conscious of one's sinfulness" (94).

concerning the affirmation of human knowing as capable of undergoing a discovery of who God is. Vatican II's *Dogmatic Constitution on Divine Revelation, Dei Verbum*, begins with the following description of divine revelation:

> In His goodness and wisdom God chose to reveal Himself and to make known to us the hidden purpose of His will (see Eph. 1:9) by which through Christ, the Word made flesh, man might in the Holy Spirit have access to the Father and come to share in the divine nature (see Eph. 2:18; 2 Peter 1:4). Through this revelation, therefore, the invisible God (see Col. 1;15, 1 Tim. 1:17) out of the abundance of His love speaks to men as friends (see Ex. 33:11; John 15:14–15) and lives among them (see Bar. 3:38), so that He may invite and take them into fellowship with Himself.[60]

The language of friendship here coheres well with an understanding that divine revelation takes place on the level of human relationality. God speaks with persons in the context of Christ's friendship with them. This friendship, which is the means of God's self-revelation, is also its goal. Here Vatican II acknowledges that human relationality is by no means an obstacle to divine revelation but is rather used and elevated by it. Alison, following Girard, emphasizes that human relationality is the necessary condition and context for human knowing and discovery.

In *Sacramentum Mundi*'s encyclopedic treatment of revelation, we also find an articulation of the positive relationship between revelation and history that resonates with Alison's view. Norbert Schiffers describes revelation as "the self-revelation of God in the OT, in Jesus and in the apostles, [which] does not define either God or man simply as 'non-world.' [Rather,] it announces that God is in the world so that men may be ordained to God in history."[61] Then citing Joseph Ratzinger's contribution to a commentary on the documents of Vatican II, Schiffers goes on to say, "Revelation as the one word of God is always there in the form of 'law and gospel', not as a timeless ideology but as a historical action of God which reaches men in this age and puts man in his place in the context of his history, as the setting of his salvation."[62] These brief statements of the developing understanding, following Vatican II, of revelation within history assert explicitly that divine revelation becomes accessible for, and discoverable by, persons precisely in their particular historical contexts. Revelation is God's action in human history to speak to persons and to reveal to them their history as the context of their salvation. Through the lens of a mimetic theory, Alison adds that acting within human history entails entering into the relational dynamics in and through which persons develop their self-understandings. Using the lens of the disciples' experience of the crucified and risen Christ, Alison adds further that this entry ultimately is the discovery of the forgiveness of sins, which becomes a new model of friendship for us.

---

[60] *Dei Verbum* 1, 2.
[61] Norbert Schiffers, "Revelation," in *Sacramentum Mundi*, Volume 5 (New York: Herder and Herder, 1970), 348. Shiffers cites Karl Jaspers' *Philosophie*, volume 2 for his use of the phrase "non-world."
[62] Schiffers, "Revelation," 348. Cf. Josef Ratzinger's entry in H. Vorgrimmler, ed. *Commentary on the Documents of Vatican II*, Volume III (Palm Publishers, Montréal, Québec Canada, 1968[1969]), 172ff.

Considering the doctrine of revelation from Alison's inductive approach, we see that, by affirming the action of God in history to speak to persons precisely in their historicity, the doctrine also affirms the context of human relationality and the process of human discovery insofar as they open persons to the possibility of transformation through an encounter with one who offers forgiveness. As I quoted Alison above, "the discovery of who God really is has happened through the human process of discovery that human beings can forgive sin: that a divine prerogative has become human without ceasing to be divine." By becoming human, the Son made the human capacity to forgive sins discoverable and, by offering forgiveness to those friends who had abandoned him, the crucified and risen Christ enabled the disciples to discover the practice of the forgiveness of sins as a path to friendship with God. Thus, the doctrine of revelation, while attesting to God's ongoing self-communication to persons in history (a communication which culminated in the life, death, and resurrection of Jesus), also strongly affirms the potential of human understanding and relationality to receive forgiveness and thereby gradually discover the vivaciousness of God. In doing so, the doctrine of revelation can be seen as a formal theological safeguard for understanding human knowing as a process of discovery initiated by the forgiveness of sins.

5.4 Conclusion

In this closing chapter, we have seen how Alison's understanding of the reciprocal relationship between conversion and theological reflection shapes not only his understanding of the theological task, but also his own practice of theological reflection and writing. In the five selected excerpts above we have glimpsed the consistency with which Alison undertakes the theological task as an explicit attempt to open persons to the possibility of new and ongoing experiences of discovering God's offer of forgiveness in Christ Jesus. He employs all disciplines of theology toward this end.

We saw that he uses a form of apologetic theology to address persons who may have become closed to seeing a particular Christian doctrine or a particular sociological or scientific discovery as potentially revelatory of the living God. He uses historical and liturgical theology to uncover past practices and understandings within the tradition that were well attuned to inviting persons to discover God's redemptive and reconciling action as moving toward them with mercy. He uses a systematic theology to draw out the coherence of the creative and eschatological imagination of Jesus and to point persuasively to what seems to him undeniable, namely, the utter vivaciousness of God, who has undertaken a never-ending project to offer persons the possibility of living without fear of death.

Alison takes a constructive or reconstructive approach in his articulation of the doctrine of original sin to uncover this doctrine's capacity to joyfully proclaim to persons the freedom that comes when they recognize that they no longer have to be bound into a perpetual framework of accusation, even though they may have spent most of their lives so bound. Taking a pastoral approach to addressing LGBTQ Catholics, Alison invites them to see themselves as an integral part of the construction of a new church, one which does not have to be defined by the old exclusions, nor by new exclusions to replace the old, but instead by choosing to live the freedom of the forgiving victim. With these excerpts as representative of Alison's practice of an inductive theology, we were able to see in greater detail how his use of mimetic theory and its associated epistemology produces a theological method that seeks to become an ongoing occasion of encounter for both those who articulate it and those who receive it.

We then saw how Alison's inductive theological method might be employed to shed light on several contemporary theological questions by beginning to articulate an Alisonian theological anthropology, a theology of doctrines, and a theology of revelation. His inductive theology provides the basis for a theological anthropology informed by mimetic theory through his theological inquiry into the disciples' experience of meeting the crucified and risen Christ. It understands human beings as desiring imitators who are always and everywhere formed according to the frameworks of desire and belonging of their most influential models. This formation is always more or less in a mode of blindness, accusation and rivalry, which is how Alison understands the dynamics of sin, or in a mode of clear-sightedness, forgiveness, and loving imitation of a forgiving model that reveals our previous sinfulness, which is how Alison understands the dynamics of grace. By focusing our attention on the disciples' discovery of the utter vivaciousness of God in their experiences of Jesus' resurrection, which exposes to them their own underlying belief in the ultimacy of death, Alison's theological anthropology also makes a significant contribution to mimetic theory. It brings into relief some of the confusion around the meanings of key terms—a confusion produced in part by the development in Girard's articulation of mimetic theory, as illustrated in Chapter 2. The invitation of the crucified and risen Christ to the disciples to imitate his peaceful imitation of his Father, who is unhindered by death, places positive or loving mimesis at the center of mimetic theory, making fully evident that mimetic desire is not identical with mimetic rivalry or positive mimesis, but that these are the two modes in which mimetic desire can operate. Mimetic desire is thereby affirmed as the given network of connectivity in which human relationality and human subjectivity become possible.

My effort to articulate a theology of doctrines and of revelation from an Alisonian perspective applies his inductive theology and his understanding of the reciprocal relationship between conversion and theological reflection to better understand Christian doctrines and revelation within the framework of discovery that characterizes human knowing. Within this framework, Christian doctrines are a fruit of communal theological reflection on the ongoing experience of encounter with the crucified and risen Christ, and they become a grammar that helps the Christian community to keep alive the active, reciprocal relationship between our theological understandings and our experiences of conversion. The doctrine of revelation from an Alisonian perspective builds on Alison's understanding of conversion through the reception of forgiveness as the means by which human beings are able to gradually come to understand and appropriate more fully the intelligence of forgiveness that makes Jesus' living, dying, and rising possible. It is a formal affirmation that the process of human discovery through relationships by which we come to receive our subjectivity as human beings must also shape our reception of the intelligence operative in the mind of Christ, which reveals to us who God is and who we are.

I would like to conclude by elaborating further Alison's view of the task and vocation of the theologian, which I developed at the end of Chapters 3 and 4. Alison's inductive theology operates according to the fundamental assumption that the task of the theologian involves using all his or her theological, historical, and pastoral knowledge, as well as all of the tools for communication at his or her disposal, to point to the forgiving and reconciling activity of God in Christ as active on behalf of all of creation, now, in this ever new, present moment. It places a strong emphasis on the "now-ness" of God's aliveness, not as already fully realized, but as already and always fully active in its offer of eternal life. His theology is inductive; that is, it seeks to act as an occasion of an encounter with Christ that enables forgiveness, which in turn inducts persons into the living of forgiveness and into becoming witnesses of the living, always active nowness of God's offer of forgiveness in Christ. Of course, Alison's inductive theology does not end with this proclamation, but it must begin with it and it must always keep it at the fore if the one reflecting is to participate in God's act of communication to persons.

From proclamation, this inductive theology must move to participate in the redemption of language. Through the gradual transformation of his or her own perception, memory, imagination, and patterns of belonging, the theologian becomes increasingly empowered to take language formed in a mode of accusation, rivalry, and death and re-form words into vessels of the utter vivaciousness of God, who offers forgiveness to all persons simply because this is what God desires.

Alison recognizes that theological reflection capable of participating in God's activity of communication cannot be separated from the transformation of the mode of perceiving, remembering, imagining, and belonging of the one reflecting, nor can it be separated from the modes of perceiving, remembering, imagining, and belonging of those who are able to receive those reflections. Only as our human capacities begin to be formed according to the utter vivaciousness of God can we learn to participate in the reception of forgiveness and the intelligence of the forgiving victim. Only as we become such receivers, in imitation of Jesus' imitation of the Father, can we participate in God's ever-present and always active offering of forgiveness to all persons and, indeed, to all of creation.

As we saw in Chapter 4, Alison is clear that the "place" of potential encounter with the Spirit of Christ cannot be made any narrower than *"wherever there are humans to be reconciled—the field of opportunity is universal."*[63] The human need for reconciliation is the only necessary condition for the Spirit of Christ to begin inducting persons into forgiven forgivers and self-accepted witnesses to, and imitators of, the crucified and risen Christ. And through their appropriation and articulation of an intelligence of forgiveness, they become potential occasions of encounter for others.

---

[63] Alison, *The Joy of Being Wrong*, 92; my emphasis.

Bibliography

1. Primary Sources for René Girard (Original French Editions Follow in Parentheses)

Deceit, Desire, and the Novel: Self and Other in Literary Structure. Translated by Yvonne Freccero. Baltimore/London: Johns Hopkins University Press, 1976. (*Mensonge romantique et vérité Romanesque*. Paris: Grasset, 1961).
Violence and the Sacred. Translated by Patrick Gregory. Baltimore: Johns Hopkins University Press, 1977. (*La Violence et le Sacré*. Paris: Grasset, 1972).
"To Double Business Bound": Essays on Literature, Mimesis and Anthropology. Baltimore: Johns Hopkins University Press, 1978.
The Scapegoat. Translated by Yvonne Freccero. Baltimore: Johns Hopkins University Press, 1986 [Reprinted: 1989]. (*Le Bouc émissaire*. Paris: Grasset, 1982).
Job: The Victim of His People. Stanford, CA: Stanford University Press, 1987. (*La Route Antique des hommes pervers; Essais sur Job*. Paris: Grasset, 1985).
Things Hidden since the Foundation of the World. Research undertaken in collaboration with Jean-Michel Oughourlian and Guy Lefort. Translated by Stephen Bann and Michael Metteer. Stanford, CA: Stanford University Press, 1987. (*Des Choses caches depuis la foundation du monde*. Paris: Grasset, 1978).
"The Founding Murder in the Philosophy of Nietzsche." In Paul Dumouchel, ed. *Violence and Truth*. Stanford, CA: Stanford University Press, 1988, 227–46.
A Theater of Envy: William Shakespeare. New York/Oxford: Oxford University Press, 1991. [Reprinted: Gracewing Press, 2000].
Girard, René and Rebecca Adams. "Violence, Difference, Sacrifice: A Conversation with René Girard." *Religion and Literature* 25.2 (1993): 11–33.
Girard, René and James Williams. "The Anthropology of the Cross: A Conversation with René Girard." In James Williams, ed. *The Girard Reader*. New York: Crossroad Herder, 1996, 262–88.
Resurrection from the Underground: Feodor Dostoevsky. Edited and Translated by James G. Williams. New York: Crossroad Herder, 1997. (*Dostoievski: Du double a l'unité*. Paris: Plon, 1963).
I See Satan Fall Like Lightning. Translated by James G. Williams. New York: Orbis Books, 2001. (*Je vois Satan tomber comme l'éclair*. Paris: Grasset, 1999).
Celui par qui le scandala arrive. Paris, France: Desclée de Brouwer, 2001.
Oedipus Unbound: Selected Writings on Rivalry and Desire. Stanford, CA: Stanford University Press, 2004.
Girard, René, with Pierpaolo Antonello and Joao Cezar de Castro Rocha. *Evolution and Conversion: Dialogues on the Origins of Culture*. London/New York: T&T Clark Continuum, 2007. (*Le origines de la culture*. Paris: Desclee de Brouwer, 2004).
Girard, René and Robert Doran. "An Interview with René Girard." *SubStance*, issue 115, 37.1 (2008): 20–32.

Mimesis and Theory: Essays on Literature and Criticism, 1953–2005. Stanford, CA: Stanford University Press, 2008.

2. Primary Sources for James Alison

Knowing Jesus. Springfield, IL: Templegate Publishers/London: SPCK Publishing, 1994.
"Girard's Breakthrough." *The Tablet* (June 29, 1996): 848–9.
Raising Abel: The Recovery of Eschatological Imagination. New York: Crossroads, 1996. [Reprinted: *Living in the End Times*. London: SPCK Publishing, 1997].
"The Man Blind from Birth and the Subversion of Sin." *Theology and Sexuality* 7 (Summer 1997): 83–102.
The Joy of Being Wrong: Original Sin through Easter Eyes. New York: Crossroad Herder, 1998.
"Theology amid the Stones and Dust." *Theology and Sexuality* 11 (Summer 1999): 91–114.
Faith beyond Resentment: Fragments Catholic and Gay. New York: Crossroads/London: DLT, 2001.
On Being Liked. New York: Crossroads/London: DLT, 2004.
Undergoing God: Dispatches from the Scene of a Break-in. New York: Continuum/London: DLT, 2006.
"Violence Undone: James Alison on Jesus as Forgiving Victim." *Christian Century* 123.18 (September 5, 2006): 30–5.
"Blindsided by God." *Anglican Theological Review* 89.2 (Spring 2007): 195–212.
"God's Self Substitution and Sacrificial Inversion." In Brad Jersak and Michael Hardin, eds. *Stricken by God? Nonviolent Identification and the Victory of Christ*. Grand Rapids, MI: Eerdmans Publishing, 2007, 166–79.
"Taking the Plunge: Immersed in Theology." *Christian Century* 124.4 (February 20, 2007): 8–9.
"Wrath and the Gay Question: On Not Being Afraid, and Its Ecclesiastical Shape." *St. Mark's Review* 202 (2007): 10–18.
Broken Hearts and New Creations. New York: Continuum/London: DLT, 2010.
Jesus the Forgiving Victim: Listening for the Unheard Voice. Glenview, IL: DOERS Publishing, 2013.
"This Is Pope Francis…" *The Tablet* (September 28, 2019): 14–16.

3. Select Secondary Sources on Girard and Alison

Alberg, Jeremiah. *Beneath the Veil of the Strange Verses: Reading Scandalous Texts*. East Lansing: Michigan State University Press, 2013.
Bailie, Gil. *Violence Unveiled: Humanity at the Crossroads*. New York: Crossroads, 1995.
Bellan-Boyer, Lisa. "Conspicuous in Their Absence: Women in Early Christianity." *Cross Currents* 53.1 (Spring 2003): 48–63.
Cowdell, Scott. *René Girard and Secular Modernity: Christ, Culture, and Crisis*. Notre Dame, IN: Notre Dame University Press, 2013.
Daly, Robert J. *The Origins of the Christian Doctrine of Sacrifice*. Philadelphia, PA: Fortress Press, 1978.
Daly, Robert J. "Is Christianity Sacrificial or Anti-Sacrificial?" *Religion* 27 (1997): 231–43.

Daly, Robert J. "Violence and Institution in Christianity." *Contagion* (Spring 2002): 4–33.
Daly, Robert J. *Sacrifice Unveiled: The True Meaning of Christian Sacrifice*. New York: Continuum, 2009.
Davies, Oliver. "Soundings: Towards a Theological Poetics of Silence." In Oliver Davies and Denys Turner, eds. *Silence and the Word: Negative Theology and Incarnation*. Cambridge/New York: Cambridge University Press, 2002, 201–22.
Depoortere, Frederiek. *Christ in Postmodern Philosophy: Gianni Vattimo, Rene Girard, and Slavoj Zizek*. New York: Continuum, 2008.
Dumouchel, Paul, ed. *Violence and Truth: On the Work of Rene Girard*. Stanford, CA: Stanford University Press, 1988.
Edwards, John P. "The Self Prior to Mimetic Desire: Rahner and Alison on Original Sin and Conversion." *Horizons* 35.1 (Spring 2008): 7–31.
Edwards, John P. "Being Freed from the Illusion of the Enemy: James Alison on Contemplative Prayer and Eucharistic Liturgy." In *Who Is My Enemy? Religious Hope in a Time of Fear. Selected Papers from the Theology Institute* 42 (Villanova, PA: Villanova University Press, 2011): 1–16.
Edwards, John P. "From a 'Revealed' Psychology to Theological Inquiry: James Alison's Theological Appropriation of Girard." *Contagion, Journal of Violence, Mimesis, and Culture* 21 (2014): 121–31.
Fleming, Chris. *Rene Girard: Violence and Mimesis*. Cambridge/Oxford: Polity, 2004.
Fraser, Giles. *Christianity and Violence: Girard, Nietzsche, Anselm, Tutu*. London: Darton, Longman and Todd, 2001.
Galvin, John P. "Jesus as Scapegoat? *Violence and the Sacred* in the Theology of Raymund Schwager." *The Thomist* 46 (1982): 173–94.
Galvin, John P. "The Marvellous Exchange: Raymund Schwager's Interpretation of the History of Soteriology." *The Thomist* 53 (1989): 675–91.
Golsan, Richard J., ed. *René Girard and Myth: An Introduction*. New York/London: Garland Publishing Inc., 1993.
Hamerton-Kelly, Robert G. *Sacred Violence: Paul's Hermeneutic of the Cross*. Philadelphia, PA: Fortress Press, 1991.
Hamerton-Kelly, Robert G. *The Gospel and the Sacred: Poetics of Violence in Mark*. Philadelphia, PA: Fortress Press, 1993.
Hamerton-Kelly, Robert G., ed. *Politics and Apocalypse*. East Lansing, MI: Michigan State University Press, 2007.
Hefling, Charles C. "A View from the Stern: James Alison's Theology (So Far)." *Anglican Theological Review* 81.4 (Fall 1999): 689–710.
Hefling, Charles C. "About What *Might* a 'Girard-Lonergan Conversation' Be?" *Lonergan Workshop* 17 (2002): 95–123.
Heim, S. Mark. *Saved from Sacrifice: A Theology of the Cross*. Grand Rapids, MI: Eerdmans Publishing Company, 2006.
Henrichs, Albert. "Loss of Self, Suffering, and Violence: The Modern View of Dionysius from Nietzsche to Girard." In Shackleton Bailey and David Roy, eds. *Harvard Studies in Classical Philology*, 88. Cambridge: Harvard University Press, 1984, 205–40.
Hunsinger, George. "The Politics of the Nonviolent God: Reflections on René Girard and Karl Barth." *Scottish Journal of Theology* 51.1 (1998): 61–85.
Jordan, Trevor L. "Scapegoating Girard: Violence and the Future of Religion." *St. Mark's Review* 202 (2007): 31–8.
Kaplan, Grant. *Unlikely Apologist: René Girard and Fundamental Theology*. Notre Dame, IN: University of Notre Dame Press, 2015.

Kerr, Fergus. "Rescuing Girard's Argument?" *Modern Theology* 8.4 (October 1992): 385–99.

Kerr, Fergus. "Revealing the Scapegoat Mechanism: Christianity after Girard." In Michael McGhee, ed. *Philosophy, Religion and the Spiritual Life*. New York/Cambridge: Cambridge University Press, 1992, 161–75.

Kirwan, Michael. *Discovering Girard*. London: DLT, 2004; Cambridge: Cowley Publications, 2005.

Kirwan, Michael. *Girard and Theology*. London/New York: Continuum, 2009.

Kofman, Sarah. "The Narcissistic Woman: Freud and Girard." In Toril Moi, ed. *French Feminist Thought: A Reader*. Oxford, UK; New York, NY: Blackwell Publishing, 1987, 210–26.

Lagarde, François. *René Girard ou la christianisation des sciences humaines*. New York: Peter Lang, 1994.

Livingston, Paisley. *Models of Desire: Rene Girard and the Psychology of Mimesis*. Baltimore: Johns Hopkins University Press, 1992.

Marr, Andrew. "Violence and the Kingdom of God: Introducing the Anthropology of René Girard." *Anglican Theological Review* 80.4 (Fall 1998): 590–603.

Moi, Toril. "The Missing Mother: The Oedipal Rivalries of René Girard." *Diacritics* 12 (1982): 21–31.

Mongrain, Kevin. "Theologians of Spiritual Transformation: A Proposal for Reading René Girard through the Lenses of Hans Urs von Balthasar and John Cassian." *Modern Theology* 28.1 (2012): 81–111.

Nowak, Susan. "The Girardian Theory and Feminism: Critique and Appropriation." *Contagion* (Spring 1994): 19–29.

Oughourlian, Jean M. *The Puppet of Desire*. Stanford, CA: Stanford University Press, 1991. (*Une Mime Nommé Desir*. Paris: Grasset, 1982).

Palaver, Wolfgang. *René Girard's Mimetic Theory*. East Lansing, MI: Michigan State University Press, 2013.

Pius Ojara, S. J. and Patrick Madigan. *Marcel, Girard, Bakhtin: The Return of Conversion*. New York: Peter Lang, 2004.

Rike, Jennifer. "The Cycle of Violence and Feminist Construction of Selfhood." *Contagion* 3 (Spring 1996): 21–42.

Robinette, Brian D. *Grammars of Resurrection: A Christian Theology of Presence and Absence*. New York: Crossroads, 2009.

Ross, Suzanne. "The Montessori Method: The Development of a Healthy Pattern of Desire in Early Childhood." *Contagion* 19 (2012): 87–122.

Schwager, Raymund. *Jesus of Nazareth: How He Understood His Life*. New York: Crossroads, 1998.

Schwager, Raymund. *Jesus in the Drama Salvation*. New York: Crossroads, 1999.

Schwager, Raymund. *Banished from Eden: Original Sin and Evolutionary Theory in the Drama of Salvation*. Leominster, Herefordshire: Gracewing Publishing, 2006.

Shanks, Andrew. *Against Innocence: Gillian Rose's Reception and Gift of Faith*. London: SCM Press, 2008.

Skerrett, K. Roberts. "Desire and Anathema: Mimetic Rivalry in Defense of Plentitude." *Journal of the American Academy of Religion* 71.4 (December 2003): 793–809.

Taylor, S. J. "Save Us from Being Saved: Girard's Critical Soteriology." *Contagion* 12–13 (2006): 21–30.

Wallace, Mark I. "Postmodern Biblicism: The Challenge of René Girard for Contemporary Theology." *Modern Theology* 5 (1989): 309–25.

Wallace, Mark I. and Theophus H. Smith, eds. *Curing Violence: Essays on Rene Girard*. Sonoma, CA: Polebridge Press, 1994.

Watson, P. J. "Girard and Integration: Desire, Violence and the Mimesis of Christ as Foundation for Postmodernity." *Journal of Psychology and Theology* 26.4 (Winter 1998): 311–21.

Weaver, Darlene Fozard. "How Sin Works: A Review Essay." *Journal of Religious Ethics* 29.3 (Fall 2001): 473–501.

Webb, Eugene. *Philosophers of Consciousness: Polanyi, Lonergan, Voegelin, Ricoeur, Girard, Kierkegaard*. Seattle: University of Washington Press, 1989.

Webb, Eugene. *The Self Between: From Freud to the New Social Psychology of France*. Seattle: University of Washington Press, 1993.

Williams, James G. *The Bible, Violence, and the Sacred: Liberation from the Myth of Sanctioned Violence*. San Francisco, CA: HarperSanFrancisco, 1991.

Williams, James G., ed. *The Girard Reader*. New York: Crossroads, 1996.

Wilson, Bruce. "What Do We Want and Why Do We Want It? Chasing after the Wind: Coquetry, Metaphysical Desire and God." *St. Mark's Review* 202 (2007): 3–9.

Wohlman, Avital. "René Girard et saint Augustin: anthropologie et théologie." *Recherches augustiniennes* 20 (1985): 257–303.

4. General Secondary Sources

Baldovin, John. *Bread of Life, Cup of Salvation: Understanding the Mass*. Lanham, MD/Oxford: Rowman and Littlefield Publishers, 2003.

Bauckham, Richard. *Jesus and the Eyewitnesses: The Gospels as Eyewitness Testimony*. Grand Rapids, MI: Eerdmans, 2006.

Baum, Gregory. *Man Becoming: God in Secular Experience*. New York: Seabury Press, 1979.

Baum, Gregory. *Religion and Alienation*. 2nd ed. New York: Orbis Books, 2001.

Brown, Raymond. *An Introduction to New Testament Christology*. Mahwah, NJ: Paulist Press, 1994.

Burridge, Richard. *What Are the Gospels? A Comparison with Graeco-Roman Biography*. Cambridge: Cambridge University Press, 1992.

Carr, Anne. "Theology and Experience in the Thought of Karl Rahner." *The Journal of Religion* 53.3 (July 1973): 359–76.

Chauvet, Louis Marie. *The Sacraments: The Word of God at the Mercy of the Body*. Collegeville, MN: Liturgical Press, 2001.

Conn, Walter. *Conversion: Perspectives on Personal and Social Transformation*. New York: Alba House, 1978.

Conn, Walter. *The Desiring Self: Rooting Pastoral Counseling and Spiritual Direction in Self-Transcendence*. New York: Paulist Press, 1998.

Conn, Walter. "From Oxford to Rome: Newman's Ecclesial Conversion." *Theological Studies* 68.3 (Fall 2007): 595–617.

Doran, Robert M. *Psychic Conversion and Theological Foundations*. 2nd ed. Milwaukee, WI: Marquette University Press, 2006.

Dunn, James D. G. *Jesus Remembered*. Grand Rapids, MI: Eerdmans Publishing, 2003.

Ford, David F. *Self and Salvation: Being Transformed*. Cambridge/New York: Cambridge University Press, 1999.

Greenberg, Steven. *Wrestling with God and Men*. Madison, WI: University of Wisconsin Press, 2005.

Haight, Roger. *Dynamics of Theology*. New York: Orbis Books, 2001.

Hauerwas, Stanley and L. Gregory Jones, eds. *Why Narrative? Readings in Narrative Theology*. Grand Rapids, MI: Eerdmans Publishing Company, 1989.

Hefling, Charles C. *Why Doctrines?* Cambridge: Cowley Publications, 1984.

Hengel, Martin. *Crucifixion: In the Ancient World and the Folly of the Message of the Cross*. Translated by John Bowden. Philadelphia, PA: Fortress Press, 1977.

Lindbeck, George. *The Nature of Doctrine*. Philadelphia, PA: Westminster Press, 1984.

Lonergan, Bernard. *Method in Theology*. 2nd ed. Toronto/Buffalo: University of Toronto Press, 1990.

McKelway, Alexander. "The Systematic Theology of Faith: A Protestant Perspective." In James Lee, ed. *Handbook of Faith*. Birmingham, AL: Religious Education Press, 1990, 164–200.

Michener, Ronald. *Postliberal Theology: A Guide for the Perplexed*. London/New York: T&T Clark, 2013.

Milbank, John. *Theology and Social Theory*. Oxford, UK; New York, NY: Blackwell Publishing, 1993.

Polyani, Michael. *The Tacit Dimension*. Chicago: University of Chicago Press, 1966.

Rahner, Karl., ed. *Sacramentum Mundi*, Volume 5. New York: Herder and Herder, 1970.

Rahner, Karl. "Theology and Anthropology." In *Theological Investigations*, Volume 9. London: DLT, 1972.

Rahner, Karl. "Considerations on the Active Role of the Person in the Sacramental Event." In *Theological Investigations*, Volume 14. Translated by David Bourke. New York: Seabury, 1976.

Ricoeur, Paul. *From Text to Action: Essays in Hermeneutics*, II. Evanston, IL: Northwestern University Press, 2007.

Schleiermacher, Friedrich. *Brief Outline on the Study of Theology*. Edinburgh: T&T Clark, 1850.

Schreiter, Robert. *Constructing Local Theologies*. New York: Orbis, 1985.

Tillich, Paul. *Systematic Theology*, Volume I. Chicago: University of Chicago Press, 1951.

Tillich, Paul. *Systematic Theology*, Volume II. Chicago: University of Chicago Press, 1957.

Tracy, David. "The Foundations of Practical Theology." In Don S. Browning, ed. *Practical Theology: The Emerging Fields in Theology*. New York: HaperCollins, 1982, 61–82.

Index

Alberg, Jeremiah 142–4
Alison, James
  biography 2–6, 108–9, 133–4, 146–7
  On Being Liked 5, 152–5
  Broken Hearts and New Creations 5, 83, 110, 166–71
  Faith beyond Resentment 103, 104, 107–9, 133–4
  Jesus the Forgiving Victim 5, 73
  The Joy of Being Wrong 1, 9–11, 72–3, 88–9, 92, 95–6, 99, 130–1, 160–2, 163–6, 188
  Knowing Jesus 4, 12, 67, 72–5, 77–80, 89, 98, 124–7, 129, 175
  Raising Abel 4, 70–3, 80, 87–8, 90–1, 96, 102, 106–7, 113–14, 121, 129
  Undergoing God, 156–9
animals 21, 37–9, 51
anthropology 9–10, 13–14, 21, 37–8, 50–1, 55–6, 58, 66
  literary-cultural 19, 35, 49, 177, 179–80
  theological 12, 19, 61–2, 72–3, 87, 150, 171–4, 179–80, 186–8, 189, 191
apologetics 15, 59–60, 111, 113–18, 120, 123, 138, 153, 172
ascension 129–31, 139

Balthasar, Hans Urs von 58
Barker, Margaret 155–7
Barth, Karl 137
Bauckham, Richard 16, 84–6
belonging 9, 82–3, 93, 103, 130–1, 171, 173–6, 179, 185, 191
Benedict XVI, pope 166–8

Cervantes, Miguel 21, 24, 31
Chauvet, Louis-Marie 94 n.84
Christ
  conversion to 8–9, 12, 15, 62, 65, 73, 76, 86, 95, 181

  crucified and risen 62, 65–6, 92, 94, 98, 118, 126, 129, 132, 142
  encounter with 52–3, 61, 83, 102, 107–8, 120, 128, 137, 145, 155, 158–9, 162, 168–9, 175–6, 191–2
  Spirit of 134, 137, 138, 141, 145, 146, 150, 160, 169
communion of saints 16, 59, 123–4, 129
conversion
  as a collapse 103–4, 107–9, 117, 119, 123, 149–50
  definition of 8–10, 12, 171–2, 174, 190–2
  and knowledge 95, 119, 123, 164–5, 185
  obstacles to 116, 118, 155, 159
  as reception of faith 12, 57, 61, 98, 114–15, 117–20, 124, 127, 159, 171, 181
  and subversion 94–5, 101–2, 105, 115, 149 (*see also* Christ, conversion to *and* grace and conversion)
Cowdell, Scott 10, 14, 42 n.83
creation 32, 109, 113, 151–4, 156–8, 186, 192
cross 80, 128, 163

death
  Alison's experiences of 3, 7
  and atonement 155–8
  belief in/fear of 89–93, 118, 127–9, 159–62, 171, 173, 176, 179, 182, 185, 186, 190
  disciples' experiences of Jesus' 76–80, 87–102, 106, 129, 142, 178
  Girard's treatment of 23–5, 30–2, 47 (*see also* intelligence of death)
doctrines 73, 111, 113–18, 120, 153–5, 180–6, 191
dominance patterns 39, 51

Dostoyevsky, Fyodor 21, 25, 29–31, 46
　The Brothers Karamazov 30
　Eternal Husband 24
　Notes from the Underground 30
　The Possessed 31–2

ecclesial 83–84, 86, 112, 114, 117–18, 140, 146, 149, 151, 153–5, 163–5, 168–71, 180
ecclesiology 11, 146, 172
encounter
　via a text 6–9, 82, 133–6, 142, 150
　via a witness 81, 83, 126–9, 136–9 (*see also* Christ, encounter with)
eschatology, eschatological 72, 121, 161–2, 190
Eucharist 23, 109, 146, 156

faith as *fides qua/fides quae* 57, 62, 114–15, 119–20, 123, 145, 185
Flaubert, Gustave 21, 24
Francis, pope 5 n.8, 168
forgiveness
　vs accusation 172–4
　and knowledge 185–6, 188–92
　and memory 70–1, 122–3
　offered by Christ 1, 9, 80, 127, 137–9, 142, 149
　received by believers 103–104, 109–15, 117–19, 169–71
　received by the disciples 16, 66, 76, 78, 88–9, 92–4, 97–9, 101, 106–8, 124–5, 162
　via texts 143–5, 112 (*see also* intelligence of forgiveness)
　and victims 130–2, 147, 163–5, 186
fundamental theology 11–13, 16, 21, 60, 172 (*see also* theological method)

Girard, René
　biography 21–4
　on conversion 31–5, 47–9, 52–5
　Deceit, Desire and the Novel/DDN 22–35, 52, 74–5
　Evolution and Conversion 21, 49–55, 72 n.15, 75 n.27
　on founding murder 40, 42 *I See Satan fall Like Lightning* 21, 49–57, 59
　on myth 41, 43, 45–6
　on prohibitions 39, 41–3
　on ritual 41–2, 46
　on rivals 33, 38–9, 43
　on scapegoats/scapegoating 20, 24, 46, 53, 60, 65
　Things Hidden since the Foundation of the World 6–8, 21, 35–49, 51–2, 74, 133–4 (*see also* mimetic theory)
God
　Father of Jesus 50, 53, 73, 79, 91, 95–97, 103–7, 128–9, 142, 146, 160–2, 178–9, 189, 191–2
　vivaciousness/deathlessness of 69, 91–3, 96–8, 106, 151, 158–62, 170–1, 173, 176–7, 182, 185, 190–2
grace
　christoformity of 130, 139
　and conversion 59–60
　and ethics 166–7, 169
　as forgiveness 12, 171–4, 179, 191

heaven 113, 131, 139
Hefling, Charles 181–3 hope 70 (*see also* eschatology)

imagination
　of the disciples 86–7, 91, 94, 104, 138, 169, 176–7
　as a human capacity 8, 70–72, 118, 121, 138, 141, 143, 169, 173
　Jesus'/eschatological 157–62, 170
incarnation 59, 91, 162
induction 8–9, 12, 16, 146, 162, 165, 171, 181, 184
intelligence
　behind the text of Scripture 56
　of death 70, 98–101, 143, 181, 186
　operative 68–71, 90, 94, 188
　of the lie 98–101, 109
　of the victim/of forgiveness 66, 95–7, 101, 105–7, 111, 117–18, 125, 132, 134, 138, 140, 145–7, 149, 170, 175–7, 181–2, 185–6, 191–2

Jesus
　as disciples' friend and teacher/rabbi 1, 57, 61, 74, 76–7, 79–80, 82, 88, 94, 98, 105, 165, 176, 178, 190

as forgiving victim, 12, 70, 86, 106, 116, 130–1, 142, 146, 169, 171, 191–2
Johnson, Elizabeth 16

Kaplan, Grant 10–12, 14, 50, 59–62, 84 n.56, 187 n.55, 188 n.56, 188 n.59
kerygmatic 83–4, 86
Kirwan, Michael 10

language
  biblical/Christian 90, 95, 118, 130, 138, 151, 156, 169–71, 182, 185, 192
  and human culture/consciousness 40–1, 117–18, 151, 169–71, 182, 184, 192
LGBTQ/gay 3–5, 108, 151, 153, 166–8, 172
Lindbeck, George 183–5

memory
  Alison on 9, 67, 70–2, 108–9, 185, 188, 192
  Christian/collective 122
  Girard on 33–4, 41–2
mimetic desire
  and acquisitive mimesis 20, 36–40, 42–3, 47–8, 51
  vs appetite 36, 38–9, 41–2, 46, 50
  external/internal mediation 26–7, 31
  and hominization 21, 36–42, 1
  vs instinct 36, 39–42, 50–1
  vs metaphysical desire 20, 27–29, 31–7, 42, 44–8, 50–1
  vs mimesis 20–1, 36–8, 41–2, 47, 51
  model/mediator of 13, 24, 26–34, 46, 48, 50–1, 53–5, 59, 104–5, 165, 173–4, 179, 183, 185, 189, 191
  modes of 20–1, 26, 37, 62, 125–6, 142, 155, 179
  as network connectivity 25, 28–9, 46, 49, 54–5, 77–8, 80, 104, 130, 180, 191
  object of 26–7, 31, 33, 36–43, 46–8, 50–1, 110, 137
  obstacle to 31, 43, 118, 151, 169
  pacific/peaceful/positive 9–10, 13, 21, 36, 38, 49–53, 55, 59, 62, 96, 102–3, 170–1, 174, 178–9, 188, 191

rivalry/rivalrous 2, 20, 24, 26–7, 31–3, 35–6, 38–43, 46, 48, 50–1, 57, 62, 65, 71, 75, 99–100, 160–2, 171, 177, 182, 184, 187, 191–2
  triangular/imitative 21–6, 30, 32–5, 53–5, 99, 173, 187
mimetic theory
  Alison's appropriation of 74, 87, 118–23, 171–5, 177–80, 187, 189, 191
  and Girard 19–21, 35, 38, 51
  summary of 1, 7
  and theological method 10–14, 16, 56, 60–2, 118–23, 150, 171–5, 177–80, 187, 189, 191
Mongrain, Kevin 50, 58–61
Moore, Sebastian 5

novel/novelist 1, 21–32, 34–5, 47, 74–5
novelistic 30–1, 49

order of discovery 8–9, 15, 115–16, 119–20, 149–62, 166, 180, 185, 187
  and order of logic 111–14
Oughourlian, Jean-Michel 29, 35, 44–5, 72

Palaver, Wolfgang 5, 10, 12, 14, 19, 20 n.5, 50, 59–60
Paul, the Apostle 52, 95, 107, 126
perception
  as a human capacity 8, 13, 67–8, 70–2, 86, 94, 115, 149, 174, 185, 188, 192
Peter, the Apostle 52, 142
prayer 58–9, 104, 132, 185
Proust, Marcel 21, 24–5, 29–30, 33, 47–8
  The Past Recaptured 33, 52
psychoanalytic 56–7, 78 n.36

Rahner, Karl 3, 130 n.37
reconciliation 43, 130–1, 138–9, 160, 166, 182, 186
redemption/salvation 11, 93, 95, 102, 113, 119, 123, 152–4, 156, 158–9, 163–4, 181–3, 186, 189, 192
  salvation history 58, 113, 187
resurrection
  disciples
    experience of 8, 13, 15, 66, 69, 72–8, 80–93, 98, 101, 107, 121, 124–7, 171–2, 174, 179

Girard on 57, 60
as historical event 80
Sadducees' denial of 96
theology of 11, 102, 154, 156, 164–5, 178–9
revelation
Christian theology/doctrine of 112, 115, 122, 150, 163, 165, 175–80, 187–91 (*see also* Scriptures)
and/as discovery 101, 118, 129, 137
Judeo-Christian/biblical 16, 61, 37, 43–5, 47, 58–9, 66, 72, 74, 96, 98, 121, 174
self-revelation of God 45, 93, 121, 130, 154, 157–8, 189
Ricouer, Paul 16, 111, 133–8, 144
Robinette, Brian 10, 95 n.86, 136 n.55, 141 n.62

sacraments 23, 126, 170
sacrifice 140–1, 144, 155–6, 158
satan/satanic 53, 69
scapegoat mechanism 7, 20
Schleiermacher, Friedrich 166 n.23
Scriptures
Judeo-Christian 7, 13–14, 23, 35–6, 43–5, 47, 57, 62, 73, 175, 177
New Testament 15–16, 52, 59, 65–6, 73–5, 77, 80–4, 87, 90, 96, 121, 123, 128, 172–3, 180
Old Testament/Hebrew 43, 82, 158, 176 (*see also* revelation)
self/selves 28–31, 34–5, 54–5, 90 n.74, 71, 105–6, 135, 179 soteriology 10, 12, 72, 171 (*see also* redemption/salvation)
Stendhal 21, 24, 26 n.29, 29 n.39, 30 n.40
subject 9, 26–35, 49, 53–5, 68–70, 103–5
communal 145–6, 149
and God/Christ 109–13, 115, 117, 127, 137, 141, 147, 165
intersubjectivity 25, 133
subjectivity 37, 54–5, 68–69, 104–5, 136, 179–80, 191
subversion from within 15, 66, 94–5, 97, 101–5, 108–9, 115, 142, 149, 170, 175

sin
as accusation 109, 163–5, 169–74, 179, 190, 192
as blindness 76, 101, 106, 142, 162, 164, 181, 185, 186
as complicity in violence 106, 109–10, 131, 140, 163–5, 188
original 56–7, 59, 62, 161–6, 172, 186, 190
and rivalry 7, 24, 31, 43, 46, 71, 75, 99, 100, 174, 177, 179, 182, 187, 192
as victimage/victimization 4, 35, 38–47, 49–50, 53–7, 62, 93, 96 n.92, 99, 103, 106, 131, 140–1, 146, 149, 188

teleology/teleological 56–7, 61–2, 175
theologians
task of 118–19, 149, 158, 171
theological method 10, 61, 172
Alison's 2, 6–9, 12–14, 62, 72–3, 75, 122, 150, 163, 172, 184, 187, 191 (*see also* fundamental theology and induction)
theological reflection
as activity of Christian believer 107, 109, 114–18, 122, 145
Alison on 75, 146–7
Alison's practice of 6, 16, 19, 72, 74, 149–71
criteria for 73, 106, 109, 114
definition of 8–10, 12, 110–11, 149, 171–2, 174, 190–2
of the disciples 93–5, 101
and doctrines 181–3
and theological texts 131–3, 136–44
Trinity 11, 159–61

victims 71, 130–1, 133, 140–1, 164–5, 186

Webb, Eugene 14, 56, 78 n.36
witness
act of 16, 81–4, 110, 124–6, 145–6, 149, 175

apostolic/NT 16, 44 n.90, 76–7, 81, 83–4, 121–2, 124, 175
Christian witnesses 86, 110, 125–9, 131–3, 138, 145–6, 149, 168, 181, 184, 192
eyewitness 84–6, 127

false 139–45
reception of a 16, 66, 123–9, 145–6, 149
texts as 131–3, 135, 137–8, 143–6
world in front of the text 135–6, 144